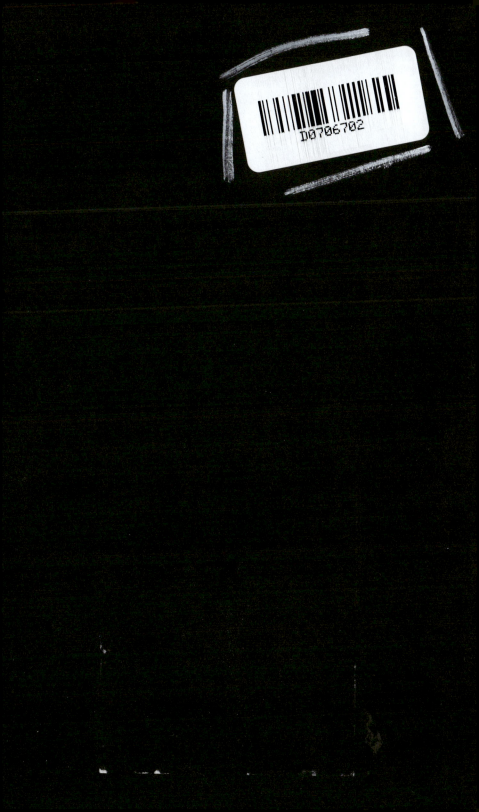

THE PROFESSION OF PLAYER
IN SHAKESPEARE'S TIME, 1590-1642

PRINCETON UNIVERSITY PRESS

The Profession
of Player in
Shakespeare's Time
1590-1642

GERALD EADES BENTLEY

Publication of this book has been aided by the
Whitney Darrow Fund of Princeton University Press

This book has been composed in Linotron Janson
Clothbound editions of Princeton University Press books are
printed on acid-free paper, and binding materials are
chosen for strength and durability

Printed in the United States of America by
Princeton University Press, Princeton, New Jersey

For G.E.B., Jr.

Contents

Preface

THIS BOOK is planned as a companion to *The Profession of Dramatist in Shakespeare's Time*. Its purpose, like that of its predecessor, is to set forth, as fully as I can, what was normal in the conduct of one of the two major components in that phenomenal creative outburst we call the "Elizabethan Drama." Most of the great flood of modern studies concerning that astounding florescence are confined to single dramatists or single plays or single themes in a limited group of writings for the theater during the reigns of Elizabeth, James, and Charles. Too many such studies simply assume conditions of composition or performance for their plays that would have been highly abnormal, if not impossible, in the theatrical milieu of late sixteenth- and early seventeenth-century London. If these two studies can help to indicate the *usual* conduct of the Elizabethan playwrights and their employers, they will have accomplished their purpose.

My use of the word "player" instead of "actor" may seem eccentric to some readers; indeed, I had at first injudiciously intended to use the title "The Profession of Actor in Shakespeare's Time." But the more I went over my notes and pored over contemporary documents, especially lawsuits and parish records, the more it was borne in upon me that such a choice would be somewhat anachronistic as well as inaccurate. Since the word "actor" has been the term in most common usage for a theatrical performer for more than three centuries now, it is understandable that we should assume that the usage was the regular Elizabethan, Jacobean, and Caroline one. It was not. "Player" and "playing" are the standard usages in these three reigns. Though "actor" is sometimes used by the printers and occasionally in the texts of plays, in the profession itself "player" was the normal term. The evidence for this seems to me overwhelming, and I set it forth here.

The most extensive single document concerning theatrical dealings of the time is the so-called Diary of Philip Henslowe. Since the majority of Henslowe's diversified dealings were with theater people, he seldom found it necessary to record their occupations; even so, he—or his witnesses—use the term "player" or "players" more than a score of times, never "actor."

Probably our best index to common usage is the London parish registers. Most of the theatrical performers in London during the reigns of Elizabeth, James, and Charles appeared in these registers sooner or later, and the entries were set down by a variety of parish clerks during the fifty-two-year period 1590-1642. Usually the extant registers are mere lists of names under the headings "Marriages," "Christenings," and "Burials," but in at least three parishes the clerks normally gave the occupations of male parishioners. In the registers of the populous parish of St. Giles Cripplegate, where so many of the performers at the Fortune theater lived, the different parish clerks used the term "player" to designate the occupation of a parishioner over 150 times, but I did not encounter "actor" at all. At St. Saviour's Southwark, home of so many of the performers at the Globe, the Hope, the Swan, and the Rose, the registers call them "players" more than 80 times, but never "actors." At St. Botolph's Aldgate, different clerks used "player" about 30 times, sometimes varied to "stage-player," but never "actor."[1] Since these records were set down by a variety of parish clerks over a period of more than half a century in different parts of London, "player" was evidently the standard professional designation in the parishes.

The government official most constantly engaged with all professional players and their performances was the Master of the Revels. Few records of the Masters before 1622 are extant, but for 1622 to 1642 there are copious extracts from the Office Book of Sir Henry Herbert. In his accounts, though, he usually calls the acting troupes "The King's Men" or "The Queen's Servants"; he calls them "players" over 50 times, "actors" never.

Even in papers written after 1660 when he was trying to reestablish himself in his old office and when the word "actor" was in more general use, Sir Henry writes "player" five or six times as often as he writes "actor." Thus Sir Henry Herbert, the man in most constant contact with all affairs theatrical during the latter part of our period, uses, like all the parish clerks noted, the standard popular term "player" and not "actor."

The common use of the term "player" was by no means confined to the metropolis. Giles Dawson studied the local records of thirteen towns in the County of Kent and found many hundreds of payments to entertainers of one sort or another.[2] In these various records the term "player" is used between 700 and 800 times; "actor" not at all.

[1] "Records of Players in the Parish of St. Giles Cripplegate," *PMLA* 44 (1929), 789-826; "Shakespeare's Fellows," *Times Literary Supplement*, 15 November 1928, p. 856; "Actors' Names in the Registers of St. Botolph's Aldgate," *PMLA* 41 (1926), 91-109.

[2] "Records of Plays and Players in Kent, 1450-1642," *Malone Society Collections* 7 (1965).

This invariable usage in the thirteen towns of Kent was not peculiar to the South. The practice in Yorkshire and in the great houses of the North was the same as in the borough records of Kent. Professor Lawrence Stone published "Companies of Players Entertained by the Earl of Cumberland and Lord Clifford, 1607-39."[3] These thirty-one records were set down by different stewards in three northern castles of the family. In 29 of the accounts the stewards used the designation "player" for the visiting entertainers; "actor" does not appear in these records at all.

Professor Bernard Beckerman has called my attention to the fact that the few casts or lists in the quartos and folios before 1642 all use the word "actor" except Ben Jonson's early editions, which use either "Tragœdians" or "Comœdians." Of course these examples are very few compared with the many hundreds of uses of the term "players." I can only guess that "actor" seemed less tainted with the contemporary commercial theater and that it was perhaps preferred by some printers. Nevertheless, the accumulated evidence seems to me to be clear that "player" was the word in normal use by the profession and by the general public from 1590 to 1642.

In my consideration of the profession of player I have considered the apprentices of the major London troupes, but not the children of the boy companies who were so prominent around the turn of the century. Good as these boys may have been for short periods, they were not true professional players, they were not paid for their acting. Most of them were singers who were pressed to act by certain masters. Or they were schoolboys whose performance of plays was not their primary activity. There is no evidence that these boys ever had anything to do with the administration of their activities, the selection of their plays, or any profit which might accrue from their endeavors. The boy companies were an astonishing activity of their time, and they certainly had an influence on the adult professional companies for a period, as the famous

[3] *Malone Society Collections* 5 (1960), 17-28.

passage in the Folio edition of *Hamlet* shows; however, they were not really professionals, though a few of them, like Nathan Field, later became professionals.

This book is not designed as a collection of contemporary records concerning players, but as an organization and interpretation of these documents, though there are a fair number of previously unpublished contemporary records transcribed. In order to make these records as clear as possible, I have generally modernized the spelling, capitalization, punctuation, and abbreviations in the transcriptions of lawsuits, financial records, letters, contracts, charters, court reports and such. For literary work of major writers there may be some risk in modernization, but I see few hazards, and I hope it will be a boon for many readers for me to regularize Philip Henslowe's play title "The Jeylle of dooges" to "The Isle of Dogs" or "the sute of Tho: Woodford compl^t againste Aaron Holland def^t vpon the mocon . . ." as copied by the clerk of the Jacobean Court of Requests, into "the suit of Thomas Woodford, complainant, against Aaron Holland, defendant, upon the motion. . . ."

There is an exception to this modernization rule in the appendix. In the extant early casts (especially in the Plots and prompt manuscripts), abbreviations, nicknames, and eccentric spellings are common, and sometimes mutilation leaves names incomplete. In view of the resulting uncertainties it has seemed less misleading to reproduce the original than to rely on my own solution to a puzzle.

My principle of organization has been to consider first the relations between the player and his company; then the three components of all adult companies—sharers, hired men, and apprentices; then three aspects of the players' activities—managing, touring, and casting; and then an attempt to draw some of the material together in a summarizing statement.

For hospitality during the pleasant task of accumulating evidence I am grateful to the Public Record Office, the Guildhall Library, the Bodleian Library, the Huntington Library, the Folger Library, and to the Clark Library, which made me a Fellow.

For help in the more onerous chore of selecting and organizing this evidence I have received suggestions and advice from Bernard Beckerman, Mary Ann Jensen, William A. Ringler, Jr., and especially from David Bevington, whose unstinted help has gone far beyond scholarly obligations.

In the many stages of book-making from manuscript revision to proofreading under difficult conditions I have enjoyed the shrewd and patient help of my wife.

G.E.B.

Princeton
13 December 1983

THE PROFESSION OF PLAYER
IN SHAKESPEARE'S TIME, 1590-1642

CHAPTER I

Introduction

THE PHENOMENAL popularity of English theatrical entertainment in the half century from 1590 to 1642 is vaguely
known to many, though perhaps not fully realized even by
many writers on dramatic subjects. During these years there
were professional performances of English plays *in English* not
only all over Britain, from Folkstone and St. Ives to Aberdeen
and Edinburgh, but in Germany, Holland, Belgium, Den-
mark, Poland, and even in France.

This unusual popularity of the London theater was recognized at the time by travellers. Fynes Moryson wrote in the
second part of his *Itinerary*, licensed for printing on 14 June
1626:

> The City of London alone hath four or five companies of
> players with their peculiar theatres capable of many thou-

sands, wherein they all play every day in the week but Sunday, with most strange concourse of people. . . . as there be, in my opinion, more plays in London than in all the parts of the world I have seen, so do these players or comedians excel all others in the world.[1]

Though there were many amateur performances, especially in the schools, at local fetes, at noblemen's houses, and in nearly all the thirty or forty colleges at Oxford and Cambridge, the vast majority of the performances were in the hands of professionals. During this half century more than a thousand players are known by name.[2] And it is likely that there were many others, for more than one hundred of these thousand named players are identified as such from the chance survival of only a single record. That record, usually a citation in a lawsuit or a parish register, sets down the profession of the man as "player" or "stage-player." New names keep turning up, and they are often those of men of some achievement in their profession. Simon Jewell, a sharer in Queen Elizabeth's company, was unheard of until Mary Edmonds published his will in 1974.[3] Two sharers in Queen Anne's company were totally unknown until references to them were discovered in the testimony of the dramatist Thomas Heywood and of the distinguished player Richard Perkins in the 1623 Chancery suit of *Ellis Worth and Thomas Blaney v. Susan Baskervile and William Browne*. (See Chapter III, "Sharers.")

An enterprise so popular and so allegedly profitable as this inevitably developed certain standards or customs of organization, of procedure, of remuneration, of division of labor, of conduct, of hierarchy, of the acquisition of property, and even

[1] Charles Hughes, ed., *Shakespeare's Europe: A Survey of the Condition of Europe at the End of the 16th Century, Being Unpublished Chapters of Fynes Moryson's Itinerary (1617)*, 2nd ed., New York, 1967, p. 476.

[2] See Edwin Nungezer, *A Dictionary of Actors and of Other Persons Associated with the Public Representation of Plays in England before 1642*, New Haven, 1929; supplemented by G. E. Bentley, *The Jacobean and Caroline Stage*, 7 vols., Oxford, 1941-1968, II.

[3] *Review of English Studies* 25 (1974), 129-36.

of providing for the widows of deceased members. These customs and the evidence for them are the subject of this book.

Generally speaking, the London professional players in the time of Elizabeth, James, and Charles were poor men, as they have been in almost all ages of the theater. This basic fact, reflected in the constant breaking up of companies and in the flight to provincial or foreign fields, has been somewhat obscured because a few widely celebrated players—perhaps twenty out of approximately one thousand performing in the time—are known to have accumulated respectable estates. One who amassed a proper fortune was Edward Alleyn, a very famous player.[4] He retired from the stage before he was forty and spent the next twenty years or so building and renting theaters; buying and selling costumes, play scripts, houses, and land; running the Bear Garden as Master of the Royal Game of Bears, Bulls, and Mastiff Dogs; and administering Philip Henslowe's estate, most of which he inherited. He bought the manor of Dulwich and established Alleyn's College of God's Gift at Dulwich, furnishing it with an endowment that still supports it. Alleyn, however, was unique.

No other player is known to have amassed such a fortune in these years, though wills and various property transactions show that several players managed their investments well: John Heminges, Henry Condell, William Shakespeare, Christopher Beeston, Michael Bowyer, John Shank, Augustine Phillips, Thomas Greene.[5] These men who are known to have

[4] John Payne Collier, *The Alleyn Papers*, London, 1843, pp. xxi-xxvi.

[5] For evidence of the estates accumulated by these players, see their wills. John Heminges: James Boswell, ed., *The Plays and Poems of William Shakespeare . . . By the Late Edmund Malone*, London, 1821, III, 191-96; Henry Condell: John Payne Collier, *Memoirs of the Principal Actors in the Plays of Shakespeare*, London, 1846, pp. 145-49; William Shakespeare: S. Schoenbaum, *William Shakespeare: A Documentary Life*, Oxford, 1975, pp. 243-48; Christopher Beeston: Leslie Hotson, *The Commonwealth and Restoration Stage*, Cambridge, Mass., 1928, pp. 398-400; Michael Bowyer: Bentley, *The Jacobean and Caroline Stage*, II, 635-36; John Shank: Bentley, *The Jacobean and Caroline Stage*, II, 646-48; Augustine Phillips: George Chalmers, *An Apology for Believers in the Shakespeare Papers*, London, 1797, pp. 431-35; Thomas Greene: F. G. Fleay, *A Chronicle History of the London Stage, 1559-1642*, London, 1890, pp. 192-94.

accumulated respectable estates, it must be noted, were all sharers, not hired men. At least six of the eight were house-keepers, i.e., owners of shares in theater buildings, as well as sharers; it is not unlikely that Thomas Greene also owned shares in the Red Bull, but no such direct evidence has sur-vived. Furthermore, they had all belonged to major London companies: the Lord Admiral's men, the Lord Chamberlain-King's men, or the Queen's men. They did not come from the score or more minor London companies, nor from the many struggling provincial troupes.

The few "Elizabethan" players who became prosperous were not only members of the superior companies and usually housekeepers in theaters, but none of them is known to have been a hired man for any length of time. Hired men of all companies, members of minor troupes, and provincial players made up the bulk of actors in this period, and most of them were poor.

Though there was no London guild of players like those of the Cordwainers or Drapers or Stationers, the players used the general principles of guild organization common to the time. The organized acting companies of London did not em-ploy the same names for their ranks as the Grocers, Station-ers, or Merchant Tailors did. They divided themselves into apprentices, hired men, and sharers; the basic hierarchy was nevertheless similar to that of the guilds.

The players also differed from the older London guilds in that they had no central organization of all troupes in the profession, like that of the Lord Mayor and Council, and nothing like the tight organization of the regular guilds such as the Ironmongers or Stationers with their own system of Master and Court and set regulations for all units of the same trade. Of course they had nothing like the prestige of the Goldsmiths or Grocers and no Hall of their own.

One of the consequences of this lack of professional organ-ization and structure is that material concerning players of the time is not to be found in one place but is exasperatingly scattered through lawsuits, parish registers, licenses, plays, contracts, correspondence, financial accounts, letters, court orders, joke books, pamphlets, wills, prefaces, commendatory verses, prompt manuscripts, and sessions of the peace records.

WHERE THE PLAYERS LIVED

In London there were certain neighborhoods that were popular with players. A few are easy to identify because the clerks of those parishes frequently wrote the occupations of parishioners into their registers. As one would expect, the parishes favored by the players were close to theaters, and this proximity must have made rehearsals, special summonses, play readings, and new member consultations convenient.

The most certain of such districts was the Bankside, especially Paris Garden and the Clink, convenient to the Globe, the Hope, the Rose, the Swan, and rather less so to Newington Butts. The parish church was St. Saviour's, sometimes still called St. Mary Overies. The registers contain the names of many players, scores of them with their occupations named. This parish still preserves its old token books, so that for many players it is possible to ascertain the exact houses in which they lived.

Another popular players' neighborhood was St. Giles without Cripplegate, a very populous parish just outside the city walls, which included the Fortune theater. In the registers of this church the clerks also frequently mentioned the occupations of players, members of whose families were christened, married, or buried there. And so in St. Botolph's Aldgate. This parish was popular with players in the early period rather than the later because its nearby playing places fell into disuse early—the Bull Inn, the Bell Inn, the Cross Keys, The Theatre, and the Curtain.

Later a fairly popular area was the parish of St. Giles in the Fields, where in 1616 Christopher Beeston built the Phoenix, a playhouse which struggled on into the Restoration. A number of players lived near this theater, tenanted at different times by the Lady Elizabeth's men, Prince Charles's (I) company, Queen Henrietta's men, and for the last few years of the period by the King and Queen's Young company. Since the parish clerks at St. Giles in the Fields did not record occupations, the players can be identified with less certainty than in three of the other parishes, but several of the names of actors at the Phoenix or Cockpit are distinctive, and a number of others with less distinctive names probably represent players who are known to have performed at Beeston's house.[6] Other parishers in which several players have been found to reside are St. James's Clerkenwell, St. Leonard's Shoreditch, St. Mary's Aldermanbury, and St. Anne's Blackfriars.

THE STATUS OF PLAYERS

A great deal has been written about the low status of the players' profession in Shakespeare's time, mostly bolstered by quotations from the moralists and some of the preachers of the sixteenth century. Of course the opposition to plays and playing cannot be doubted, but not quite so familiar is the fact that the status of players rose notably before the closing act of 1642; the general attitude toward the profession was not the same in 1635 as it had been in 1580.

In the late years of the reign of Elizabeth and throughout those of her two successors most of the players were no longer "masterless men," "rogues," and "vagabonds," though their enemies often called them so. All the London companies and a great many of the provincial ones held licenses or patents or charters which established their connections with some noble or royal household and assigned to them rights and privileges

---

[6] "Shakespeare's Fellows," *Times Literary Supplement*, 15 November 1928, p. 856; William Ingram, *A London Life in the Brazen Age: Francis Langley, 1548-1602*, Cambridge, Mass., 1978, p. 301 n. 24; Emma Marshall Denkinger, "Actors' Names in the Registers of St. Botolph's Aldgate," *PMLA* 41 (1926), 91-109; "Players in the Parish of St. Giles in the Fields," *Review of English Studies* 6 (1930), 2-18; "Records of Players in the Parish of St. Giles Cripplegate," *PMLA* 44 (1929), 789-826.

that could not have been claimed by the wanderers of the early sixteenth century.[7] Opposition to the players had always been heard from certain elements in the city as well as in the country. But performers who carried a document with the seal of a great nobleman, like the Lord Chamberlain or (after 1603) that of the King or Queen or Prince, were not generally treated with the contempt some of the Puritan preachers or William Prynne would have liked.

Not without influence in the somewhat improved status of the players was the great increase in the number of times they were called to perform before royalty and the assembled court. While Elizabeth in the last decade of her reign summoned the companies to play before her four to eight times a year, twenty or more performances in a season were not exceptional in the time of James and Charles.[8] Such displays at Whitehall and St. James's and Hampton Court were not unknown to the London populace, and the status of the performers was not lowered thereby.

Perhaps the most tangible impetus to the slowly altering status of the players was the publication of the Jonson folio in 1616. For many years the normal form of publication for those plays that did achieve print was cheap pamphlets looking like joke books, almanacs, coney-catching pamphlets, and other such ephemera, frequently with no author's name on the title page. In contrast this handsome Jonson folio volume was set up like a collection of sermons or *The Works of King James*, printed in the same year. Furthermore the individual plays were dedicated to persons of standing, like the great historian Camden and Lord Aubigny, Lady Wroth and the

---

[7] The procedure of obtaining a patent is set out and fourteen examples of such document for dramatic companies are transcribed by E. K. Chambers and W. W. Greg in "Dramatic Records from the Patent Rolls: Company Licenses," *Malone Society Collections* 1, pt. 3 (1909) 260-84.

[8] See E. K. Chambers, *The Elizabethan Stage*, 4 vols., Oxford, 1967, IV, 104-130; and Bentley, *The Jacobean and Caroline Stage*, I, 94-100 and VII, 16-128.

Earl of Pembroke. Never before had English plays been treated with such dignity.[9]

But even more significant for the players was another innovation in the Jonson folio. Each of the nine tragedies and comedies in the volume was accompanied by a list of the names of the players who had created the principal roles; they are called either "Comœdians" or "Tragœdians." Such formal recognition for the lowly players had never been shown in an English book before. It was followed in a different form in the Shakespeare folio of 1623 and in the second Beaumont and Fletcher folio of 1679.

Possibly of some influence in the gradual improvement of the status of the players was Thomas Heywood's *An Apology for Actors* in 1612 and Nathan Field's "Field the player's letter to Mr. Sutton, preacher at St. Mary Overs, 1616." Both works of these player-dramatists were reasonable and informed. Heywood's is bolstered with a good deal of classical evidence. Field's letter, first printed separately by Halliwell-Phillips in an issue of twenty-five copies in 1865, is pious with a good display of Biblical knowledge.

Another event that tended to enhance the status of the players in these years was Edward Alleyn's deed of foundation of his College of God's Gift at Dulwich in 1619. This deed was read before a gathering of notables in London. The influence of such an event was recognized by the contemporary histo-

---

[9] It should be noted, however, that to some writers the Jonson volume seemed pretentious, especially the use of the designation "Works." George Fitz-Geoffry, Thomas Heywood, John Suckling, John Boys, and an anonymous writer in *Wits Recreation* all twit Jonson, generally by the easy quibble on "play" and "work." See Jesse Franklin Bradley and Joseph Quincy Adams, *The Jonson Allusion Book*, New Haven, 1922, pp. 119, 167, 175, 196, 271, and G. E. Bentley, *Shakespeare and Jonson: Their Reputations in the Seventeenth Century Compared*, 2 vols. in 1, Chicago, 1969, II, 35.

Of course in the milieu of London publishing in 1616 the Jonson volume *was* rather ostentatious. But there it was, displayed on the bookstalls for all to see, and there were the names of the noble dedicatees for individual plays and the conspicuous list of players for each comedy or tragedy.

rian, Sir Richard Baker. In his *Chronicle of the Kings of England* he wrote:

> About this time also *Edward Allen* of *Dulwich* in *Surrey* founded a fair hospital at *Dulwich*. . . . This man may be an example, who having gotten his wealth by stage playing converted it to this pious use, not without a kind of reputation to the Society of Players.[10]

The rising status of the players—especially the King's men— is reflected about this same time in Ralph Crane's *The Works of Mercy*, 1621, in which the scrivener says:

> And some employment hath my useful pen
> Had 'mongst those civil, well-deserving men,
> That grace the stage with honor and delight,
> Of whose true honesties I much could write,
> But will compress 't (as in a cask of gold)
> Under the Kingly service they do hold.
>
> [A₆]

It should be remembered, of course, that these remarks apply primarily, if not exclusively, to a few superior companies and their leading sharers, like Heminges and Condell who were longtime churchwardens at St. Mary's Aldermanbury. Though the whole profession of players was less vilified in the later days of James and the reign of Charles I, the hundreds of hired men and most of the provincial players were far from enjoying positions of dignity.

[10] *A Chronicle of the Kings of England*, London, 1684, p. 423.

CHAPTER II

The Player and His Company

FOR THE PROFESSIONAL player in London during the years 1590-1642, the primary focus of his life was usually the theatrical troupe to which he was attached at the moment. One must say "at the moment," for life in the theater is always precarious. Only one troupe, the Lord Chamberlain's-King's company, had a continuous existence throughout the period; other troupes came and went, usually overwhelmed by their debts but sometimes dispersed because a theater landlord like Henslowe or Beeston or Meade or Langley had reason to expel them from the playhouse he owned. Since about twenty different commercial companies performed in London during this period at one time or another, the failure rate is striking. Even so, not nearly all the commercial companies were primarily metropolitan ones. Well over a hundred troupes are known to have been touring in the provinces at some time during these years, and the majority of them are never heard of in London.[1]

All normal London commercial companies of adult players in these years were made up of the same three groups: sharers, hired men, and boys or apprentices. Of course there were many changes as the years passed and prosperity and inflation increased. Since all troupes were repertory companies whose principal assets were their costumes and their exclusive library of dramatic scripts, most of the plays were kept out of print—at least until they were obsolete or the failing company was forced to sell its most precious assets in order to eat. The Red Bull and the Blackfriars theaters in the Caroline period tended to draw the preponderance of their audiences from different social classes, so there were differences in the play

[1] In the first decade of this century Professor John Tucker Murray made a somewhat superficial survey of the records of provincial towns in England from 1558 to 1642. (J. T. Murray, *English Dramatic Companies 1558-1642*, 2 vols., London, 1910, II, *passim*.) He found well over a hundred named dramatic companies which visited provincial towns in his period.

Recently a much more thorough survey of provincial records has been undertaken by a Canadian group. In a preliminary report on the records of the town of Leicester, Alice B. Hamilton notes:

I have counted over fifty different companies of actors that came to Leicester in the sixteenth and seventeenth centuries, who were rewarded for playing or for not playing at the Town Hall. They came sporatically between 1531 and 1547, but not all borough records exist for these years and visits by actors may have occurred more frequently than appears from the surviving fiscal rolls. The hosts of companies come after 1560. (*Records of Early English Drama*, Toronto, 1979, I, 18)

Even these astonishing numbers are too small, for the records of many provincial towns have not yet been thoroughly examined, and many of the records that have been examined neglect to give the name of the company that was paid, but simply say "to the players." The clerk was interested in the money spent, not in the identity of the company—unless there had been trouble. Nor do these numbers include the many troupes of English players touring the continent, especially Germany and the Low Countries, and playing in English. Truly the rage for theatrical entertainment was astounding, though most of these companies could never have been very profitable.

requirements of different theaters and in the requisites of their performers. Jig dancers were long in demand at the Fortune, seldom if ever at the Blackfriars.[2]

In spite of these differences, however, there was a norm— witness the fact that there are scores of examples of players who transferred from one troupe to another during these years,[3] and the fact that in several instances the same play is known to have been performed at different times by different companies, Kyd's *Spanish Tragedy* and Marston's *Malcontent*, for instance. It is possible, therefore, to outline what was usual in a London professional adult acting troupe during the period.

It was normal for a company to be attached to a single theater owned by a landlord or a group of landlords—speculators, not players. The company's rent was not a fixed sum but a percentage of the take at each performance.

To this normal arrangement there were one or two exceptions, most conspicuously, as usual, the Lord Chamberlain-King's company. In the early nineties they were playing at The Theatre, a playhouse built by the father of their great actor Richard Burbage and inherited by Richard and his brother Cuthbert. In 1598 they transported The Theatre, timber by timber, across the river, embellished and enlarged it, named it the Globe, and vested the ownership of the house in the Burbage brothers and several leading fellows or sharers of the company: William Shakespeare, Augustine Phillips, Thomas Pope, John Heminges, and William Kempe. These men were the "housekeepers," and they received the rent that other companies paid to their real estate landlords.

In 1608 this company took over the Blackfriars, a private

---

[2] For the reputations of audiences at the Fortune and Red Bull theaters, see Edmund Gayton's *Pleasant Notes upon Don Quixote* (1654); relevant passages are quoted in my *Jacobean and Caroline Stage*, 7 vols., Oxford, 1941-1968, II, 690-91. See also the section on "The Reputation of the Red Bull Theatre," ibid., VI, 238-47.

[3] See E. K. Chambers, *The Elizabethan Stage*, 4 vols., Oxford, 1967, II, 295-350; and Bentley, *The Jacobean and Caroline Stage*, II, 343-628.

theater (small and expensive), which they owned and operated by the same sort of combination: the Burbage brothers, four sharers, John Heminges, William Shakespeare, Henry Condell, William Sly, and a former lessee, Thomas Evans. The Lord Chamberlain-King's theatrical troupe was the only company operating two theaters and maintaining over a long period of time the same system of ownership.

There is some evidence that Edward Alleyn was trying to work out a similar system of cooperative ownership for the Palsgrave's men at the Fortune in the early twenties; but it did not last long and the company disintegrated in a few years.[4]

None of the other score or more of London theatrical troupes in the period is known to have enjoyed the control of its own playhouse. Troubles with owners were common. A long list of the grievances of the Lady Elizabeth's company in 1615 against their landlord and financial agent Philip Henslowe is still extant among Edward Alleyn's papers.[5] The list of grievances, mostly financial, is long and complex, and few of them can be checked now, but it is clear that at the time there was bad blood between theater owner and company. The Lady Elizabeth's men conclude their list, "Also within 3 years he hath broken and dismembered five companies." It is not surprising that the Lady Elizabeth's company shortly disappears from London records for the next several years and is found in provincial accounts only.[6]

Such troubles as these were one of the conditions leading to another feature in the lives of all players except the Lord Chamberlain-King's men, namely the moving about from theater to theater or from London to the provinces as conditions became intolerable at one house or a better bargain was offered at another. Thus Thomas Heywood's company, the Earl of Worcester-Queen Anne's men, moved from the Rose to the Curtain to the Boar's Head to the Red Bull and to

---

[4] See Bentley, *The Jacobean and Caroline Stage*, I, 141ff.
[5] W. W. Greg, ed., *Henslowe Papers*, London, 1907, pp. 86-90.
[6] See Bentley, *The Jacobean and Caroline Stage*, I, 176-80.

Beeston's new Phoenix, all between 1603 and 1617. At the latter end of our period Prince Charles's (II) company moved from the Salisbury Court to the Red Bull to the Fortune in a period of ten years. Probably neither series of flittings is a record, but they do illustrate again the rather precarious life of most London players and the unique stability and profitability of the premier troupe of the time.

This constantly threatening departure or disintegration of the London theatrical companies was a hazard to most of the London theater owners and managers as well as to the players. Not only were desertions or transfers frequent, but several records of attempts to forestall such withdrawals survive.

According to a suit brought in the Court of Requests in November 1597, Francis Langley persuaded five leading members of the Earl of Pembroke's company to sign bonds forfeiting £100 if they left his Swan theater to play elsewhere. There are other charges in the complaint and answer, but both parties agree that such bonds were signed.[7] For a variety of reasons the bonds did not accomplish their purpose, and the players involved went to Henslowe's nearby Rose theater.

But Henslowe too was worried about retaining his players. From 1597 to 1600 he persuaded a dozen or more of the leading sharers and hired men of the Admiral's company to sign bonds according to which they forfeited from 100 marks to £40 if they left Henslowe's theater in the course of the next three, or in some instances two years.[8]

Two or three decades later, in 1624, Richard Gunnell, manager of the Fortune, tried to hold together the faltering Palsgrave's company by persuading six of the sharers to sign a bond to continue playing together at the Fortune.[9]

[7] C. W. Wallace, "The Swan Theatre and the Earl of Pembroke's Servants," *Englische Studien* 43 (1911), 345-55; supplemented by William Ingram, *A London Life in the Brazen Age: Francis Langley, 1548-1602*, Cambridge, Mass., 1978, pp. 151-66.

[8] The various agreements, all recorded and witnessed, generally by other players of the company, are conveniently assembled from Henslowe's Diary in Chambers, *The Elizabethan Stage*, II, 151-55.

[9] The agreement is known only from a Chancery suit of 1654, long after the closing of the theaters, when Gunnell's heirs tried to collect. See Leslie

The same managerial purpose to forestall disintegration or desertion is apparent in 1639 in Richard Heton's proposal for a new Queen Henrietta's company patent giving him exceptional powers. One of his "intentions for the rest" has the same binding purpose as Henslowe's agreements of forty years before and Gunnell's bonds of fifteen years before, namely to ensure that Queen Henrietta's men stayed together and remained under his direction at their present theater.[10]

Managers, owners, and players all suffered from this instability of most of the acting troupes of the time, though each group generally thought the other the guilty party. An example of the players blaming the owner for their desertion of his theater is seen in a letter written some time in the winter of 1616-1617 to Edward Alleyn and signed by the seven principal sharers. They had been performing at the Hope theater on the Bankside, a convertible playhouse and bear-baiting arena, and they explain why they had deserted. Their arrangement as to the days on which they should play had been violated, they say, in favor of the bears, and they ask Alleyn's help:

> Sir:
> I hope you mistake not our removal from the Bankside: we stood the intemperate weather, till more intemperate Mr. Meade thrust us over, taking the day from us which by course was ours; though by the time we can yet claim none, and that power he exacted on us. For the prosecution of our further suit in a house we entreat you to forethink well of the place (though it crave a speedy resolution) lest we make a second fruitless pains. . . .[11]

After the Restoration, Davenant was still trying by agreement in 1660 to keep his players together at the Cockpit. Of

---

Hotson, *The Commonwealth and Restoration Stage*, Cambridge, Mass., 1928, pp. 52-53; and Bentley, *The Jacobean and Caroline Stage*, II, 148-49.

[10] From an unidentified manuscript transcribed by Peter Cunningham in *The Shakespeare Society Papers* 4 (1849), 95-100, reprinted in Bentley, *The Jacobean and Caroline Stage*, II, 684-87.

[11] Greg, ed., *Henslowe Papers*, p. 93. For a discussion, see Bentley, *The Jacobean and Caroline Stage*, I, 200-201 and VI, 207-209.

course many conditions had changed by that time, but managers or owners still had the same problems of holding their players at their theaters.

Though his company attachment often caused trouble for the player, it was also the source of his income and often provided other satisfactions.

To the player who was a sharer, his company, if it was one of the major London ones, gave a certain prestige. In the reign of Elizabeth he wore the badge of the nobleman who was his master—perhaps patron would be the better term, since there is little evidence of any connection with the master's household except for occasional entertainments and even more occasional petitions for privileges or protection in difficult situations. But now and then an extant example does show the influence of an Elizabethan company patron, as when Lord Hunsdon wrote to the Lord Mayor in 1598 requesting that his company be allowed to play at the Cross Keys.[12]

After James came to the throne and the principal London companies were all officially licensed as servants of members of the royal family, the sharers wore the livery of the King or the Queen or the Prince or the Princess and were identifiable on the street as superior to the ordinary apprentice or craftsman or shopkeeper. In a time when court influence was of great value not only in individual transactions but in casual street encounters, not to say assaults and brawls, such advertisement of influencial connections could be of value.

Quarrelling and petty jealousies in performing organizations in all times are notorious, but there is evidence that friendship and trust were not uncommon among the members of London theater troupes. Perhaps the best evidence is to be seen in a few of the extant wills. Of course, most players were too poor to have much to leave and they made no last testament, but quite a number of the extant wills specify remembrances for fellow players, or special confidence in making them executors or trustees. Shakespeare's remembrances

[12] See below, pp. 79-80.

to Burbage, Heminges, and Condell, made years after he had
retired from London, are well known, but similar bequests to
their theatrical associates are made by Thomas Basse, Michael
Bowyer, Richard Cowley, John Honeyman, Henry Condell,
Thomas Greene, Nicholas Tooley, and especially Augustine
Phillips. There are various others. And often fellow players
of the company are witnesses to the signature of the testator,
suggesting that in several cases they were present at the death-
bed.[13]

Most eloquent of this affection for his co-workers in the
King's company is the will of Augustine Phillips, made on
the 4th of May 1605. The bulk of his estate he divided among
his wife and his two daughters, but a surprising number of
his colleagues are remembered:

> Item, I give and bequeath unto and amongst the hired men
> of the company which I am of, which shall be at the time
> of my decease, the sum of five pounds of lawful money of
> England to be equally distributed among them.

> Item, I give and bequeath to my fellow [i.e., fellow sharer]
> William Shakespeare a thirty shilling piece in gold; to my
> fellow Henry Condell one other thirty shilling piece in gold;
> to my servant, Christopher Beeston, thirty shillings in gold;
> to my fellow Lawrence Fletcher, twenty shillings in gold;
> to my fellow Robert Armin, twenty shillings in gold; to my
> fellow Richard Cowley, twenty shillings in gold; to my fel-
> low Alexander Cook, twenty shillings in gold; to my fellow
> Nicholas Tooley, twenty shillings in gold. . . .

[13] The will of each of these players is in print. Thomas Basse: Bentley, *The
Jacobean and Caroline State*, II, 631; Michael Bowyer: ibid., II, 635-36; Richard
Cowley: *Notes and Queries*, ser. 10, 6 (1906), 368; John Honeyman: Bentley,
The Jacobean and Caroline Stage, II, 645; Henry Condell: John Payne Collier,
Memoirs of the Principal Actors in the Plays of Shakespeare, London, 1846, pp.
145-49; Thomas Greene: F. G. Fleay, *A Chronicle History of the London Stage,
1559-1642*, London, 1890, pp. 192-94; Nicholas Tooley: James Boswell, ed.,
The Plays and Poems of William Shakespeare . . . By the Late Edmond Malone,
London, 1821, III, 484-89; Augustine Phillips: George Chalmers, *An Apology
for Believers in the Shakespeare Papers*, London, 1797, pp. 431-35.

Item, I give to Samuel Gilborne, my late apprentice, the sum of forty shillings, and my mouse-colored velvet hose, and a white taffeta doublet, a black taffeta suit, my purple cloak, sword and dagger, and my bass viol.

Item, I give to James Sands, my apprentice, the sum of forty shillings and a cittern, a bandore, and a lute to be paid and delivered unto him at the expiration of his term of years in his indenture of apprenticehood. . . .

[His wife Anne is made executrix] . . . if the said Anne my wife do at any time marry after my decease that then and from thenceforth she shall cease to be anymore or longer the executrix of this . . . and that then and from thenceforth John Hemings, Richard Burbage, William Slye, and Timothy Whithorne shall be fully and wholly my executors of this my last will and testament as though the said Anne had never been named. And of the execution of this my present testament and last will I ordain and make the said John Hemings, Richard Burbage, William Slye and Timothy Whithorne, overseers of this my present testament and last will and I bequeath unto the said John Hemings, Richard Burbage, and William Slye, to either of them my said overseers for their pains herein to be taken a bowl of silver of the value of five pounds apiece. . . .

One of the two witnesses to the will is Robert Goffe or Gough, who was one of the fellows or sharers in Shakespeare's plays listed in the first Folio. This special remembrance of all the hired men, most of the fellows, and two of the apprentices plus the trust imposed of Heminges, Burbage, and Slye suggest the importance of the company in the life of this player as well as his affection for his associates in the troupe. Of course such affection for colleagues was not universal, but a few of the remaining wills of players show a similar regard for certain of the testator's company associates, though not so many as Augustine Phillips named.

Three of Thomas Heywood's fellow sharers in Queen Anne's

company wrote commendatory verses for his *Apology for Actors* in 1612, and each advertised his company connection by addressing his verses to "To my loving Friend and Fellow, Thomas Heywood" or "To my good Friend and Fellow, Thomas Heywood." There are two or three elegies by players on the deaths of their colleagues, like Thomas Jordan's on the death of Richard Gunnell or William Rowley's elegy on his fellow in Prince Charles's company, Hugh Attwell.

Of course all was not sweetness and light among the players of these dramatic troupes: everyone remembers that Ben Jonson fought a duel with his fellow actor Gabriel Spencer and killed him, in 1598. And the long row between William Bankes and the members and managers of his company in 1635[14] are also examples of the contrary. Yet the many evidences of confidence and affection among fellows of several of the Elizabethan, Jacobean, and Caroline theatrical troupes seem to me to be noteworthy.

We have noticed that in the course of the period twenty or so different troupes played in London, but not, of course, all at the same time. Usually there were four or five companies playing simultaneously in town. There are several allusions to the number of companies playing in competition: the number varies from four to five, but four seems to be the number usually officially recognized.

On 29 March 1615 the Privy Council ordered one of their messengers to bring before them John Heminges, Richard Burbage, Christopher Beeston, Robert Lee, William Rowley, John Newton, Thomas Downton, Humphrey Jeffes, for performing during Lent in spite of the order of the Master of the Revels.[15] These eight players were leading members of four London companies: Heminges and Burbage, the King's Men; Beeston and Lee, Queen Anne's company; Rowley and Newton, the Palsgrave's company; and Thomas Downton and

[14] See below, pp. 41-45.

[15] E. K. Chambers and W. W. Greg, "Dramatic Records from the Privy Council Registers, 1603-1642," *Malone Society Collections* 1, pt. 4 (1911), 372.

Humphrey Jeffes, Prince Charles's (I) company. These four were evidently the officially recognized London companies in 1615.

Four is also the number of companies recognized in 1618 by Sir George Buc, then Master of the Revels. Among his extracts from the lost Office Book of Sir George's successor, Sir Henry Herbert, Edmond Malone copied:

> Of John Heminges, in the name of the four companies for toleration in the holy-days, 44s. January 29, 1618. "*Extracts from the office-book of Sir George Buc. MSS Herbert*"[16]

Other notes made by Edmond Malone and by George Chalmers from now lost manuscripts testify to the number of companies playing in London at a given time. In his *Supplemental Apology for the Believers in the Shakespeare Papers* in 1799 George Chalmers wrote: "When the sceptre of the stage was delivered into his [Henry Herbert's] hands, there appears from the record of his office to have been four established companies of players; exclusive of strangers, who sometimes invaded their territories" (p. 211). Malone wrote in his Variorum edition of Shakespeare, apparently using the same lost manuscript:

> Soon after his [Shakespeare's] death, four of the principal companies, then subsisting, made a union, and were afterwards called The United Companies; but I know not precisely in what this union consisted.[17]

> It appears from the office-book of Sir Henry Herbert, Master of the Revels to King James the First, and the two succeeding kings, that very soon after our poet's [Shakespeare's] death, in the year 1622, there were but five principal companies of comedians in London; the King's Servants, who performed at the Globe and in Blackfriars; the Prince's Servants, who performed then at the Curtain; the Pals-

---

[16] Joseph Quincy Adams, *The Dramatic Records of Sir Henry Herbert, Master of the Revels, 1622-1673*, New Haven, 1917, p. 48.

[17] Boswell, *Plays and Poems*, III, 224.

grave's Servants, who had possession of the Fortune; the players of the Revels, who acted at the Red Bull, and the Lady Elizabeth's Servants, or, as they are sometimes denominated, the Queen of Bohemia's players, who performed at the Cockpit in Drury Lane.[18]

These variations between four companies and five companies I interpret as meaning that though Londoners in these years had their choice among five different companies of players, four of them had special status and certain privileges. This interpretation is confirmed by two or three occasional phrases used by the Master in connection with various of his regulatory actions.

On 12 September 1623 Sir Henry made an entry which has apparently been garbled in later transcriptions,[19] but only the straightforward part of his notation concerns us here, ". . . It was acted at the Red Bull, and licensed without my hand to it; because they were none of the four companies." Whatever was meant by "the four companies," it is apparent that five were acting in London in these later years, though one did not belong to the four officially recognized "United Companies." When Richard Kendall, wardrobe keeper at the Salisbury Court theater, told Thomas Crosfield about the London companies in July 1634, he listed five companies, naming their theaters and their principal players.[20]

Sir Henry Herbert also said a number of years later that there were five companies operating in London in his time. In 1662 when Sir Henry was trying to reassert his old claims to be Master of the Revels in opposition to Sir William Davenant, he submitted to the Lord Chancellor a list of the fees he had received from the companies before the wars. One item reads: "For a share from each company of four companies of players (besides the late King's company) valued at

[18] Ibid., III, 57-59
[19] See Bentley, *The Jacobean and Caroline Stage*, III, 30-32.
[20] Fredrick S. Boas, ed., *The Diary of Thomas Crosfield*, London, 1935, pp. 71-73.

£100 a year, one year with another, besides the usual fees, by the year.[21]

Such a large number of competing London theatrical troupes not only testifies to the appetite for drama of a population of under 300,000 (in the 1590s far less) but it offered greater opportunities for employment to the players. When a London company broke up, there was always a chance that the unemployed player could get a job as a hired man in another London troupe and a greater chance that he could arrange to eke out a living with one of the many companies touring in the provinces. But there is no evidence that touring was ever very profitable, and it was certainly uncomfortable in the mire and the rain.

[21] Adams, *Dramatic Records of Sir Henry Herbert*, p. 121.

CHAPTER III

Sharers

THROUGHOUT THE PERIOD the ranking players in the adult companies were the sharers, so called because their remuneration was not a weekly wage, as in the case of the hired men, or valuable training as in the case of the apprentices, but a share in the receipts for each performance by the company. Other terms for the same status were in common use: "patented member" because only the sharers were named in the royal patents for the companies; "fellow" in the first sense given in the *Oxford English Dictionary*, "One who shares with another in a possession, official dignity, or the performance of any work: a partner, a colleague, or co-worker." "Fellow" is the term commonly used by the leading players in referring to each other. Shakespeare's usage in his will was characteristic. He bequeathed money to buy rings to "my ffellowes John Hemynge, Richard Burbage, & Henry Cundall." The same usage of this title of familiarity and respect is found in the wills of other actors: John Bentley, Alexander Cooke, Thomas Greene, John Heminges, John Honeyman, Simon Jewell, Augustine Phillips, John Shank, and John Underwood.[1]

Not only were the sharers the leading players in the company, but in the eyes of the law and of the regulatory agencies they *were* the company, and all the others in the troupe merely their employees. The extant patents for theatrical companies usually name each of the sharers in the official document, but the minor players, the apprentices, and all the many necessary theatrical functionaries are simply blanketed under the phrase, "and the rest of their associates."[2]

The fact that the sharers were the official company is apparent in other theatrical records. When in 1624 the King's men performed a now lost play called *The Spanish Viceroy* without having had it officially licensed for performance by the Master of the Revels, they were in serious trouble; not only had they violated the law, but they had offended their immediate supervisor; Sir Henry Herbert was very jealous of his prerogative. Sir Henry kept in his records their letter of abject apology:

[1] These wills have all been printed. John Bentley's can be found in *Modern Philology* 29 (1931), 111-12; Alexander Cooke's in George Chalmers, *An Apology for the Believers in the Shakespeare Papers*, London, 1797, pp. 447-49; Thomas Greene's in F. G. Fleay, *A Chronicle History of the London Stage, 1559-1642*, London, 1890, pp. 192-94; and John Heminges' in James Boswell, ed., *The Plays and Poems of William Shakespeare . . . By the Late Edmond Malone*, London, 1821, III, 191-96; John Honeyman's in G. E. Bentley, *The Jacobean and Caroline Stage*, 7 vols., Oxford, 1941-1968, II, 645; Simon Jewell's in *Review of English Studies* 25 (1974), 129-30; Augustine Phillips' in Chalmers, *An Apology for Believers in the Shakespeare Papers*, pp. 431-35; John Shank's in Bentley, *The Jacobean and Caroline Stage*, II, 646-48; John Underwood's in John Payne Collier, *Memoirs of the Principal Actors in the Plays of Shakespeare*, London, 1846, pp. 229-32.

[2] E. K. Chambers and W. W. Greg, "Dramatic Records from the Patent Rolls: Company Licences," *Malone Society Collections* 1, pt. 3 (1909), 260-83.

. . . we do confess and hereby acknowledge that we have offended, and that it is in your power to punish this offense, and are very sorry for it; and do likewise promise hereby that we will not act any play without your hand or substitute's hereafter, nor do any thing that may prejudice the authority of your office: So hoping that this humble submission of ours may be accepted, we have thereunto set our hands. . . .

The letter is signed by eleven sharers or patented members of the King's company.[3]

In the same way the sharers were the legal Lord Admiral's company in 1598. The debt of the company to Philip Henslowe was acknowledged by the signatures of ten sharers of the company, J. Singer, Thomas Downton, William Bird, Robert Shaw, Richard Jones, Gabriel Spencer, Thomas Towne, Humphry Jeffes, Charles Massey, and Samuel Rowley.[4] Similarly on 20 March 1615/16 the sharers of Prince Charles's (I) company acknowledged to Edward Alleyn and Jacob Meade that they stood indebted to Philip Henslowe, deceased, and Jacob Meade for £400 for loans and "playinge apparell" and they would repay £200 out of the takings from the gallery at the Hope theater, and would continue to play at that theater. Ten sharers signed the agreement.[5]

In Jacobean and Caroline times when the major London companies were all under the sponsorship of some member of the royal family—the Lady Elizabeth, the Duke of York, Prince Charles, as well as the King and Queen—it was ordinarily only the sharers and not the lesser members of the troupe who

[3] Joseph Quincy Adams, *The Dramatic Records of Sir Henry Herbert*, New Haven, 1917, p. 21. Two patented members did not sign, John Heminges and Henry Condell, though they were named first in the new patent for the company issued six months later. I can only conjecture that they had somehow purged themselves of the offense.

[4] R. A. Foakes and R. T. Rickert, eds., *Henslowe's Diary*, Cambridge, 1961, p. 87.

[5] W. W. Greg, ed., *Henslowe Papers*, London, 1907, pp. 90-91.

were given the special status of Grooms of the Chamber in Ordinary and who had the liveries and exemption from arrest attached to that status.[6]

The sharers in the theatrical companies of the period 1590 to 1642 are commonly said to have been made up of the most distinguished and popular performers in the troupe excepting, of course, those boys who attained fame while they were still apprentices, like Salmon Pavy, Nicholas Burt, and Richard Robinson. To a certain extent this identification of sharers and superior players is valid. Of course the sharers of different companies included their most popular performers, men like Burbage and Alleyn and Kempe and Tarleton and Field and Thomas Greene and Robert Armin and Richard Perkins and John Shank and Andrew Cane and Joseph Taylor. But a good many sharers never attained any special distinction for their performances. The best-known example is William Shakespeare. Nor were John Heminges and Henry Condell, though of immense value to the company and sharers for a good many years, ever distinguished players, and for more than a decade of their active careers they were certainly inconspicuous in performances, if they were on stage at all.

In other London companies several of the known sharers lacked distinction as actors. Thomas Heywood was a long-time sharer in Worcester-Queen Anne's company though there is no evidence that he ever made much of an impression as an actor, and the same is true of Richard Gunnell and Charles Massey and John Cumber and Christopher Beeston and John Townsend. Sometimes we can tell why these undistinguished players remained sharers: obviously William Shakespeare and Thomas Heywood were valuable to their companies as writers, but certainly a share was not the common way of paying a devoted playwright. There is no evidence that John Fletcher or Philip Massinger or Thomas Dekker or Thomas Middleton

[6] E. K. Chambers, *The Elizabethan Stage*, 4 vols., Oxford, 1923, I, 311-13; and G. E. Bentley, "The Troubles of a Caroline Acting Troupe: Prince Charles's Company," *Huntington Library Quarterly* 41 (1978), 233-35.

or James Shirley (who each wrote almost as many plays for their companies as Shakespeare did for his) were ever sharers. William Rowley was a sharer in the Duke of York-Prince Charles's (I) company, but he was a well-known comedian as well as a writer. Heminges and Beeston and Gunnell were obviously of value as managers or treasurers or business agents, and all of them, like Shakespeare, began as actors.[7]

But there was a financial element involved in becoming a sharer in a dramatic company of the time. Any successful troupe required capital, mostly for costumes, but also for wages for hired men and other theatrical functionaries—wardrobe keepers, stagekeepers, gatherers, musicians, bookkeepers, or prompters—for new plays, for licensing fees, and for travelling expenses, if only to Hampton Court or Greenwich or Windsor or Whitehall. Some of this capital evidently came from sharers. There are a number of indications of this fact, but the most fully known case is that of William Bankes and his experiences in becoming a sharer in Prince Charles's (II) company in the mid-1630s. The details of the affair are known only from a Bill of Complaint brought in the Court of Requests in February 1634/35 by William Bankes, a sharer in Prince Charles's (II) company, against the leaders of that company, the well-known actors Andrew Cane (or Keyne) and Ellis Worth, and from the joint answer of Keyne and Worth.[8] Both parties agree that Bankes paid £100 to become a sharer in the company, and they agree that he was promised that as a sharer he would be made a Groom of the Chamber.

This investment of sharers in the "stock" of the company is alluded to in the affairs of other companies. According to the widow of the prominent player Thomas Greene who died in 1612, he had laid out for the company £37, and at his death the company (Queen Anne's) owed her £80 in payment for

---

[7] See below, Chapter VI, for a discussion of managers of theatrical troupes in the period.

[8] See Bentley, "The Troubles of a Caroline Acting Troupe," pp. 217-49.

his full share, as was customary with the company.[9] The leading sharers of the same company in a Chancery suit of 1618 had said that when their fellow sharer, Robert Lee, left the organization they agreed to pay him £60 as soon as he returned some of the company property. And in his will of 31 December 1635 John Shank, a sharer and principal comedian of the King's company, admonished his fellows to pay to his widow the £50 which was due "for my share in the stock, books, apparel, and other things according to the old custom and agreement amongst us."[10]

That this sort of deposit by the sharers in the chief company of the time was not unusual is shown by a statement in a Chancery suit of 1655 brought by Theophilus Bird, who about 1640 had become a sharer in the King's company after a career with Queen Henrietta's men, against Thomas Morrison who has married the widow of Bird's old colleague in both companies, Michael Bowyer.[11] Bird says in his Chancery Bill of Complaint that

> . . . the said company being at the time of your Orator's said admission thereinto, possessed of a stock consisting of apparel, books [i.e., play mnuscripts], hangings, and other goods of the value of £3,000 and upwards, your Orator at his said admission into the said company disbursed and deposited the sum of £200 towards the said apparel, books, goods, and other things, being £150 at least more than others

[9] See the Answer of Susan Baskervile and William Browne, 23 May 1623 in the Chancery suit of *Worth, Cumber, and Blaney v. Baskervile and Brown*, transcribed in Fleay, *A Chronicle History of the London Stage*, pp. 279-92.

[10] See the will of John Shank, in Bentley, *The Jacobean and Caroline Stage*, II, 646-48.

[11] This Chancery suit was discovered and transcribed by the Wallaces before World War I, but never printed. Without knowledge that the Wallaces had used the documents before him, Leslie Hotson rediscovered and published a few quotations and a reference in *The Commonwealth and Restoration Stage*, Cambridge, Mass., 1928, pp. 31-34 and 315. My quotations come from the full transcriptions in the Wallace Papers in the Huntington Library, San Marino, California.

of the said company had done, and was more than his proportion of the said clothes and stock did amount unto. . . .

In their answer to Bird, the Morrisons disagree, of course, about the sums of money involved, but in the suits of the time it is usual for one party to maximize and the other to minimize cash values and payments. For our present purposes the more significant point is that there is no disagreement about the fact that as a new sharer in the major company of the time Theophilus Bird did deposit a sum of money in the treasury of the rich and successful King's men, just as William Bankes had made a deposit with Prince Charles's (II) troupe, one of the poorer and more struggling theatrical organizations.

That money was involved in becoming a sharer in a London theatrical troupe ought not to be surprising, though it is seldom considered. Play production had become vastly more expensive since the early days when four or five men and a boy trudged the country roads beside a wagon loaded with theatrical gear. Bird claimed in his Bill of Complaint that the royal company's stock of apparel, books, hangings, and other goods was worth £3,000, and though the defendants claim, naturally, that this sum is too large, it does not seem unreasonable to me. In August 1641 the company claimed exclusive rights to over sixty *unpublished* plays, and their entire repertory (most of which they tried to control) consisted of 170 *identifiable* titles.[12] Since many extant documents, such as Henslowe's accounts, indicate that the costumes cost the companies more than plays, £3,000 does not seem an excessive evaluation for a long-established troupe which had frequently to display itself before royalty.

A similar statement about the value of the company stocks was made fifteen or more years earlier when the King's men, though rich and powerful, had not yet accumulated the assets they had in 1640. This estimate comes in a complaint of Thomas Hobbes, a player who had been a sharer in Prince Charles's company during the reign of James. When his pa-

[12] See Bentley, *The Jacobean and Caroline Stage*, I, 65-66 and 108-134.

tron succeeded as Charles I, Hobbes was one of those who became a King's man. For some reason, however, he had apparently not been made a Groom of the Chamber as the others were, and this distressed him. In the notes of Sir Edward Coke for an audience at Whitehall is an item under the head, "King Charles His Servants": "Thomas Hobbes comedian, now left out of the number new sworn, being engaged for the stock debt of their company in £500, desireth to be sworn as the rest are or disengaged.[13] The difference in the sums cited by Hobbes and Bird could be accounted for by the accumulations and inflation of fifteen years, or Bird may have exaggerated somewhat. At any rate each statement is evidence of the great value of the possessions of King Charles's company.

Thus the contribution of capital as well as histrionic ability was a requirement for the sharers in those dramatic companies that entertained the London subjects of Elizabeth, James, and Charles. In at least one known instance, and one suspects in others, the money was more important than the acting ability. In the case of William Bankes, who brought suit against his colleagues of Prince Charles's (II), there is no evidence that he was ever a player of any note at all, but the company of Prince Charles obviously needed his £100. How often this situation was repeated we shall never know; one would guess not infrequently in the minor London companies but less often with the major and more solvent ones.

Even with Henslowe's companies in the early days, the situation did not differ in its essentials. Though Henslowe bought the costumes and the plays, the company had to pay him back. And a new sharer joining after the troupe was well established enjoyed the benefits of the plays, costumes, and hangings already owned, and it was fair enough that he should contribute something for the assets his colleagues had already paid for.

It was customary for this financial stake of a sharer in the

[13] *Historical Manuscripts Commission*, 12th Report Appendix 1 (London, 1888), p. 198.

company to be recognized as part of his estate, and a payment was supposed to be made to him when he left the company or to his wife at his death. About 1613 Charles Massey was trying to borrow money from Philip Henslowe and wrote about his security. He said

> . . . for sir I know you understand that there is the composition between our company that if any one give over with consent of his fellows, he is to receive three score and ten pounds (Anthony Jeffes hath had so much); if any one die his widow or friends whom he appoints is to receive fifty pounds (Mrs. Pavy and Mrs. Towne hath had the like). . . .[14]

In his will of December 1635, John Shank, a leading sharer in the King's company, desires that his fellow sharers in the company "do not abridge my said wife and executrix in the receiving of what is due unto me and my estate amongst them, as namely fifty pounds for my share in the stocks, books, apparel, and other things according to the old custom and agreement amongst us."[15]

The situation was similar in the company of Prince Charles (II); both plaintiff and defendants agree that George Stutville was paid £30 for his share in the stock when he left the company about the same time.[16] Twenty years earlier the arrangement for fellows leaving the company prevailed with Queen Anne's men, a troupe once more prosperous than Prince Charles's men. In the Chancery suit of *Perkins &c. v. Lee* the plaintiffs say that when Robert Lee, one of the sharers, left the organization, he received £60 provided he return the playbooks, clothes, and other goods belonging to the company.[17]

Apparently there were exceptions to this custom of returning money to widows, at least in Queen Anne's troupe, possibly because of the deterioration in the affairs of those play-

[14] Greg, ed., *Henslowe Papers*, p. 64.
[15] See Bentley, *The Jacobean and Caroline Stage*, II, 647.
[16] See Bentley, "The Troubles of a Caroline Acting Troupe," pp. 217-49.
[17] Wallace Papers.

ers. In a suit in Chancery in 1623, *Ellis Worth and John Blaney v. Susan Baskervile and William Browne*,[18] two well-known sharers in the company, Thomas Heywood and Richard Perkins, testified. Richard Perkins of St. James Clerkenwell aged "44 or thereabouts" testified that

> He knew one John Thayer who was a half sharer in the company of players at the Red Bull who departed this life about 11 years since, and sayeth he did also know Thomas Albanes who was a [?] quarter sharer in the company who died about five or six years agone and this deponent sayeth that he is well assured that neither the wives nor executors or administrators of the said Thayer and Albanes [had] anything allowed of the remainders or survivors of the said company in [?] of the said Thayer and Albanes' shares. And this deponent also saith that he knoweth Thomas Heywood and Francis Walpole who were sharers in the company left the same and yet he saith that neither Heywood, Walpole, nor himself this deponent ever had afterwards any allowance from the said company. Neither doth this deponent know any reason that anything should be demanded in that kind for he saith there was never any agreement made between the company for the allowing to the executors or administrators of such as should die or to such as should depart the company any sum or money whatsoever. . . .
>
> R. Perkins

The testimony of Richard Perkins is corroborated by his fellow sharer, the dramatist Thomas Heywood. Thomas Heywood of the parish of St. James's Clerkenwell aged 49 years or thereabouts told the interrogators:

> That within these 14 or 15 years he hath known one John Thayre who was one half sharer amongst the company of players at the Red Bull and who had bought it with his money and afterwards died and yet there was not one penny or other recompense paid or allowed to the executor or any

---

[18] London, Public Record Office C 24/500/103.

other in recompense [?] thereof and this deponent saith that
he doth also know Richard Perkins and Francis Walpole
two of the said company who left the company and had no
allowance albeit they were sharers at the time of their departure from the said company. Also he saith that himself
this day being a full sharer in the company did depart from
them but yet had no allowance of the said company so that
this deponent verily believeth that there was no agreement
in writing made by the said whole company for the payment of any sum of money if any sharer should die or
otherwise depart the company. . . .   Thomas Heywood

This authoritative contradiction in 1623 of the agreement
made a decade earlier when Robert Lee left this troupe is
puzzling. It may well have been that the rapidly declining
fortunes of Queen Anne's men after Beeston left them had
made it impossible to continue the old custom. It should be
remembered also that the action of which this testimony is a
part derived from Susan Baskervile's attempts to force the disintegrated Queen Anne's men to pay her money she claimed
they owed her as chief legatee of their former manager, Thomas
Greene, who had died eleven years before.

In any case it is apparent that this custom of buying out a
sharer's interests was a theater custom, like so many others,
which could be forgotten or ignored in times of adversity.

Not only did sharers need to have some capital to contribute, but their obligations to the troupe were not wholly discharged on the stage. Money had to be collected for the company's performances at court. The receipts for such payments
were always signed by certain sharers. In the earlier days different sharers seem to have performed this chore. In March
1594/95 the payment for the performance of two plays at court
in the previous Christmas season was made to three sharers
of the Lord Chamberlain's company, William Kempe, William Shakespeare, and Richard Burbage; in the following year
two other fellows of the company, John Heminges and George
Bryan, collected. In the subsequent years of Elizabeth's reign

the receipts were signed by Thomas Pope and John Heminges, but for more than thirty years thereafter Heminges, as
manager, was payee.

The collection of fees for royal performances was similar in
the other companies of sufficient distinction to be commanded
to perform at court: fees for the Queen's men were collected
by John Dutton, John Laneham, and Lawrence Dutton; for
the Earl of Nottingham's company by Robert Shaw and
Thomas Downton; for the Lord Admiral's company by Martin Slater and Edward Alleyn, mostly Alleyn.[19]

HALF SHARES

Various allusions in documents of the period establish the fact
that some of the sharers of a theatrical troupe owned only half
a share. No doubt the most familiar of such allusions is the
one in the third act of *Hamlet*. It will be remembered that
after the success of the play scene, Hamlet, in high excite-
ment about the success of the performance he has arranged,
cries to Horatio,

> Would not this, sir. . . .
> get me a fellowship in a cry of players, sir?

And Horatio replies soberly

> Half a share

and Hamlet

> A whole one I.

Philip Henslowe also refers in his Diary to the half shares
of certain players. On the first of June 1595 he loaned to his
improvident and frequently imprisoned nephew, Francis
Henslowe, ". . . In ready money to lay down for his half
share with the company which he doth play withal to be paid

[19] Chambers, *The Elizabethan Stage*, IV, 163-67. See Chapter VI below on
managers.

unto me when he doth receive his money which he lent to
my lord Burt or when my assigns doth demand it . . . £9."
The company cannot now be identified, but the transaction
is witnessed by "Wm Smyght player, gorge Attewell, player,
Robard Nycowlles player."

Two and one half years later Henslowe had an accounting
of money received on the half share of Humphry Jeffes, a
Lord Admiral's man for several years. Sir Walter Greg inter-
prets this transaction as an incompleted attempt on the part
of the company to buy back a half share from Jeffes, who is
known to have continued with the company for several years
after this. "A just account of the money which I have received
of Humphry Jeffes' half share beginning the 14 of January
1597 [98] as followeth."[20] There follows a list of seven payments of a few shillings each in the next three months. Then
Henslowe goes on, "This sum was paid back again unto the
company of my Lord Admiral's players the 8th of March 1598
and they shared it amongst them. I say paid back again the
sum of £3."[21] The reason for this attempt is by no means
clear, but it is obvious enough that Humphry Jeffes held a
half share.

In 1623 in their testimony in the suit of *Ellis Worth and John
Blaney v. Susan Baskervile and William Browne* both the experienced players, Richard Perkins and Thomas Heywood, refer
to the half share of Thomas Albanes in the company.[22]

There is even evidence that on occasion a full sharer was
reduced to half a share. In a letter of Richard Jones to Edward
Alleyn, probably of 1591/92, Jones writes that "I am to go
over beyond the seas with Mr. Browne and the company but
not by his means, for he is put to half a share, and to stay
here, for they are all against his going. . . ."[23] The wording
clearly suggests the company's disapproval of Browne but not

---

[20] W. W. Greg, ed., *Henslowe's Diary*, 2 vols., London, 1904-1908, II, 287.

[21] Foakes and Rickert, eds., *Henslowe's Diary*, pp. 9 and 71.

[22] See the more extended testimony of these witnesses quoted above, pp.
34-35.

[23] Greg, ed., *Henslowe Papers*, p. 33.

why. We can glean only the presumption that it was possible for a troupe to reduce a full sharer to a half sharer.

These scattered pieces of evidence are enough to show that the companies did make use of half sharers and that the public—at least theater audiences—were expected to be aware of the fact.

Why these men had only half shares one can only guess. Neither Francis Henslowe nor Humphry Jeffes much less John Thayer and Thomas Albanes were performers of any distinction, and Horatio's remark to Hamlet is evidently intended to be belittling. I would surmise that these half-share holders had paid only half the entrance fee subscribed by the whole-share holders; certainly the £9 which Philip Henslowe loaned his nephew is much less than any other sharer's fee known. I am aware of no evidence as to how their half-sharer status affected the function of these men in the councils of the company.

There seems to have been a growing tendency in the reigns of James and Charles for the companies to concentrate financial and managerial functions in the hands of one, two, or three sharers. In some troupes this concentration approached the managerial system of the Restoration companies. That development can be treated more conveniently in Chapter VI.

Selection of Plays

Another responsibility of the sharers had to do with additions to the repertory. Precisely what the procedure was in the judging of new manuscripts offered for production cannot yet be determined; probably it differed from troupe to troupe and from period to period. Certainly, in the 1590s when fewer actable old plays were available for revival, the players whose purchases were underwritten by Philip Henslowe had to buy more new manuscripts than did the King's men in the 1630s when they already owned all Shakespeare, nearly all Beaumont and Fletcher, and most of Massinger, Middleton, and Jonson.[24]

There is enough evidence to show that the sharers often had to assemble to listen to the reading of a new composition and to pass judgment on it. There are various references to this practice. On 3 December 1597 Henslowe recorded in his diary a payment of twenty shillings to Ben Jonson "upon a book which he showed the plot unto the company. . . ." After several payments to Drayton, Dekker, and Chettle for a play called *The Famous Wars of Henry I and the Prince of Wales*, Henslowe recorded on 13 March 1597/98 that he lent the company "for to spend at the reading of that book" at the Sun in New Fish street, five shillings. On 8 November 1599 Robert Shaw wrote to Henslowe that "we have heard their book and like it" and requested Henslowe to advance £8 to Wilson for it. In May 1602 Henslow recorded in his Diary what he had paid out for wine for the company "when they read the play of Jeffa."[25]

Several years later, in 1613, half a dozen letters from the playwright Robert Daborne refer to this play-reading custom. On 8 May Daborne wrote to Philip Henslowe that the play he was working on would be ready soon, so that when the company finished with "this new play they are now studying" Henslowe would please to "appoint any hour to read to Mr. Allin." Again on the 16th he wrote that he would read some of the new play to Henslowe and Alleyn, "for I am unwilling to read to the general company till all be finished." About a month later he wrote that the company would not have to delay for him because that same week he would deliver in the last word . . . "& will that night they play their new play read this. . . ." In December 1613, Daborne, still wanting money, wrote that the new play he was working on would make "as good a play for your public house as ever was played"

[24] See Bentley, *The Jacobean and Caroline Stage*, I, 108-134.
[25] Foakes and Rickert, eds., *Henslowe's Diary*, pp. 85, 88, 201; Greg, ed., *Henslowe Papers*, p. 49.

and that "upon the reading it" the company would have Henslowe pay out for them £20 rather than lose such a fine play. To a letter of 31 December 1613 Daborne adds a postscript "on Monday I will come to you & appoint for the reading the old book & bringing in the new."[26]

One cannot be certain, of course, that this custom of reading a new manuscript to all sharers was universal, but evidently it was common. The chore must have consumed a deal of the time of sharers, especially in the early days when so many more new plays were required than later.

What happened when the sharers listened to the plays must be mostly a matter for conjecture. Surely not every play offered could have had a complete reading before all the patented members; they would have had time for little else. Presumably someone had done a preliminary reading, but who? I have found no answer to this question. There are a few records of the rejection of play manuscripts by the players, but they do not tell us much.[27]

And what happened with play manuscripts submitted by the regular attached dramatists for their companies, like the plays Thomas Heywood wrote for Queen Anne's company or James Shirley for Queen Henrietta's or William Rowley for the Prince's men or Richard Brome for the Salisbury Court players or Shakespeare, Fletcher, Philip Massinger, and James Shirley during their different periods of attachment to the Lord Chamberlain-King's company?[28] Since these playwrights were so intimately associated with the companies of players for which they were writing, the sharers may well have known in advance what was being composed and could even have been consulted about particular scenes or characters or stagings while the new manuscript was in process of composition. For such attached dramatists the usual reading be-

---

[26] Greg, ed., *Henslowe Papers*, pp. 69-81.

[27] See G. E. Bentley, *The Profession of Dramatist in Shakespeare's Time*, Princeton, 1971, "Rejections," pp. 79-82.

[28] Ibid., *passim*, esp. pp. 30-37.

fore the sharers may have been omitted. Or perhaps it became something more in the nature of a meeting of the ways and means committee than of an assessment committee.

Yet in at least one instance a play written by an attached dramatist for the company to which he was contracted was rejected by the sharers. Richard Brome had signed a contract in 1635, renewed in 1638, with the sharers of Queen Henrietta's company and the owners of the Salisbury Court theater to write plays exclusively for them. Troubles developed, and the ten sharers in Queen Henrietta's company and the owners of the Salisbury Court brought suit in the Court of Requests against Brome. In the usual fashion of lawsuits, the two parties make numerous charges against each other. In his answer Richard Brome says:

> . . . before Easter term 1639 this defendant brought them another new play written all but part of the last scene. But this defendant found that divers of the company did so slight the last-mentioned plays and used such scornful and re- proachful speeches concerning this defendant and divers of them did advise the rest of them to stop all weekly pay- ments towards this defendant. . . .[29]

One could wish for more evidence of the deliberations of the sharers before they accepted a proffered manuscript and turned it over to the prompter for annotation and the prepa- ration of sides. And who was in charge of the casting? I can- not answer this question with confidence. Presumably casting was discussed with attached dramatists while their plays were being composed, but many plays written by free-lance dram- atists were performed. Surely such dramatists as Henry Shir- ley, Robert Davenport, Lodowick Carlell, Arthur Wilson, William Berkeley, or Jasper Mayne, who had a play or two produced by the King's men, were not consulted about the casting. One can only speculate that such casting may have

[29] See Ann Haaker, "The Plague, the Theatre, and the Poet," *Renaissance Drama*, n.s. 1 (1968), 304.

been done by the manager or leader of the company in consultation with the sharers.[30]

RECRUITMENTS AND DISMISSALS

The sharers of the company must also have had much of the responsibility for recruitment to their ranks and for the dismissal of unsatisfactory members. The number of sharers in a troupe seems to have remained more or less constant at ten or twelve,[31] and commonly a new sharer was acquired only when an old one died, retired, or gave up his fellowship for one in another troupe. But there were exceptions. Will Kempe, who was the most famous comedian of his day and the subject of numerous allusions,[32] left the company apparently in 1599, about the time of his spectacular dance from London to Norwich, one of the most notorious feats of the period. The popular Kempe ceased to be a member of the Lord Chamberlain's company and at that time sold his shares in the new Globe theater, then abuilding, to Shakespeare, Heminges, and Augustine Phillips.[33] There is no evidence that he ever returned to the Lord Chamberlain's company; he seems to have spent some months doing other dancing feats. He was succeeded as principal comedian by Robert Armin, and not long after had become a member of the Earl of Worcester's company, a troupe clearly inferior to the Lord Chamberlain's.

It is odd for an actor as famous as Kempe to leave the lead-

[30] See below, Chapter VI, "Managers."

[31] See T. W. Baldwin, *The Organization and Personnel of the Shakespearean Company*, Princeton, 1927, pp. 46-89. Actually the number of sharers even for the King's company was not quite so rigorously maintained as Baldwin contends, but in general his arguments for a fairly constant group are well taken.

[32] See Edwin Nungezer, *A Dictionary of Actors and of Other Persons Associated with the Public Representation of Plays in England before 1642*, New Haven, 1929, pp. 216-22.

[33] See the suit of *John Witter v. John Heminges and Henry Condell* in the Court of Requests, C. W. Wallace, "Shakespeare and His London Associates," *University of Nebraska Studies* 10 (1910), 54.

ing company of the time; and, so far as we know, it is unparalleled for an actor to go off on solo feats of his own like the dance to Norwich and the alleged dance over the Alps into Italy. Was he dropped because of his long absence? Were the dancing spectacles motivated by a break with the company?

There is no reliable evidence, but the departure of Kempe, one of the principal attractions at the Globe, surely presented a problem to the sharers. The selection of Robert Armin as their new comedian and sharer was obviously a matter of great concern and must have required protracted discussions among the patented members.

A more fully documented disciplinary action by a group of sharers is that of Prince Charles's (II) company against William Bankes. Again the affair is known through a suit in the Court of Requests, *William Bankes v. Andrew Keyne and Ellis Worth* in 1635. Both parties agree that Bankes became a sharer by paying into the "stock of the company" £100. But Bankes complains that he has been assessed for the purchase of costumes, though he asserts that he had been promised exemption from such levies; that he has not been paid his dividends; that he has not been made a Groom of the Chamber as the other sharers were and as he was promised. He claims that all his dealings were with Worth and Keyne hence he makes them defendants in his suit.

A very different story is told in the Answer of Worth and Keyne, which, on analysis, is much more in accord with facts and customary practices.[34] The defendants say that Bankes had introduced himself

> unto these defendants and to the rest of the company of the Prince's players of the private playhouse in Salisbury Court in the bill mentioned (they being in all eleven in number) that he the complainant might enter into the said company the complainant paying into the stock of the said company

[34] See Bentley, "The Troubles of a Caroline Acting Troupe" for both the quotations from the documents of the suit and a discussion of the accuracy of the statements of the two parties.

the sum of one hundred pounds, whereunto these defendants and the rest of the said company assented. And thereupon the complainant did agree to pay to the said company one hundred pounds and to become an actor with the defendants in the said exercise of stage playing and to bear his ratable and proportionable part of the charges of apparel and other necessary charges incident thereunto from time to time and to be conformable to the orders of the said company. And thereupon and not otherwise the said whole company of players of that house (and not the said defendants alone) did agree to and with the complainant that he should have and enjoy his proportionable part and share of such profit and benefit as should accrue and arise unto the said company and that they would employ themselves as actors in the said company.

This answer of Worth and Keyne indicates what from other sources would appear to have been the normal practice, though not elsewhere so explicitly stated. And consideration of Bankes and his money by the eleven sharers of Prince Charles's company was one of the normal extrahistrionic activities of the patented members of a troupe.

But the problems of the sharers with Bankes went far beyond this initial consideration. Further along in their Answer Worth and Keyne deny some of his complaints and explain others. They say that some three weeks before Bankes's complaint he had departed from the company:

And since his departure his share is set apart for him and he may have it if he will rejoin himself to the said company according to the said agreement. But these defendants say that the complainant hath not been conformable to the orders of the said company but hath broken the same orders by his disorderly behavior to the very great prejudice of the said company whereof these defendants doubt not but that they shall be able to make due proof to this honorable court.
. . .

Worth and Keyne say further that if Bankes will come back and behave himself they are ready and willing

> to go with the complainant to speak for him that he might be sworn his Majesty's servant in ordinary, the complainant being at the charge thereof and paying such fees and duties as were to be paid for the same which these defendants have been and are ready to do so as he [Bankes] rejoin himself again to these [sic] company and be conformable thereto.
> . . .

Bankes did come back, as is proved by the fact that ten months later he and three others were sworn Grooms of the Chamber "to attend the Prince his highness in the quality of player."

This suit in the Court of Requests tells us nothing of what Bankes's offenses had been, but serious they evidently were, and protracted discussions among the sharers must have been required.[35]

The company of Prince Charles was greatly inferior to the King's men at the Blackfriars and the Globe and to Queen Henrietta's troupe at the Phoenix. Those troupes would never, so far as we can tell, have made a full sharer of a man like William Bankes. But the responsibilities of the sharers were similar.

[35] The dismissal of a sharer was evidently not too unusual, since it had been explicitly provided for in the contract, probably of 1613, between Henslowe and Meade on the one hand and Nathan Field representing the company (Lady Elizabeth's?) on the other.

. . . And further that the said Philip Henslowe and Jacob Meade shall and will at all times upon request made by the major part of the sharers of the said company under their hands remove and put out of the said company any of the said company of players if the said Philip Henslowe and Jacob Meade shall find the said request to be just and that there be no hope of conformity in the party complained of. . . . (Greg, ed., *Henslowe Papers*, p. 24)

The fact that the sharers were to take the initiative suggests to me that difficulties with a nonconforming sharer had prompted expulsions in London companies before. This clause is evidently not another example of Henslowe's attempts at dominance.

45

Finally, there is one method of recruitment of which I know only a single example, but which should be noticed. On the 6th of May 1633, the Lord Chamberlain addressed a warrant to John Lowin and Joseph Taylor, who had been the leaders or managers of the King's company since the death of John Heminges:

> Whereas the late decease, infirmity, and sickness of divers principal actors of His Majesty's company of players hath much decayed and weakened them, so that they are disabled to do His Majesty's service in their quality, unless there be some speedy order taken to supply and furnish them with a convenient number of new actors. His Majesty having taken notice thereof and signified his royal pleasure unto me therein, these are to will and require you and in His Majesty's name straightly to charge, command, and authorize you and either of you to choose receive and take into your company any such actor or actors belonging to any of the licensed companies within and about the city of London as you shall think fit and able to do his Majesty service in that kind. Herein you may not fail. And this shall be your sufficient warrant and discharge in that behalf. Court at Whitehall the 6th of May 1633. To John Lowen and Joseph Taylor, two of the company of his Majesty's players.[36]

The drafting of players was not wholly without precedent, but the earlier example is outside the scope of this work and rather different in character. It is best recounted by Edmund Howes in his continuation of Stowe's *Annales*.

> Comedians and stage-players of former time were very poor and ignorant in respect of these of this time; but being now grown very skillful and exquisite actors for all matters, they were entertained into the service of divers great lords; out of which companies there were twelve of the best chosen,

[36] "Dramatic Records: The Lord Chamberlain's Office," *Malone Society Collections* 2, pt. 3 (1931), 361.

and, at the request of Sir Francis Walsingham they were sworn the Queen's servants and were allowed wages and liveries as grooms of the chamber. And until this year 1583 the Queen had no players.[37]

The unique order of 6 May 1633 to the leaders of the King's company to draft any London player or players they thought they needed is another example of the dominance of the royal troupe in London theatrical affairs. Probably any player in London would have been happy to be so drafted, for increased income and prestige would normally follow. What was the attitude of the managers of the other London companies whose players were so drafted is another matter.[38]

DUTIES OF SHARERS

What were the regular duties and responsibilities of sharers? So far as I know there is only one extant document that outlines them in detail. This agreement is far from a normal one, but though it stipulates excessive fines, and is an attempt to establish a dictatorship (which soon failed) the duties and responsibilities enumerated can, I think, be taken as normal.

In August 1613 Philip Henslowe joined with Jacob Meade in a builder's contract to transform the Bear Garden into a dual purpose house, namely the Hope theater, for the exhibition of both bear-baiting and playacting. The enterprise did not last long: the first company deserted in about a year, and Henslowe died in two or three years.[39]

As a part of this project an agreement was drawn up with one of the players, Robert Dawes. Presumably there were agreements with other players of the company as well, but no trace of them has been found. The articles between Henslowe

---

[37] Stowe, *Annales*, 1615, p. 697, as quoted in Chambers, *The Elizabethan Stage*, II, 104-105.

[38] See below, Chapter VI, on managers.

[39] See Chambers, *The Elizabethan Stage*, II, 448-71; and Bentley, *The Jacobean and Caroline Stage*, VI, 200-214.

and Meade on the one hand and the player Robert Dawes on the other were clearly designed to establish Henslowe as a theatrical dictator rather in the fashion of the attempt of Richard Heton twenty-five years later. Henslowe failed, and the agreement can scarcely have been wholly typical of most companies. Nevertheless the duties and responsibilities enumerated appear to be those expected of a sharer in a normal London troupe.

The document, now lost, was formerly among Henslowe's papers; it is dated 7 April 1614.[40] I have excerpted these papers, I hope judiciously, because of the number of provisions that apply to the payment of rents or special obligations to Henslowe and Meade and not to the duties and responsibilities that may be taken to be more typical of most sharers.

[Articles of Agreement,] made concluded and agreed upon and which are to be kept and performed by Robert Dawes of London Gent. unto and with Phillip Henslowe Esquire and Jacob [Meade Waterman] in manner and form following, that is to say

Imprimis. The said Robert Dawes for him his executors and administrators doth covenant promise and grant to and with the said Phillip Henslowe and Jacob Meade their executors administrators and assigns in manner and form following, that is to say that he the said Robert Dawes shall and will play with such company as the said Phillip Henslowe and Jacob Meade shall appoint for and during the time and space of three years from the date hereof for and at the rate of one whole share according to the custom of players; and that he the said Robert Dawes shall and will at all times during the said term duly attend all such rehearsal which shall the night before the rehearsal be given publicly out; and if that he the said Robert Dawes shall at any time fail to come at the hour appointed, then he shall and will pay to the said Phillip Henslowe and Jacob Meade their executors or assigns twelve pence; and if he come not

[40] Greg, ed., *Henslowe Papers*, pp. 123-25.

before the said rehearsal is ended then the said Robert Dawes
is contented to pay two shillings; and further that if the
said Robert Dawes shall not every day whereon any play
is or ought to be played be ready apparelled and—to begin
the play at the hour of three of the clock in the afternoon
unless by six of the same company he shall be licensed to
the contrary, that then he the said Robert Dawes shall and
will pay unto the said Phillip and Jacob or their assigns
three [shillings] and if that he the said Robert Dawes happen to be overcome with drink at the time when he [ought
to] play, by the judgment of four of the said company, he
shall and will pay ten shillings, and if he [the said Robert
Dawes] shall [fail to come] during any play having no license or just excuse of sickness he is contended to pay twenty
shillings. . . . and likewise shall and may take and receive
his other moity . . . the moneys received at the galleries
and tiring house due toward the paying to them the said
Phillip Henslowe and Jacob Meade of the sum of one
hundred twenty and four pounds [being the value of the
stock of apparel furnished by the said company by the said
Phillip Henslowe and Jacob Meade] . . . the one part of
him the said Dawes or any other sums . . . to them for any
apparel hereafter newly to be bought by the [said Phillip
Henslowe and Jacob Meade until the said Phillip Henslowe
and Jacob Meade] shall thereby be fully satisfied contented
and paid. And further the said Robert Dawes doth covenant [promise and grant to and with the said Phillip Henslowe and Jacob Meade that if he the said Robert Dawes]
shall at any time after the play is ended depart or go out of
the [house] with any [of their] apparel on his body, or if the
said Robert Dawes [shall carry away any property] belonging to the said company, or shall be consenting [or privy to
any other of the said company going out of the house with
any of their apparel on his or their bodies he the said] Robert Dawes shall and will forfeit and pay unto the said Phillip and Jacob or their administrators or assigns the sum of
forty pounds of lawful [money of England]. . . .

49

. . . [In testimony] for every such whereof I the said Robert Dawes have hereunto set my hand and seal this [sev]enth day of April 1614 in the twelfth year [of the reign of our sovereign lord &c.]   Robert Dawes

Since this detailed agreement is the only one of its kind that has been preserved, it is not easy to distinguish those provisions which may be taken as typical from those which are peculiar to Henslowe and Meade and their attempt to establish an autocracy at the Hope. Dawes's agreement to attach himself permanently to the Hope and its owners no matter what troupe occupied the theater was not, so far as one can tell, usual at the Globe, the Blackfriars, the Red Bull, the Phoenix, or the Fortune. The sharer's allegiance was ordinarily to his company and not to the theater or its owner. It is true that in 1624 Richard Gunnell persuaded six sharers of the Palsgrave's company to sign a bond to continue to play together at the Fortune, but this was an attempt to preserve a faltering troupe, not to tie individuals to a theatrical entrepreneur.[41]

The provision about attendance and punctuality at rehearsals I take to be common, though fines for violations in most companies would be paid not to the owner of the theater but to the company treasury.[42] Similarly I take the fines for absence, tardiness, or drunkenness at performances to be common, though again the money would ordinarily go not to the theater owner but to the company.

The responsibility of Dawes as a sharer for the company debt for supplies and for further purchases of costumes and properties is a common obligation,[43] but except for those companies financed by Philip Henslowe or Edward Alleyn the payment of the sharer for his interest in past purchases and

[41] See Bentley, *The Jacobean and Caroline Stage*, 1, 148-49.

[42] The passage in *Histriomastix* (Act IV 1610 quatro), in which Posthaste is fined one shilling for coming late to rehearsal indicates that the custom was familiar. The two cases are not, however, precisely parallel since Posthaste is the poet and not an actor.

[43] See above, pp. 29-32.

for new ones as they were made seems to have been due to the company and not to the theater owner.

The problem of actors making off with costumes or sometimes with play scripts is alluded to in other contexts. Perhaps the most revealing is in the agreement between Martin Slater and his company recited in a Chancery Bill of Complaint of 9 February 1608/09.

> It is . . . agreed that all such apparel as is abroad shall be brought in . . . it is further . . . agreed . . . that if at any time hereafter any apparel, books, or any other goods or commodities shall be conveyed or taken away by any of the said parties without the consent and allowance of the said residue of his fellow sharers and the same exceeding the value of two shillings, that then he or they so offending shall forfeit and lose all . . . benefits . . . besides the loss of their places and all other interests which they may claim amongst us. . . .[44]

Although these duties, obligations, and punishments specified for Robert Dawes cannot be demonstrated to be the same as those of all sharers in all companies of the time, it seems to me likely that other established troupes had similar understandings. The irregularities listed are those which would be troublesome in other Jacobean and Caroline companies, and most of them are referred to in Henslowe's and Alleyn's papers and in various suits of the time, though not elsewhere grouped together and specifying penalties.

Sharers' Incomes

As we have seen, the sharers in Elizabethan, Jacobean, and Caroline dramatic companies were not paid wages as the hired

---

[44] *Transactions of the New Shakespeare Society*, Vol. 1887-92, pt. 3, p. 276. In May 1598 Henslowe had bought from this same Martin Slater five plays for the Admiral's men. All five had formerly belonged to the company. Had Slater made off with them when he left the company about a year before? (Foakes and Rickert, eds., *Henslowe's Diary*, pp. 89 and 93.)

men were; they were directors of the organization, and their recompense was a share in the profits.

There is plenty of evidence that the sharers did receive a portion of the take at each performance, but until the reign of Charles I almost no direct and reliable evidence of how much money this might be. Henslowe's Diary shows clearly enough in various entries that sharers were paid from the receipts but not how much per sharer. In a few instances sharers assigned to Henslowe the income from their shares, but only occasionally does the entry record what the sum was or, if a sum is set down, what proportion of the share it constituted. Probably most specific is the record of 1 April 1598, "Received of Gabriel Spencer at several times of his share in the galleries as followeth beginning the 6 of April 1598." There follow the records of five payments, but they were made at irregular intervals of from eight to forty-three days apart and there is no indication as to whether the sums—from four to seven shillings—were Spencer's total share for that day or only the sum he chose to pay to Henslowe.

Well known is Henslowe's entry about the player and poet Ben Jonson.[45]

> Received of Benjamin Jonson's share as
> followeth   1597
>
> Received the 28 of July 1597 . . . 3s 9d

The entry is, however, ambiguous, since "share" could mean either a share in the receipts of the company or a share in the payment for a play or for the revisions in a play. Though there is evidence elsewhere in the Diary that Jonson was a player, there is none that he was ever a sharer.

It would be interesting and useful to know how much a share might be expected to produce in the course of a year. Until the last decade of the period, however, the evidence is too scattered, too contradictory, and too inferential to allow any sound generalizations for all companies. Such slippery

---

[45] Foakes and Rickert, eds., *Henslowe's Diary*, pp. 67-68 and 52.

evidence is used in Appendix II, "Finance in the Shakespearean Company," of T. W. Baldwin's *The Organization and Personnel of the Shakespearean Company* but even for this best-known
troupe of London players the conclusions seem to me to be
totally unreliable.

The variations in the compensation reaching sharers during
the period 1590-1642 must have been great. First, there are
the variations according to date. The cash rewards available
to a major player in 1591 would fall far short of those available
to sharers in almost any London troupe in 1639 when all had
royal patents and inflation had soared. Again there are large
discrepancies between the receipts of a minor troupe like Prince
Charles's (II) men and those of a major company like the players of King Charles. This discrepancy between the incomes
of fellows of minor and major organizations is due not only
to the comparative receipts of playhouses like the Blackfriars
and the Globe on the one hand and the lowly Red Bull on
the other, but also to the fact that extratheatrical fees such as
those for court performances, guilds, and Inns of Court performances, and individual rewards for participation in guild
and royal pageantry are paid in nearly all recorded examples
to players in the major troupes like the King's men and the
Queen's men. Finally the theater receipts, upon which the
dividends of the sharers depended, fluctuated wildly from
season to season. In plague years of 1593, 1594, 1603, 1604,
1625, 1630, 1631, 1636-37, and 1640 there were no London
gate receipts for significant periods. In 1625 the plague was
so severe and the closing so protracted that all London companies except the King's went bankrupt. The plague of 1636-
37 was less severe but more protracted, and again all London
theaters were closed for months on end.[46] Such fluctuations
compound the difficulties raised by the paucity of evidence of
direct payments.

The most reliable figures on a sharer's annual income derive

[46] See Bentley, *The Jacobean and Caroline Stage*, II, 652-72; and F. P. Wilson,
The Plague in Shakespeare's London, Oxford, 1927.

from a series of petitions to the Lord Chamberlain.[47] These petitions ("The Sharers' Papers") primarily concern the holdings of actors and others in two playhouses, the Blackfriars and the Globe; the figures about acting shares are mentioned only incidentally, but they come from reliable sources. As may be remembered, three leading sharers in the King's company were trying to persuade the Lord Chamberlain to force John Shank, Cuthbert Burbage, Winifred Burbage, and young William Burbage to sell them part of their housekeepers' shares in the Blackfriars and Globe theaters. The three complaining sharers, Robert Benfield, Eyllaerdt Swanston, and Thomas Pollard, assert that

> . . . upon a medium made of the gains of the housekeepers and those of the actors one day with another throughout the year, the petitioners will make it apparent that when some of the housekeepers share the 12 shillings a day at the Globe the actors share not above 3 shillings. And then what those gain that are both actors and housekeepers and have their shares in both your Lordship will easily judge. . . .

To these assertions John Shank, the veteran comedian and longtime sharer in the comapny, replies:

> That whereas the petitioners in their complaint say that they have not means to subsist, it shall by oath (if need be) be made apparent that every one of the three petitioners for his own particular hath gotten and received this year last past of the sum of £180 which, as your suppliant conceiveth is a very sufficient means to satisfy and answer their long and patient expectation, and is more by above the one half than any of them ever got or were capable of elsewhere. . . .

This surprisingly large sum is verified and made slightly more explicit by the three Burbages in their own reply to the Lord Chamberlain, supplementary to John Shank's:

[47] "Dramatic Records: The Lord Chamberlain's Office," pp. 362-73.

Then to show your Honor against these sayings that we eat the fruits of their labors, we refer it to your Honor's judgment to consider their profits, which we may safely maintain, for it appeareth by their own accounts for one whole year last past beginning from Whitsun-Monday 1634 to Whitsun-Monday 1635 each of these complainants gained severally as he was a player and no housekeeper £180. Besides Mr. Swanston hath received from the Blackfriars this year as he is there a housekeeper above £30, all which being accounted together may very well keep him from starving.

This large sum of £180 which "might very well keep them from starving" includes, of course, sizable amounts that were each sharers' portion of the "rewards" paid the company for court performances.[48] One hundred eighty pounds is truly a surprising amount for a player to receive; it must be remembered, however, that no other troupe handled anything like the large receipts that came to the King's men.

No comparatively precise and authoritative figures are available for other companies or other times, but one of almost the same date as the reports of John Shanks and the Burbages shows how different the situation was in one of their rival troupes, Prince Charles's (II) men. In the Court of Requests suit of *Bankes v. Worth and Keyne*, Ellis Worth and Andrew Keyne, managers of the company, reply on 18 February 1634/35 to the complaint of William Bankes that he had not received returns that were his right as a sharer.

that the complainant hath been and is allowed such particular share and benefit of the gain and profit gotten at the said playhouse called the Red Bull as was or is due unto him by the agreement made between the company and the complainant in that behalf. And the complainant or his wife did usually attend the sharing of the gains of the said playhouse from time to time at the end of every play and did receive all such moneys as were due the complainant for his

[48] See Bentley, *The Jacobean and Caroline Stage*, I, 97-98.

share together with an allowance of six pence by the day for every day they acted over and above the complainant's share, which did amount to twenty nobles [six shillings and eight pence, or one-third of a pound] per annum or thereabouts . . . these defendants do believe that the complainant or his wife for his use hath received for the complainant's share of the said stage playing about the sum of one hundred pounds with the said six pence per day and five pounds for progress money.

By analyzing this statement and noting that the sum covers a period of two years, it can be deduced that Bankes's income as a sharer was approximately £40 per year. Of course it was to the advantage of Worth and Keyne to exaggerate the payment of the company to the complainant, but even so it is clear that the sharers in Prince Charles's company received far less than the patented members of the King's company at about the same date.[49] It must be remembered that these figures come from late dates when the profitable court performances were far more numerous than in the days of Elizabeth, and when inflation had greatly diminished the value of the Elizabethan pound sterling.

Then there were various additional payments for special occasions for the better companies and for certain individuals—payments at noble houses, at the Inns of Court, or at guild halls. Probably lucrative were performances at great houses, but very few records have been unearthed. The only extensive account so far in print is the one Lawrence Stone made from the papers of the Earl of Cumberland and Lord Clifford.[50] But these records really apply to companies on tour; the houses concerned are so far from the capital that they could not have been visited by a regular London company unless it were touring. Nevertheless, the frequency of the vis-

[49] For the suit and for an analysis of the figures, see Bentley, "The Troubles of a Caroline Acting Troupe," esp. pp. 241-42.

[50] *Malone Society Collections* 5 (1960), 17-28. Also see below, Chapter VII, "London Companies on Tour."

its recorded and the sums paid to the players are suggestive of what London companies might have received for performances at noble palaces in or near town.

These figures on the income of sharers are most unsatisfying, except for Prince Charles's (II) men and for the King's players toward the end of the period, when we can be sure that prices and payments were much greater than in the 1590s. During the reigns of Elizabeth and James the evidence is too spotty and too uncertain for me to hazard estimates of the usual incomes of sharers in the London companies.

OCCASIONS FOR PAYMENT OF SHARERS

There are several references to the occasions when sharers were paid their dividends, and they seem to indicate roughly the same methods in different London companies and at different times. To us the method seems oddly primitive and direct. At the end of each regular performance (except for court and private performances, when payment was often long deferred) there seems to have been a simple dividing up of the cash.

This nightly division of receipts seems to be required in the mutilated contract (presumably of 1613) between Nathan Field for the Lady Elizabeth's company and Jacob Meade and Philip Henslowe. ". . . And they the said Philip Henslowe and Jacob Meade . . . grant and agree that there shall be due account given every night to any one that shall by the company be appointed thereunto. . . ."[51]

Of course the receipts from the parts of the house reserved for housekeepers were deducted and the wages for the hired men would, one would assume, also have been set aside. But the cash from the players' parts of the theater seem to have been literally parcelled out on a board or a table.

This custom of payment at the end of every performance was evidently in vogue by Prince Charles's (II) company in

[51] Greg, ed., *Henslowe Papers*, p. 24.

1635; it is explicitly referred to by Worth and Keyne in their Answer in the suit of Bankes referred to before. These defendants reply to the complaint of Bankes that he had received no money: "And the complainant or his wife did usually attend the sharing of the gains of the said playhouse from time to time at the end of every play and did receive all such moneys as were due the complainant for his share. . . ."[52]

The same systems of dividend payments is indicated in the epilogue for Richard Brome's play, *The English Moor, or the Mock Marriage*, performed by Queen Henrietta's company in 1637, though not published until 1659 in the collection *Five New Plays*. The epilogue, speaking of the dodges to which this author (Brome) refuses to resort, says:

> Now let me be a modest undertaker
> For us the players, the play, and the play-maker
> ....
> And all that in defense the Poet can say
> Is that he cannot mend it by a jest
> I'th epilogue exceeding all the rest
> To send you off upon a champing bit,
> More than the scenes afforded of his wit.
> Nor studies he the art to have it said
> He skulks behind the hangings as afraid
> Of a hard censure, or pretend to brag
> Here's all your money again brought in i'th bag
> If you applaud not, when before the word
> 'Twas parcel'd out upon the sharing-board.

This primitive method of handling dividends of sharers seems rather crude for well-organized companies like Queen Henrietta's and for the King's men; one would suppose that Beeston and Heminges could have improved upon it. But I have been able to find references to no other method of paying the sharers their regular dividends.

[52] Bentley, "The Troubles of a Caroline Acting Troupe," p. 241.

SHARERS' EXTRAS

In addition to the payments to the sharers for their regular performances as a full troupe, there are records of payments to individual sharers for participation in the festivities of the London livery companies.

The records of the City guilds have been combed by Jean Robertson and D. J. Gordon in their "A Calendar of Dramatic Records in the Books of the Livery Companies of London, 1485-1640;"[53] but though the feasts and pageants of the guilds often used players, the accounts seldom give names as well as amounts paid.

In 1611 John Lowin, who became a prominent sharer in the King's company, had a large role in the Lord Mayor's pageant, and according to the Goldsmiths' records agreed that "himself should provide a horse and furniture for himself and the horse, and for his paines therein is referred to the consideration of Master Wardens."[54] Lowin was a little different from the others in that he had served an apprenticeship under a goldsmith, but in 1611 he was a King's man. How much the "Master Wardens" decided to pay Lowin for himself, his horse, and its furniture is not recorded.

In the following year the new Lord Mayor was Sir Thomas Swinnerton, Merchant Tailor. In the pageant which his company prepared in his honor, John Lowin's fellow, John Heminges, had an even larger part. The company accounts carry the entry:

> Item paid to Master Heminges and Master Thomas Dekker, the Poet, for the device of the land shows, being a sea chariot drawn by the sea horses, one pageant called Neptune's throne, with seven liberal sciences, one castle called Envy's Castle, one other pageant called Virtue's Throne, and for the printing of the books of the speeches, and for

[53] *Malone Society Collections* 3 (1954).
[54] Ibid., p. 81.

the persons and apparel of those that went in them, the sum of . . . £197.0.0[55]

Unfortunately this sum is not itemized, but the opening statement sounds as if Heminges had a principal part in the composition. When the pageant, *Troia-Nova Triumphans*, was printed in 1612, however, only Dekker's name appeared on the title page. Heminges had been employed by the Merchant Tailors several years before in training his apprentice John Rice to deliver a speech at the Merchant Tailors' dinner for royalty.

Much later, in 1639, William Hall of the King's Revels company was paid by the Drapers' Guild for his part in preparing their pageant *Londini Status Pacatus*. The entry reads:

Item paid to William Hall the player for his music and actions in Cheapside the sum of . . . £13.6.8[56]

The very scattering of these records suggests that there may have been other examples of players being paid for their parts in traditional shows. But the only generalization one can make is that it seems likely that various sharers in the major companies made a little money on the side by helping in the pageantry for Lord Mayor's shows and other City occasions.

For the leading companies there were occasional grants of assistance in times of distress, such as those given the King's men near the end of the severe plague of 1603 and again during the plague of 1636-37. In the Revels accounts at the beginning of the reign of James I is the entry:

To Richard Burbage one of his Majesty's comedians upon the Council's warrant dated at Hampton Court 8 February 1603 [/04] for the maintenance and relief of himself and the rest of his company being prohibited to present any plays publicly in or near London by reason of great peril that might grow through the extraordinary concourse and as-

[55] Ibid., p. 85.
[56] Ibid., p. 130.

sembly of people to a new increase of the plague till it shall please God to settle the city in a more perfect health: by way of his Majesty's free gift . . . £30.[57]

In the later protracted plague of 1636-37 King Charles was even more generous. During that plague a warrant was issued on 13 December 1636:

> . . . the King having commanded his servants the players to assemble their company and keep themselves together near the Court, gives them an allowance of £20 per week, which is to be paid to John Lowen and Joseph Taylor, on behalf of their company; such allowance to commence from the 1st November last, to continue during his Majesty's pleasure, and to be taken as of his princely bounty.[58]

Individual members of the King's company also achieved special recognition to which some monetary reward must have been attached. In 1632 Queen Henrietta decided that she and several of her ladies would give a performance of Walter Montague's *The Shepherd's Paradise*. There was much talk about the enterprise both before and after the performance. On 15 September 1632 John Pory wrote to Viscount Scudamore:

> The Queen's Majesty with some of her ladies, and maids of honor is daily practicing upon a Pastoral penned by Mr. Walter Montague. And Taylor the prime actor at the Globe goes every day to teach them action.

Six weeks later the same correspondent wrote Scudamore: ". . . Mr. Taylor, the player, hath also the making of a knight given him for teaching them how to act the Pastoral."[59]

So far as I know this use of a professional player as a coach

[57] Peter Cunningham, *Extracts from the Accounts of the Revels at Court in the Reigns of Queen Elizabeth and King James I, from the Original Office Books of the Masters and Yeomen*, Shakespeare Society, vol. 7, London, 1842, p. xxxv.

[58] *Calendar of State Papers, Domestic*, London, 1636-37, p. 228.

[59] Quoted from the Scudamore Papers by J. P. Feils, *Shakespeare Survey* 11 (1958), 109-110.

for amateur performances at court is unique. Considering the social status of Queen Henrietta and the ladies of her court versus that of a professional player, as well as the jealousies usual among court ladies, one marvels at the tact which must have been required of Taylor. His selection for the post is no surprise, for at the time he was probably the most distinguished player in London as well as a manager of the premier company. He must have been rewarded liberally for his services.

Taylor received other court rewards, but too much later to seem related to his coaching activities. In the Lord Chamberlain's Warrant Books under date of 29 September 1639 occurs the entry: "A warrant to swear Mr. Joseph Taylor, yeoman of the Revels to His Majesty in the place of William Hunt, deceased." And six weeks later Taylor's patent confirming him in his new office was copied into the Warrant Books. It is too long and verbose to quote in full, but it provides that Taylor is to have the office for life; he is to receive a fee of six pence a day; he is to receive yearly a royal livery coat "such as the yeoman officers of our household have of us"; and he is "to have and enjoy one sufficient house or mansion as shall hereafter be assigned to the said Joseph Taylor for the sure better and safe keeping of our said vestures, apparels, and Trappers together with all manner of other commodities and advantages to the said offices to be due and accustomed. . . ."[60] In spite of his new position Taylor appears to have remained active in the King's company, receiving payments for court performances with Lowin and Swanston on several occasions.

John Lowin, another prominent sharer of the company and later a co-manager with Taylor, also received an honor and no doubt profits from a court appointment. In the notes by one of the Masters of Requests, Sir John Coke, prepared for his first audience with Charles I on 12 May 1625, occurs the following: "King James's servants . . . John Lowen, porter,

[60] "Dramatic Records: The Lord Chamberlain's Office," pp. 391 and 343-46.

who bought his place, being a player, for £200, to be continued in it. . . . His Majesty's comedians to be sworn again in ordinary. . . ."[61]

All these extra fees might suggest at first glance that one way and another the players had a fairly lucrative profession, but such a conclusion would be very far from the truth. It should be noted that only five players are named, John Lowin, Joseph Taylor, John Heminges, John Rice, and William Hall. There were hundreds of other stage people in London in these years, none of whom is known to have received any of these perquisites. It should be further noted that all but one of these players, William Hall, belonged to the Lord Chamberlain-King's company. Even the odd, wholly undramatic, payment of William Shakespeare and Richard Burbage for painting the shield and devising the motto of the Earl of Rutland for the anniversary of the accession of James I, though it seems to have no theatrical connection at all, involved two more fellows of the King's company.[62] Again the records testify to the overwhelming dominance of the King's company and the fallacy of taking anything that happened to its members as typical of the lives of London players.

[61] *Review of English Studies* 1 (1925), 184. From *Historical Manuscripts Commission*, Cowper MSS., p. 194.

[62] See E. K. Chambers, *William Shakespeare: A Study of Facts and Problems*, 2 vols., Oxford, 1930, II, 153. On 31 March 1613, Shakespeare was paid forty-four shillings for devising the impressa, and Burbage the same for painting it.

CHAPTER IV

Hired Men

"HIRED MEN" is the term commonly used in the reigns of Elizabeth, James, and Charles for those theater people who were not named in the patents and did not share in the profits but were paid weekly wages by the sharers. The term was used by both players and laymen. In the anonymous late Elizabethan play *Histriomastix* one of the soldiers says: "Come on Players, now we are the Sharers, and you the hired men." A leading actor in the King's company, Augustine Phillips, in his will of May 1605 leaves £5 to be distributed amongst "the hired men of the company." In 1623 the actor Richard Baxter testified in a Chancery suit that he had come to the players of the Red Bull "as an hired man to the company." Three sharers of the King's company complained in 1635 that out of the sharers' dividends there is "defrayed all wages to hired men." In 1640 the Master of the Revels issued a special pass to "the

Prince's Players' hired men." And after Parliament's abolition of all theatrical enterprises, the anonymous author of *The Actors' Remonstrance*, 1643/44, a former sharer of some dramatic troupe, complained that "our Hired-men are dispersed, some turned Soldiers and Trumpeters, and others destined to meaner courses or depending on us, whom in courtesy we cannot see want for old acquaintance sake."[1]

The distinction between sharers and hired men or servants or "hirelings" of the players was clearly explained in July 1634 to Thomas Crosfield, a Fellow of Queen's College, Oxford. On the 18th, Crosfield was visited by one of a troupe of touring players whom he calls "The company of Salisbury Court at the further end of Fleet Street against the Conduit." Crosfield noted in his diary what had been explained to him about the London theatrical troupes. After listing nine members of his own company, the informant, Richard Kendall, continued, "These are the chief, whereof seven are called sharers, i.e., such as pay wages to the servants and equally share in the overplus: other servants there are as two clothes keepers, Richard Kendall and Anthony Dover."[2] As Kendall implies, though he mentions only "clothes keepers" or tiremen or wardrobe keepers, the basic distinction is that hired men did not, like the major actors, or sharers, receive a percentage of the profits from the theater, nor did they work for their keep and their training and a fee for their masters as did the boys or apprentices. All hired men, whatever their duties, worked for weekly wages. The distinction is clearly implied in two of the tickets of privilege granted to the hired men of the King's company. On 27 December 1624 the Master of the Revels listed twenty-one names and said that they "are all employed by the King's Majesty's servants in their quality of playing as

[1] Several examples of the use of the terms "hired men," "hirelings," or "journeymen" in the nondramatic literature of the time are given in E. K. Chambers, *The Elizabethan Stage*, 4 vols., Oxford, 1967, I, 362n. "Hired man" is, however, the term nearly always used by the players themselves.

[2] G. E. Bentley, *The Jacobean and Caroline Stage*, 7 vols., Oxford, 1941-1968, II, 688-89.

65

musicians and other necessary attendants. . . ." Thirteen years later a similar document of 1636/37 was issued from the Lord Chamberlain's Office. It protected eleven men from arrest. Part of the sample form reads: "Whereas the bearer hereof Richard Baxter hath been and is employed by His Majesty's Servants the players of the Blackfriars and is of special use unto them both on the stage and otherwise. . . ."[3] In both documents "the King's servants" refers to the sharers of the company, the patented members, the employers of the hired men.

These employees were minor actors, musicians, prompters or book holders, stagekeepers, wardrobe keepers or tiremen, or sometimes gatherers. Of course, any of these functionaries of the playhouse could be called upon to act minor roles in performances, especially in crowd scenes. Usually the performers with few or no lines are not named in extant cast lists, but now and then the surviving play texts, especially prompt manuscripts, reveal what must have been a common practice. In the Folio text of *A Midsummer Night's Dream* in the first scene of the fifth act before the entrance of Bottom and his fellow players is the direction *"Tawyer with a Trumpet before them,"* a line evidently crept in from a prompt manuscript. Tawyer was one of the twenty-one men listed in Sir Henry Herbert's ticket of privilege of 1624 referred to above. In the British Museum manuscript of Thomas Heywood's *The Captives*, a prompt stage direction at V,2 reads, "stagekeepers as a guard." In Glapthorne's *The Lady Mother* the company musicians have an active part. Shakespeare's use of a small group of his company's musicians to take part in the action on the stage is familiar in plays like *Romeo and Juliet* and *Othello*. In the modified version of Marston's *Malcontent*, acted by Shakespeare's company in 1604, the Induction begins with the entrance of Will Sly, "a tireman following him with a stool." The tireman, or wardrobe keeper, has two or three lines.

[3] "Dramatic Records: The Lord Chamberlain's Office," *Malone Society Collections* 2, pt. 3 (1931), 380-81; and Joseph Quincy Adams, *The Dramatic Records of Sir Henry Herbert*, New Haven, 1917, pp. 74-75.

It does not seem likely that the book holder or prompter could often be spared for an acting role during a performance. The "Book-keeper" in the Induction to Jonson's *Bartholomew Fair* performed at the opening of the Hope theater in 1614, may have been the actual book keeper for the Lady Elizabeth's company, but it seems more likely that he was a regular player impersonating the company's book keeper, who would have been busy with his regular duties during the opening scene of a performance.

In their heyday a major company could have a good many of these hired men. On 27 December 1624, the Master of the Revels issued a certificate to protect from arrest, imprisonment, or other molestation the hired men of the King's company; twenty-one men are named. Several can be identified: one is the book keeper; several are musicians; several are little-known players; but six are known as theatrical personnel from this document only. The fact that half a dozen of the names in this certificate are otherwise totally unknown is suggestive. If so many of the men necessary for performances at Blackfriars and the Globe by the richest and most fully documented company of the time are lost in obscurity save for this single record, how many of the "necessary attendants" attached to the twenty or so less prominent London troupes during these fifty-two years have completely disappeared? All signs suggest that there were many more players in London than we can at present identify. Certain parish registers support this assumption.[4] Of these London "players" of whom

---

[4] Most of the parish registers of births, marriages, and burials that are extant either in print or in manuscript are little more than lists of names and dates. In a city like Tudor and Stuart London where so many names are the same it is usually impossible to identify players in these registers. But there are a few sets of parish registers, like those of St. Giles without Cripplegate, St. Botolph's Aldgate, and St. Saviour's Southwark that record the occupation of the father of the christened child and sometimes are even more explicit in a burial register; as when the clerk of St. Botolph's Aldgate recorded in November 1615, "Robert Armin free of the Goldsmiths and a Player was buried the thirteenth day." In these three unusually explicit registers there are more than twenty men called "player" by their parish clerks who are otherwise unknown in any theatrical connection.

we know only that they fathered a child or suffered the loss of a wife or child, it is likely that most were hired men. Of nearly all the sharers we know more, because they are generally named in the required legal patents for their companies, and as superior actors they are more likely to be named in allusions, financial records, or lawsuits. Boy actors were generally too young to sire children or to be named in lawsuits. Hired men probably constituted the largest class of theatrical personnel living in London in Shakespeare's time.

HIRED MEN WHO WERE PRIMARILY PLAYERS

As the tickets of privilege of 1624 and 1636/37 have shown, there were a good many hired men—certainly in the King's company and presumably in others as well—who were not primarily players. But these musicians, stagekeepers, and other helpers often appeared on the stage, as we have seen in the examples of *The Captives, A Midsummer Night's Dream, The Lady Mother, Romeo and Juliet,* and *Othello*; a good many other examples can be gleaned from the chance printing of prompters' notes in printed texts, and still more from extant prompt manuscripts like that for Massinger's *Believe as You List.*

Is it possible to identify those hired men who were primarily actors and not musicians or wardrobe keepers or tiremen or gatherers or stagekeepers? One source of information is the casts and player lists published in certain quartos and folios and listed in a few manuscript plays. Unhappily there are less than thrity of them and almost never do they give a full cast; eight to twelve players are usually named and a third to half the named roles are unassigned. Of course these unassigned roles are the ones most likely to have been filled by hired men, but the majority of them are too small to require a trained performer.

These casts give good reason for certain conclusions about hired men. They show that, at least in the companies from which we have several sets of assigned roles, the majority of the hired men cannot have been primarily players. We have seen that in December 1624 twenty-one individuals were named hired men of the King's company, yet in the seven casts for productions by this company in the years 1626-1632 (*The Roman Actor*, *The Deserving Favorite*, *The Lovers Melancholy*, *The Picture*, *The Wild Goose Chase*, *The Soddered Citizen*, and *The Swisser*) the numbers of hired men assigned roles are four, three, four or five, one, one, three, and one. These figures suggest that of the twenty-one hired men the King's company needed in 1624 to supplement the efforts of the thirteen sharers and the apprentices, not more than five or six of them needed to be primarily actors. The fact that all but three or four of these hired men who were assigned roles in the plays of the King's company became, in later years, sharers in this or some other company indicates that they were indeed players and not tiremen or stagekeepers filling in.

The persons who appeared as hired men in casts or lists (including the Jonson folio lists) of the King's company but who over a period of thirty-five years became sharers in this or some other London troupe were John Duke, Christopher Beeston, John Lowin, Alexander Cooke, William Eccleston, John Underwood, Thomas Pollard, William Penn, John Honeyman, and probably Anthony Smith. These hired men were evidently actors. Players who appeared in more than one King's cast but are not known ever to have become sharers are Patrick, Greville, Vernon, Horne, and Nicholas Underhill. Even though they are not known ever to have reached the top of their profession, I am inclined to think that these particular hired men were players and not wardrobe keepers or musicians filling in.

There is some reason to think that these dispositions of sharers and hired men in the King's company were fairly normal. The five casts for Queen Henrietta's men show similar numbers and dispositions except for a slight increase in the use of hired men: two, three, three, three, four. In Queen Henrietta's casts the hired men who later became sharers in some company are John Young, Christopher Goad, Theophilus Bird or Bourne, and George Stutfield. Hired men in Queen

Henrietta's company who never became, so far as we know, sharers in any London troupe were William Reynolds, William Shakerley, William Wilbraham, John Dobson, Robert Axen, and John Page.

HIRED MEN, NOT PLAYERS

Although, as we have seen, those hired men who were not primarily players did appear occasionally on the stage in performances, their primary activities in the theaters were not histrionic. They played music, or took care of costumes, or swept the stage and moved props, or prepared prompt manuscripts and actors' sides, or collected admissions at the door. Something is known of the activities of all these lesser theatrical folk, though in some classes tantalizingly little. Most frequently mentioned of these nonacting groups are the musicians.

HIRED MEN, MUSICIAN-PLAYERS

The fact that there exist a few instances in which a man is sometimes called musician, sometimes player in one or two parish registers is suggestive that the man concerned was probably a theater musician hence the varied designations. See Francis Hitchins, once player, once drummer in St. Giles Cripplegate registers; Edward Minshaw, gent, player, musician, and again player, St. Saviour's Southwark; Thomas Heywood, St. Saviour's Southwark, 1600-1610 four times player, once musician; Thomas Marbeck, in 1603 a musician in St. Saviour's Southwark records but in Admiral's record of 1602 as a player.[5]

Perhaps these irregularities show that those musicians who played in the theaters were often classified as players, but the answer is not clear. Some of the contradictions may reflect

[5] Bentley, *The Jacobean and Caroline Stage*, ii; "Shakespeare's Fellows," *Times Literary Supplement*, 15 November 1928, p. 856.

simple errors made by the parish clerks, or some may indicate changes of profession. It is also possible that in one or two cases different men of the same name may be involved.

In any case, these few examples from parish records are not enough to invalidate the evidence showing that theater musicians, though included in exemptions for hired men, were generally considered a separate group.

MUSICIANS

The extensive use of music in all Tudor and Stuart dramatic productions sometimes surprises modern readers. The vast majority of all extant plays of this period call for vocal or instrumental music, generally both, and there is copious evidence that the music was of a fairly high order. Even in the early sixteenth-century days of the poor touring companies of four to six men and a boy, musical demands are made of the players; even then music was an important part of English dramatic activities. David Bevington points out how common it was in the early sixteenth-century plays:

> In a remarkably high percentage of plays offered for acting, all or nearly all of the actors are required to sing, usually as a group. In *The Longer Thou Livest* all four players are on hand on two separate occasions to sing. . . . The two songs in *New Custom* are each rendered by all four actors in the troupe. *The Tide Tarieth*, with four players, has three songs and each is sung by a quartet. In *Trial of Treasure* all five players join in song. . . . In *Lusty Juventus, Like Will to Like*, and *King Darius*, the number of singers equals the number of players, and in *Three Laws* and *Mary Magdalen* all but one of the actors sing.[6]

In the nineties Henslowe was buying musical instruments for his companies as several of his entries show:

[6] David M. Bevington, *From "Mankind" to Marlowe: Growth of Structure in the Popular Drama of Tudor England*, Cambridge, Mass., 1962, p. 98.

Lent unto Richard Jones the 22nd of December 1598 to buy a bass viol and other instruments for the company . . . 40 shillings

Lent unto Thomas Downton the 13th of July 1599 to buy instruments for the company the sum of . . . 30 shillings

Lent unto the company the 6th of February 1599 to buy a drum when to go into the country . . . 11 shillings 6 pence

Received of Mr. Henslowe this 7th of February 1599 the sum of 22 shillings to buy 2 trumpets . . . 22 shillings
Robt Shaa[7]

A few years later there is a tribute to London theater music in one of the tales in *Ratsies Ghost*: "I pray you (quoth Ratsey) let me hear your music, for I have often gone to plays more for music sake than for action. . . ."[8]

A similar impression of music in the theaters is recorded in 1617 in a letter of the chaplain of the Venetian Embassy in London:

> The other day, therefore, they determined on taking me to one of the many theatres where plays are performed, and we saw a tragedy, which diverted me very little, especially as I cannot understand a word of English, though some little amusement may be derived from gazing at the very costly dresses of the actors, and from the various interludes of instrumental music, and dancing, and singing. . . .[9]

Years later theater musicians, at least in London's most distinguished playhouse, had a high reputation. Bulstrode Whitelocke wrote a set of memoirs for his children in which

---

[7] R. A. Foakes and R. T. Rickert, eds., *Henslowe's Diary*, Cambridge, 1961, pp. 102, 122, and 130.

[8] *Ratsies Ghost, or the Second Part of His Mad Pranks and Robberies* (1605), facsimile edition of the Rylands copy, ed. H. B. Charleton, Manchester, 1932, A3.

[9] *Calendar of State Papers, Venetian*, London, 1910, XVI, 67.

he tells something of his life as a young lawyer at the Middle Temple; at that time he made some of the preparations for the notorious *Masque of Peace* presented by the lawyers to the King and Queen. He says:

> I was so conversant with the musicians, and so willing to gain their favor, especially at this time, that I composed an air myself, with the assistance of Mr. Ives, and called it *Whitelocke's Coranto*; which being cried up was first played publicly by the Blackfriars music, who were then esteemed the best of common musicians in London. Whenever I came to that house (as I did sometimes in those days) though not often, to see a play, the musicians would presently play *Whitelocke's Coranto*, and it was so often called for that they would have it played twice or thrice in an afternoon.[10]

Whitelocke implies that the musicians at Blackfriars formed a permanent group and not a temporary collection of musicians. He indicates the same in his accounts for the production of Shirley's *Masque of Peace* when he assigns a chariot each to the Blackfriars music and to the Phoenix musicians (see below).

The same assumption that the Blackfriars music was a permanent unit is seen in an account of events in Barbados after the closing of the theaters.

> As for music and such sounds as please the ear, they wish some supplies may come from *England* both for instruments and voices, to delight that sense, that sometimes when they are tired out with their labor, they may have some refreshment by their ears; and to that end, they had a purpose to send for the music that were wont to play at *Blackfriars*, and to allow them a competent salary, to make them live as happily there, as they had done in *England*. And had not extreme weakness, by a miserable long sickness, made me uncapable of any undertaking, they had employed me in

[10] Charles Burney, *A General History of Music*, New York, 1935, II, 299. From Whitelocke's manuscript.

73

the business, as the likeliest to prevail with those men, whose persons and qualities were well known to me in *England*.[11]

Probably the musicians were the most distinctive and exclusive group among the hired men of the London dramatic companies—at least in the latter half of the period. Not only were they a unit but certain records suggest that some of these theater orchestras had a certain independent existence. Edmond Malone, who had the original of Herbert's Office Book, now lost, said that "From Sir Henry Herbert's Manuscript I learn, that the musicians belonging to Shakespeare's company were obliged to pay the Master of the Revels an annual fee for a license to play in the theater." And then he quotes from Sir Henry Herbert's manuscript: "For a warrant to the musicians of the King's company this 9th of April, 1627—£1.0.0."[12]

Other records show theater musicians hired as a unit for entertainments at the Inns of Court, or mention their charges for special performances outside the theater. In Bulstrode Whitelocke's account of the preparations for the Inns of Court presentation of Shirley's *Triumph of Peace* in 1633/34 he lists the various floats and chariots in the procession. He says that the second chariot carried the Blackfriars music "John Adson, Ralph Stretch, Henry Field, Ambrose Beeland, Francis Parker, Thomas Hutton, and two boys," and that "the first chariot carried the Phoenix musicians, Jeffrey Collins, Thomas Hunter, John Levasher, Nicholas Underhill, Edward Wright, John Strange, and two boys."[13]

Similarly in 1634 the Drapers' accounts for their Lord Mayor's Show for Sir Henry Garway list: "Item paid to William Hall the player for his music and actions in Cheapside the sum of £13.6.8."[14] Since William Hall was a member of Prince

[11] Richard Ligon, *A True and Exact History of the Island of Barbados*, London, 1657, p. 107.

[12] Adams, *Dramatic Records of Sir Henry Herbert*, p. 46.

[13] Andrew J. Sabol, "New Documents on Shirley's Masque, The Triumph of Peace," *Music and Letters* 47 (January 1966), 25-26.

[14] Jean Robertson and D. J. Gordon, "A Calendar of Dramatic Records in

Charles's (II) company at this time presumably his music was provided by musicians belonging to that company.

Indicative of the same custom of theater orchestras playing for fees outside their theaters is a statement of the anonymous player who published *The Actors' Remonstrance or Complaint* . . . in 1643/44; complaining of the sad state of the actors and their employees since Parliament's closing of the theaters:

> Our music that was held so delectable and precious that they scorned to come to a Tavern under twenty shillings salary for two hours, now wander with their instruments under their cloaks, I mean such as have any, into all houses of good fellowship, saluting every room where there is company with *Will you have any music Gentlemen.* . . . [A3^V–A4]

I know of no conclusive evidence of the number of musicians in a theater orchestra during this period, but there is a suggestive repetition of the number six. Whitelocke listed six names as the Blackfriars orchestra he hired and six names of musicians in the Phoenix orchestra. The same number is noted in Henry Glapthorne's play *The Lady Mother*, extant only in manuscript until 1882, but licensed for production 15 October 1635 and performed by the Revels company at the Salisbury Court theater.[15] In Act II Captain Suckett calls for the musicians to help him and when they come in, he says:

> . . . where are they? Let me see how many's of you, 1, 2, 3, 4, 5, 6. Good. Can any of you dance?[16]

In December of 1624 the Master of the Revels issued an exemption from arrest during the time of the Revels for twenty-one men "all employed by the King's Majesty's servants in their quality of playing as musicians and other necessary attendants, and are at all times and hours to be ready with their

the Books of the Livery Companies of London, 1485-1640," *Malone Society Collections* 3 (1954), 130.
[15] See Bentley, *The Jacobean and Caroline Stage*, IV, 483-85.
[16] Arthur Brown, ed., *The Lady Mother by Henry Glapthorne*, Malone Society, Oxford, 1958 (1959), ll. 694ff.

best endeavors to do his Majesty's service (during the times of the Revels)." John P. Cutts has succeeded in identifying seven of these men as musicians. Some of the other names are not yet certainly identifiable, and two or three of the musicians may have been on temporary duty for the revels. Nevertheless, the number is suggestively close to the six indicated in the other records noted.[17]

The scene just quoted from *The Lady Mother* is another of the numerous examples which might be cited in which the company musicians were called upon not only to play in their music room before, during, and after the performance, but to be on stage as a part of the action. In this scene the musicians are on for more than fifty lines and the leader has several lines to speak. Shakespeare's use of the company's musicians on stage in *Romeo and Juliet* and *Othello* is familiar to all; numerous examples from other plays might be cited. Clearly it was generally assumed that the musicians were not confined to the music room but were available whenever the playwright and the company wanted a group of instrumentalists in the action on stage.

It has been suggested to me that though there are numerous allusions to musicians playing in theaters and though the majority of the extant plays of the period call for music, it is possible that a regular orchestra may not have been part of every established dramatic company. Some theaters may have simply called in London consorts when the performance of a play required instrumental music.

The passages already quoted seem to me to rule out this expedient for the Blackfriars, the Phoenix, and the Salisbury Court at least in the 1630s. As for the public theaters in the reigns of Elizabeth and James, I cannot prove that musicians were a regular part of every theater staff, but surely the musicians who played an hour's concert before the performance

[17] John P. Cutts, "New Findings with Regard to the 1624 Protection List," *Shakespeare Survey* 19 (1966), 101-107.

at Blackfriars in 1602[18] must have been attached to that theater.

I have encountered no allusions to the summoning to a theater of an unattached group of musicians, but of course I cannot say that it never happened. For the established companies of Jacobean and Caroline London the substitution of occasional musicians on call for a regular attached orchestra would seem to me to have been a very awkward and unreliable expedient.

TRUMPETERS AND DRUMMERS

Of course the group in the music room of Elizabethan, Jacobean, and Caroline theaters did not include the drummers and trumpeters who were in such constant demand. Every theater had to have them, but they seem not to have been included in the term "musicians," at least as it was used in the theaters. The music historian, Sternfeld, points out that "The trumpeters belonged to a special guild and did not play in combination with other instruments.[19]

There must have been a good many trumpeters in London, for they were in constant use not only in all playhouses but for all sorts of state occasions. When the Iron Mongers company produced Dekker's *London's Tempe, or The Field of Happiness* as a Lord Mayor's Show, thirty-six trumpeters were employed, according to James Peller Malcolm; the accounts for Queen Anne's funeral show payments to twenty-eight trumpeters; the accounts of Shirley's *Masque of Peace* record the use of seven pairs of trumpeters.[20]

It is not extraordinary in a society so accustomed to trumpeting that three trumpet calls customarily announced the opening of theater performances. The scores of references to

[18] See Chambers, *The Elizabethan Stage*, II, 46-47.

[19] Frederick W. Sternfeld, "*Troilus and Cressida*: Music for the Play," *English Institute Essays* (1952), 121.

[20] James Peller Malcolm, *Londinium Redivivum*, London, 1803-1807, II, 45; H. C. De Lafontaine, *The King's Musicke*, London, 1909, p. 52.

this custom are so familiar that it seems unnecessary to cite any. So far as one can find, all theaters, public and private, normally used this announcement system.

But within the performance trumpets and cornets were in regular use too. The stage directions often call for a "flourish" or a "tucket" or a "sennet." Used in moderation these offstage music devices can be extremely effective, even thrilling, as a good modern performance of almost any of Shakespeare's histories and many of his tragedies have shown. But there are Jacobean and Caroline assertions that the more vulgar theaters overused their drums and trumpets.

Shortly after the Company of the Revels moved into the Red Bull theater, a house frequently charged with vulgarity, they announced in the prologue for their comedy *The Two Merry Milkmaids, or the Best Words Wear the Garland,*

> This day we entreat all that are hither come
> To expect no noise of guns, trumpets, nor drum,
> Nor sword and target; but to hear sense and words
> Fitting the matter that the scene affords.
> So that the stage being reform'd and free
> From the loud clamors it was wont to be
> Turmoiled with battles; you I hope will cease
> Your daily tumults, and with us wish peace.
>
> [1620 edition]

Years later Edward Howard in his criticism of vulgarity in the Restoration theaters reminded the players,

> . . . but we may remember that the Red Bull writers, with their drums, trumpets, battles, and heroes have had this success formerly, and perhaps have been able to number as many audiences as our theatres. . . .
>
> [*Six Days' Adventure*, 1671, A4ᵛ]

However crude the excessive use of trumpeting at the Red Bull may have been, a reading of a large number of Elizabethan, Jacobean, and Caroline plays makes it obvious that trumpets or cornets were called for in many scenes in other theaters as well. Since the London trumpeters had an organization of their own, it was probably necessary to have one or two among the hired men of any company. Besides their daily "three soundings" to announce performances, the trumpeters were called upon less constantly during most plays—especially Caroline ones—than were musicians in general. Presumably these trumpeters would often have been available for a single act as "walk-ons" or for other miscellaneous chores.

In the Caroline plays drummers are also less frequently mentioned in the dialogue or in the stage directions than they had been in earlier plays. I have found no references to professional drummers in the theaters. Tarleton, Kempe, and other comedians are known to have used drums, but drumming was certainly not their primary function. Perhaps odd players or hired men could take care of the drumming when necessary.

In the earlier years of the period when the London companies were not so far removed from the old troupes which spent much of their time touring the provinces, the use of drums and trumpets to summon audiences in London as in the country is mentioned. On 8 October 1594, Lord Hunsdon, then Lord Chamberlain and patron of Shakespeare's company, wrote to the Lord Mayor requesting toleration for his company of players in the City. His letter reads in part:

> . . . where my now company of players have been accustomed for the better exercise of their quality and for the service of her Majesty if need so require to play this winter time within the City at the Cross Keys in Gracious Street. These are to require and pray your lordship, the time being such as thanks be to God there is now no danger of the sickness, to permit and suffer them so to do. The which I pray you the rather to do for that they have undertaken to me that where heretofore they began not their plays till towards four o'clock, they will now begin at two and have done between four and five and will not use any drums or trumpets at all for the calling of people together and shall

79

be contributories to the poor of the parish where they play according to their abilities. . . . H. Hunsdon[21]

This use of drums and trumpets to summon crowds to performances in the country is familiar, but I know of no record of the use of drums as summoners for theater crowds in London after 1594. The use of drums in plays is common enough, but not their use as advertising for performances.

PROMPTER OR BOOK HOLDER OR BOOK KEEPER[22]

Though the work of the prompter was obviously important for London companies producing so many different plays each season as did troupes like the Lord Chamberlain-King's men, the Admiral-Palsgrave's men, and Worcester-Queen Anne's men, the evidence for his precise activities is meager and scattered. Much of the job description for this position must be inferential.

It has been suggested to me that the prompter's function in the metropolitan companies may have been carried on from time to time by various fellows of the troupe. Such an arrangement seems to me to be improbable, except possibly in emergencies. When companies produced as many different plays and as many revisions involving as many men and boys as did Elizabethan, Jacobean, and Caroline theater organizations, the prompter's chores must have been so multifarious

[21] E. K. Chambers and W. W. Greg, eds., "Dramatic Records of the City of London: The Remembrancia," *Malone Society Collections* 1 (1907), 74.

[22] All three terms were in regular use by theater people as well as the general public in the reigns of Elizabeth, James, and Charles. The prompt book itself was known as "the book" (see W. W. Greg, *Dramatic Documents from the Elizabethan Playhouses*, 2 vols., Oxford, 1931, I, 192-93). This general usage sometimes produces what seem odd redundancies to modern readers. Greg points out entries in the Stationers' Register: "a booke called the booke of David and Bethsaba," "A booke called the booke of the m'chant of Venyce," "a booke called The booke of Pericles Prynce of Tyre." Obviously the printer was registering a prompt copy with this title either on the manuscript or on a wrapper.

and vital and many of them so nerve-wracking that irregular substitutions would surely have produced chaos.

Though the prompters were, by the very nature of their function, not much in the public eye, they are several times referred to, twice or thrice by name. In a Court of Requests suit of 20 May 1603 concerning affairs at the Boar's Head, Oliver Woodliffe describes Israel Jordane as "of London, Scrivener, belonging unto Browne and his fellow stage-players." Of course this statement is none too specific, but C. J. Sisson thinks that it "suggests that [Jordane] was the scribe and book-keeper of Worcester's men."[23]

Much more specific is the statement made by John Taylor, the Water Poet in *Taylor's Feast*, 1638: "I myself did know one *Thomas Vincent* that was a Book-keeper or prompter at the Globe playhouse near the Bank-end in Maid Lane. . . ." There is no other known reference to Vincent; presumably he worked in the early days of the Globe, since Taylor mentions him in connection with Singer, who was dead before 1612.

As will be noted later, the Master of the Revels mentions Knight as book keeper for the King's men in 1633, but no others are specifically named, though there have been various conjectures.

Plays and essays sometimes mention obvious functions of the prompter which merely indicate the assumption that the audience was aware of his activities. The Character of an Excellent Actor, in the Overbury collection, says:

> He doth not strive to make nature monstrous; she is often seen in the same scene with him, but neither on stilts nor crutches; and for his voice, 'tis not lower than the prompter, nor louder than the foil and Target.[24]

In John Fletcher's *Maid in the Mill* of 1623, after some confusion, Bustofa says, "That's true indeed: they are out of their

---

[23] C. J. Sisson, *The Boar's Head Theatre; An Inn-Yard Theatre of the Elizabethan Age*, London, 1972, p. 73.

[24] W. J. Paylor, ed., *The Overburian Characters to which is added a Wife*, by Sir Thomas Overbury, Oxford, 1936, pp. 76-77.

parts sure, It may be 'tis the Book-holder's fault: I'll go see. *Exit*" (II,2). Similarly in Richard Brome's *Antipodes*, performed by Queen Henrietta's men at the Salisbury Court theater in 1638, a voice "within" says "Dismiss the Court," whereupon Lord Letoy says, "Dismiss the Court: can you not hear the Prompter?" (III,8). In the additions to Thomas Goffe's *The Careless Shepherdess*[25] occur the lines:

> *Loud Music sounds.*
> But hist, the Prologue enters. *Landl.* Now it chimes. All in
> to the Play, the Peals were rung before.
> *Pro.* Must always I a Hearer only be?
> *Spark. Thrift.*
> *He being out, is laughed at, by*
> *Spruce. Landl.*
> *Pro.* Pox take the Prompter. *Exit*

These samples of references to the prompter show him in functions that might be characteristic of almost any period, but for the years 1590 to 1642 he must have been more indispensable than commonly. Not only were most companies producing scores of new plays, but in the earlier years of the period, 1590-1610, rarely was a play given consecutive performances; in the later years there were seldom more than three consecutive performances. Under such conditions a letter-perfect rendition must have been unheard of, and prompting a constant necessity. Furthermore, as the notes in the few surviving prompt manuscripts show, the prompter had to carry out a good many of the functions of a modern stage manager, seeing that the props were ready to be brought on, boys were ready to sing offstage or on, offstage noises were ready, musicians were in position before they had to come on stage—all this for several different plays each week.

In addition, it must be remembered that rarely in Elizabethan and Jacobean days, and seldom after, could prompter or players have been working from printed pages. The prompter had his full text and the players had their sides. But all were

---

[25] See Bentley, *The Jacobean and Caroline Stage*, IV, 501-505.

in longhand—and in some of the extant examples very poor and messy longhand it was.[26]

Much more of the prompter's time must have been taken up in working on prompt copies and the sides for actors than in prompting at actual performances; so much time in fact that one man could scarcely have written all that a company required, and most theatrical troupes must have been forced to employ scribes for much of the copying. Even if the dramatist's "fair copy" was legible enough for prompting, the entire 2,000 lines or so had to be copied for the actors' sides.[27]

Even after the prompter had a fair copy of the new play, he had a great deal to do before it could be performed. First it had to be licensed for performance by the Master of the Revels. Usually the Master does not say what individual brought in the manuscript, but on one occasion in October 1632 Sir Henry Herbert noted that it was Knight, the book keeper for the King's company, who paid him his £2.0.0 fee for licensing Ben Jonson's *Magnetic Lady*.[28]

Next the prompter had to see that any corrections, deletions, or revisions required by the Master were made in the prompt copy and in the sides of the several players. This chore could be assumed, but we have one record of Sir Henry Herbert's specific orders. In 1633 the King's men revived Beaumont and Fletcher's *The Woman's Prize or The Tamer Tamed*, but much in the play displeased Herbert. He wrote the company prompter:

Mr. Knight,
In many things you have saved me labor; yet where your judgment or pen failed you, I have made bold to use mine. Purge their parts as I have the book. And I hope every

[26] See the facsimiles in the second volume of Greg's *Dramatic Documents from the Elizabethan Playhouses*.

[27] These sides were the most ephemeral sort of theater material; only one is known to have survived from the period, that of Edward Alleyn for the role of Orlando in Greene's *Orlando Furioso*. Greg, *Dramatic Documents from the Elizabethan Playhouses*, I, 176-81. Most of my material on prompters is derived from this book.

[28] Adams, *Dramatic Records of Sir Henry Herbert*, p. 34.

hearer and player will think that I have done God good service, and the quality no wrong; who hath no greater enemies than oaths, profaneness, and public ribaldry, which for the future I do absolutely forbid to be presented unto me in any playbook, as you will answer it at your peril. 21 October 1633.[29]

The Master seems to suggest ("in many things you have saved me labor") that Knight had done some preliminary censoring for him on previous manuscripts; at any rate he flatly orders him to do so in the future. This was another chore for the prompter and one that seems likely to have got him into disagreements with players and dramatists.

But this censorship was by no means the end of the prompter's preproduction chores. He had to add to the dramatist's fair copy, or the scribe's transcription of it, scores of directions for properties and offstage sounds. Dramatists never made such directions sufficiently specific and frequently omitted them entirely. The book keeper usually had to add anticipatory stage directions, warnings for actors to be ready, such as *"Gascoine: and Hubert below: ready to open the trap door for Mr. Taylor"* on folio 18b of the prompt manuscript of Philip Massinger's *Believe as You List*, or in the entrance direction in the plot of *Frederick and Basilea* played by the Admiral's men at the Rose in 1597: "Basilea servant: Black Dick, Dick."

Somebody had to cast the play, and though the major roles were probably set by the players in conference, the many minor roles and their doubling probably had to be worked out by the prompter and he had to remember who had been assigned what walk-on. Hence the names of players appearing in the prompt manuscripts are mostly those of hired men or boys whose assignments in that play could easily be forgotten; names of major actors usually appear only incidentally, as in the case of Joseph Taylor in the quotation from *Believe as You List*.

Another function of the prompter is somewhat problemat-

ical, namely the making of a Plot or Plat for each play produced. It is problematical, because there are only seven extant
examples, all of them dating from the first twelve years of our
period. The question is, did the theaters continue to use them
until the closing of 1642? Their obvious usefulness is such
that I am inclined to guess that they were always used, but I
know of no evidence after about 1602. Sir Walter Greg, the
great authority on the subject, says that "Theatrical Plots are
documents giving the skeleton outline of plays, scene by scene,
for use in the theatre."[30] They summarize the entrances and
other nonverbal activities. To quote Sir Walter again, ". . .
we may suppose that these were prepared for the guidance of
actors and others in the playhouse, to remind those concerned
when and in what character they were to appear, what properties were required, and what noises were to be made behind
the scenes."

The prompter would have been the obvious man to make,
or at least to supervise the making of such Plots. They were
essentially aids to him as well as to the players in getting them
on stage at the proper moment and with the proper equip-
ment, a real difficulty when the repertories were so large and
the run of each play so short. It is suggested that the Plot
hung backstage for the consultation of players uncertain about
their entrance cues.

Of course the Jacobean and Caroline use of Plots is speculative, since no example later than 1602 has been discovered,
but then most other records used inside the theaters after
Henslowe have disappeared too. Since a Plot for the play would
have been so helpful to the overworked prompter, I am inclined to think that they were used by the later companies as
by the earlier ones.

All the chores so far outlined involve the work on new plays,
but many productions in the reigns of Elizabeth and James
and probably most of those in the reign of Charles I were
revivals, plays that had been first mounted anywhere from

[30] Greg, *Dramatic Documents from the Elizabethan Playhouses*, i, 1, 3.

one to thirty years before. And a good many of these revivals, probably most of those for plays ten or more years old, involved revisions. Henslowe's Diary is full of payments to dramatists for revising or adding to old plays. Many title pages of printed plays advertise such revisions, and prologues often refer to them.[31]

All these revisions required more work, presumably done by the hard-working prompter. Not only did the revisions and deletions have to be added to the prompt copy, but changes in the personnel of the company required adjustments. Even in a troupe so stable as the King's men, boys grew too old or too tall for their old roles, and established actors died and were succeeded by sharers who might be equally competent but talented in different ways. When one notes that the repertory of the King's company in 1641 contained over sixty plays that had never been printed, to say nothing of one hundred or more which had been[32] the task of the book keeper swells to monumental proportions.

SCRIBES

Those hired copyists who accomplished part of the numerous chores of the prompters were not, so far as is known, really players or any organized part of the dramatic companies. One would guess that a number of scribes were given occasional employment, and they must have copied out thousands of pages for the various London troupes. Even Ralph Crane, the best-known of these copyists, says, as noted below, that he had "some" employment by the King's men. Presumably much of the work of these men was the writing out from the prompt manuscript the sides of the players, but the little identifiable copyists' work which has come down consists for the most part of copies of plays made for wealthy patrons.

[31] See the chapter on revisions in G. E. Bentley, *The Profession of Dramatist in Shakespeare's Time*, Princeton, 1971, pp. 235-63.
[32] See Bentley, *The Jacobean and Caroline Stage*, I, 65-66 and 108-134.

The best, almost the only one, of these copyists still identifiable is Ralph Crane, whose career has been studied by Professor F. P. Wilson.[33] Crane himself records that although he had worked chiefly for lawyers, he had sometimes worked for the King's company. In his volume of religious verse entitled *The Workes of Mercy*, which he published in 1621, he wrote:

> And some employment hath my useful pen
> Had 'mongst those civil, well-deserving men
> That grace the Stage with honor and delight,
> Of whose true honesties I much could write,
> But will compris't (as in a Cask of Gold)
> Under the Kingly Service they do hold.

A number of his transcriptions have been identified. His copy of Fletcher's *Sir John van Olden Barnavelt* has been used as a prompt book, but more of his dramatic transcriptions have been made for private collectors: Middleton's *A Game at Chess*, the version of Fletcher's *Humorous Lieutenant* entitled *Demetrius and Enanthe*, and Middleton's *The Witch*. If so much of his work with the plays of the King's men is identifiable, one is tempted to think that he may have done more of the lost prompt books and of the hundreds of lost sides which the King's company had to have.

Anyone who has rummaged through the hundreds of thousands of legal documents of this period in the Public Record Office has surely been impressed by the great number of copyists who must have been working in London from 1590 to 1642. How many of them, like Ralph Crane, earned a few extra shillings by copying plays and sides for the theatrical companies? And who were they? And were any of the regular hired men of the theatrical troupes good enough penmen to be assigned some of the endless copying?[34]

[33] F. P. Wilson, "Ralph Crane, Scrivener to the King's Players," *The Library*, 4th ser., 7 (1927), 194-215.

[34] Perhaps we should remember that John Downes, the veteran prompter in the Restoration theater, says that he did all this copying of sides himself. Downes says that from 1662 to 1706 he worked for Davenant's company,

WARDROBE KEEPERS OR TIREMEN

The theater records of this period are full of accounts of ex-
penditures for costumes; in fact, one would estimate that the
greatest expense of any company of players in the period was
the purchase of costumes. The most casual leafing through
the pages of Henslowe's Diary is enough to show that he was
putting out for his various companies a good deal more money
in the purchases of costumes and costume materials than he
was paying the dramatists for the plays in which this finery
was displayed. These proportions, of course, represented sound
economy. If the play turned out to be a complete failure, the
money paid the playwright was not recoverable, while the
costumes could be used for play after play; even after the
fabric had worn out the gold or copper or silver trimming
could be used to decorate other costumes in later plays. Color
in "Elizabethan" performances came primarily from the gor-
geous (and expensive) costumes of the actors. Foreign visitors
to London theaters almost always comment on the splendid
dresses of the actors.

The large stock of fine clothes which every company required and to which they were constantly adding must have
demanded unremitting protection and care, but there are surprisingly few references to company wardrobe keepers or
"clothes keepers" or "tiremen."

Henslowe made several payments to tiremen in the late years
of Elizabeth but most show little about the duties of these
wardrobe keepers. They do buy clothes or materials on order,
and some of the entries suggest that the tireman himself was
making part of the costumes. On 3 December 1596 Henslowe
made an entry, "Delivered unto Stephen the tireman for to

"And as Book keeper and Prompter, continu'd so, till October 1706. . . .
Writing out all the Parts in each Play; and Attending every Morning the
Actors Rehearsals, and their Performances, Afternoons" (*Roscius Anglicanus*,
London, 1708, p. A2). Even if this statement is accurate, there was much
less copying to be done at Lincoln's Inn Fields, for many of the plays pro-
duced were revivals of plays already in print.

deliver unto the company for to buy a headtire and a rebato and other things, £3.10." Henslowe paid the "tyre man" ". . . for money which he laid out to buy taffeta for the play of Cardinal Wolsey . . . 13 d." And on 4 September 1602 he wrote into the company's accounts: "paid unto your tireman for making of William Kemp's suit and the boys' . . . 8s. 8d."

One of Henslowe's regular playwrights for a few years was Wentworth Smith, who is recorded as writing or collaborating in at least fifteen lost plays, first for the Admiral's men and later for the Earl of Worcester's men. Henslowe entered several payments for costumes for one of Smith's plays, *The Two Brothers*, which he sometimes calls *The Three Brothers*; a couple of these entries seem to imply that the tireman not only bought the material but made the costumes himself. In October 1602 he recorded:

> Lent at the appointment of the company unto the tireman to buy say for the play of the 2 brothers to make a witche's gown the sum of . . . 18/

> Paid unto the tireman for making of the devil's suit and "sperethes" [?] and for the witch for the play of the 3 brothers the 23 of October 1602 the sum of . . . 10/9

For another play by Wentworth Smith, the popular *Black Dog of Newgate*, Henslowe paid out for Worcester's men later in the following year:

> Delivered unto the tireman for the company 1602 [i.e., 1602/03] to buy 8 yards and a half of black satin at 12/ a yard to make a suit for the 2nd part of the Black Dog the sum of . . . £5.2   15 February[35]

[35] Foakes and Rickert, eds., *Henslowe's Diary*, pp. 50, 180, 215, 218, 219, 224. It is difficult for us to put in perspective these sums paid out by Henslowe and other financial agents, partly because the rate of inflation differed so vastly for different commodities, and partly because we find it incredible that the Elizabethan players spent such fantastic sums for costumes. The £5.2.0 that Henslowe paid the tireman to buy black satin for a costume for the second half of *The Black Dog of Newgate* would have purchased 204 play quartos in the bookstalls that year.

There are, of course, hundreds of other costume entries in the Diary, but most of them indicate the prices of the stuffs purchased rather than particular activities of the tiremen.

The names of three other tiremen (though for a boy company not an adult one) are known from a suit of 1608 discovered by Mark Eccles. Eccles says:

> David Yeomans, a tailor who could not sign his name, testified that Kirkham, Kendall, Hawkins, and "one Gibbyns" had made an inventory of the playhouse apparel and goods when Yeomans was "taken in by the masters of the said playhouse to be tyreman in the room of one Robert Rutson and one Goffe."[36]

During the years 1612-1616 William Freshwater, Merchant Tailor, aged seventy-two in 1620, was evidently a wardrobe keeper for Queen Anne's men at the Red Bull. In the Court of Requests suit brought by John Smith against Christopher Beeston concerning old debts for materials bought for Queen Anne's company, William was called to answer interrogatories in May 1620. He testified that he had himself frequently been sent to Smith to get materials. He said:

> . . . he knoweth it so to be for that he himself being a workman to the said company hath often and diverse times gone to the plaintiff's house sometimes by direction from the said Beeston and sometimes as sent by others of the said company for divers stuffs which they had occasion to use. . . .[37]

In the passage in Crosfield's Diary concerning the information regarding London companies given him by Richard Kendall, partly quoted above (see p. 65) there is an introductory statement. The diary entry, it will be remembered, is dated 18 July 1634:

[36] Mark Eccles, "Martin Peerson and the Blackfriars," *Shakespeare Survey* 11 (1958), 102.

[37] C. W. Wallace, "Three London Theaters of Shakespeare's Time," *University of Nebraska Studies* 9 (1909), 332.

One Richard Kendall about the age of 50 or upwards, belonging to the company of players of Salisbury Court that came to Oxford this year came to see me and related unto me divers particular stories, vizt.

1. Of his particular state and education in his youth at Kirkby Lonsdall where he served his apprenticeship to a tailor, and afterward went to Cambridge where he stayed but little, and then went to London where he became servant to Sir William Slingsby—and now he is one of the two keepers of the wardrobe of the said company.

And the enumeration of the companies ends with the account of Kendall's company at Salisbury Court. The final sentence is:

These are the chief, whereof seven are called sharers, i.e., such as pay wages to the servants and equally share in the overplus: other servants there are as two clothes keepers, Richard Kendall and Anthony Dover.[38]

Two later references to wardrobe keepers or tiremen tell us little about the men or their duties, but they do indicate the public awareness of the position among the hired men of the London troupes. In 1643/44 the anonymous player who wrote *The Actors' Remonstrance* included in his lament about the plight of the theater people since the closing of the theaters: "For our tiremen, and others that belonged formerly to our wardrobe, with the rest, they are out of service: our stock of clothes, such as are not in tribulation for the general use, being sacrificed to moths. . . ."

When John Downes, prompter in the Restoration theater, wrote his *Roscius Anglicanus*, he gave some account of the beginnings of the Restoration theater:

In the year 1659 . . . Mr. Rhodes a bookseller, being Wardrobe keeper formerly (as I am informed) to King Charles

---

[38] Frederick S. Boas, ed., *The Diary of Thomas Crosfield*, London, 1935, pp. 71-72.

the First's company of comedians in Blackfriars, getting a license from the then governing State. . . .[39]

The number of these tiremen or wardrobe keepers who were tailors or had been apprenticed to tailors or who were paid for making or altering costumes is highly suggestive. Surely a third-rate company like the one at the Salisbury Court theater in 1634 did not own enough costumes to require two full-time tiremen to keep track of them, but if most wardrobe keepers were tailors making new costumes and repairing old ones, the number is easily accounted for. In this connection it will be remembered that when William Bird of the Palsgrave's men wrote to Edward Alleyn in 1617 about the dishonest John Russell who had been cheating the company as box holder, Bird declared Russell would never again be allowed to hold the box, "Yet, for your sake, he shall have his wages, to be a necessary attendant on the stage, and if he will pleasure himself and us, to mend our garments when he hath leisure, we'll pay him for that too. . . ." This offer would seem to imply that the Palsgrave's men had more mending and altering than their regular wardrobe keepers could manage.

Some slight suggestion of what the size of the wardrobe of the Palsgrave's men might have been can be derived from some miscellaneous papers of Philip Henslowe. The Lord Admiral's men, whose costumes he records, were the direct antecedents of the Palsgrave's and though some of the articles in their collection of 1592/93 had surely worn out or had been sold, it can be assumed that the troupe had bought many others in the subsequent years. Henslowe lists: "*The book of the Inventory of the goods of my* Lord Admiral's men, *taken the 10 of March in the year* 1598 [i.e., 1598/99]." With the supplementary list dated three days later over 270 items of dress are included.[40] It can be assumed that the much richer and older

---

[39] P. C1. For a discussion of men of the name see Bentley, *The Jacobean and Caroline Stage*, II, 544-46.

[40] W. W. Greg, ed., *Henslowe Papers*, London, 1907, pp. 113-16 and 118-21.

King's company of the 1620s and 1630s had more costumes than the Palsgrave's of 1592/93.

That a wardrobe keeper could also be a "necessary attendant" or even an actor on the stage is indicated by the Induction that the King's Men had John Webster write for Marston's *Malcontent* probably in 1603 or 1604. It will be recalled that the Induction appearing in the third edition of *The Malcontent* consists of a conversation among five members of the company speaking under their own names, William Sly, Richard Burbage, John Lowin, John Sinklo, Henry Condell, plus the wardrobe keeper. The opening stage direction reads: "*Enter W. Sly, a Tire-man following him with a stool.*" The tire-man has only three short speeches (within the capacity of almost any adult) and then presumably returned to his other duties. There would seem to be no reason that wardrobe keepers could not perform similarly in this or other companies, though not in their own characters.

GATHERERS OR BOX-HOLDERS

The most heterogenous group among the hired men was the gatherers; often called the box-holders for the obvious reason that they stood at the doors holding a box to receive admissions. Richard Flecknoe wrote in a melancholy piece which he dated 1652:

> From thence passing on to Blackfriars, and seeing never a playbill on the gate, no coaches on the place, nor doorkeeper at the playhouse door, with his box like a churchwarden, desiring you to remember the poor players. . . .[41]

Thirty years before in the previously noted letter to Edward Alleyn about John Russell, William Bird had said

> There is one John Russell, that by your appointment was made a gatherer with us, but my fellows finding often false to us have many times warned him from taking the box;

---

[41] Richard Flecknoe, *Miscellania*, London, 1653, I6-I6ᵛ.

and he as often, with most damnable oaths, hath vowed never to touch. Yet, notwithstanding his execrable oaths, he hath taken the box, and many times most unconscionably gathered, for which we have resolved he shall never more come to the door. . . .[42]

The gatherers were a heterogeneous group in a variety of ways; perhaps most conspicuously in that they were the only servants of the Elizabethan theaters known to have included both men and women. Various references attest to this diversity, most succinctly a passage in the newsbook *Perfect Occurrences* for 5 October 1647, describing a raid on a performance of *A King and No King*: "The Sheriffs of the City of London with their officers went thither, and found a great number of people; some young Lords and other eminent persons; and the men and women with the boxes (that took monies) fled. . . ."[43]

Perhaps the most specific and accurate record of a female gatherer is to be found in the will of Henry Condell and later of his wife, Elizabeth. In his last testament of 13 December 1627, the veteran sharer of the King's company and housekeeper in both the Globe and the Blackfriars theaters bequeathed to his old servant Elizabeth Wheaton a mourning gown, forty shillings, and ". . . that place of privilege which she now exerciseth and enjoyeth in the houses of the Blackfriars, London, and the Globe on the Bankside [for life] if my estate shall so long continue in the premises. . . ." This bequest was renewed in the will of Condell's widow, Elizabeth, eight years later: "Item. I do give and bequeath unto Elizabeth Wheaton widow, the gathering place at the Globe during my lease. . . ."[44]

In other theaters besides the Globe and Blackfriars there were women gatherers. On 11 April 1612, the player Robert

[42] Greg, ed., *Henslowe Papers*, pp. 85-86.
[43] Quoted in Leslie Hotson, *The Commonwealth and Restoration Stage*, Cambridge, Mass., 1928, p. 26.
[44] See Bentley, *The Jacobean and Caroline Stage*, II, 638-42.

Browne wrote to Edward Alleyn requesting Alleyn's good offices for his friend, an actor named Rose.

> . . . I understand that Mr. Rose is entertained among the Prince's men and means to stay and settle himself in that company and to set up his rest and to do his best endeavors only in that company. . . . In the meantime he hath requested me to be solicitous for him to you (who he knows can strike a greater stroke amongst them than this) as to procure him but a gathering place for his wife, for he hath had many crosses and it will be some comfort and help to them both, and he makes no doubt but she shall so carry herself in that place as they shall think it well bestowed by reason of her upright dealing in that nature. . . .[45]

The same assumption that gatherers were both male and female is made by the anonymous private theater actor who published *The Actors' Remonstrance or Complaint* in 1643. He recites the parlous state of all theater people since Parliament closed all playhouses more than a year before, and continues: "Nay, our very doorkeepers, men and women, most grievously complain that by this cessation they are robbed of the privilege of stealing from us with license. . . ."[46]

But the gathering was not invariably done by women or by people of low status in the company. There are allusions to senior sharers holding the box. As early as 1583 the newly formed company of Queen Elizabeth was on tour and played at Norwich. There was a fracas when a local man tried to see the performance at the Red Lion Inn without paying. A scuffle ensued; two sharers left the stage to assist the gatherer; the culprit was chased and eventually stabbed. The important detail for our present purpose is that the cheated box-holder was John Singer, a sharer and one of the founding players of Queen Elizabeth's company.[47]

[45] Greg, ed., *Henslowe Papers*, p. 63.
[46] *The Actors' Remonstrance or Complaint*, London, 1643, p. A3v.
[47] See G. M. Pinciss, "The Queen's Men, 1583-1592," *Theatre Survey* 11 (May 1970), 51-52.

Another senior player who is known to have "held the box" was Richard Errington, leader of a provincial company. In the autumn of 1627 his company was on tour and playing at Ludlow; again there was an affray, and Errington testified in the ensuing investigation:

> The information of Richard Errington of the city of London, pewterer, aged fifty years or thereabout, deposeth and saith that upon yesterday about ten or eleven of the clock at night, this deponent being one of the company of his Majesty's players who then were acting in the said house, and this deponent taking money at the door. . . .[48]

One must note that these two examples of senior players acting as gatherers both come from provincial records. I am inclined to doubt that sharers ever held the box at a London theater except in some special situation; at least, I know of no record of such activity on the part of a patented member in London.

As one might expect, a recurrent problem the sharers had with their low-paid gatherers was theft. I have found no record of any method of checking the cash in the box against the number of spectators in the house. Presumably the actor Rose had this problem in mind when in recommending his wife as a prospective gatherer, he authorized Robert Browne to assure Edward Alleyn that ". . . he makes no doubt but she shall so carry herself in that place as they [the company] shall think it well bestowed by reason of her upright dealing in that nature. . . ." Alleyn and his company were not so fortunate in their experience with other gatherers, as the previously quoted letter concerning John Russell shows.

Thomas Heywood, who had had a long experience with the problems of the London theaters and their players, wrote an epistle for his *Apology for Actors* in 1612, "To my good Friends and Fellows the City-Actors." He concluded with a

[48] John Tucker Murray, *English Dramatic Companies 1558-1642*, 2 vols., London, 1910, II, 326.

wish implying what the constant problems of the players were: "So wishing you judicial audiences, honest poets, and true gatherers, I commit you all to the fullness of your best wishes. Yours ever, T. H." It is a little surprising to see a veteran dramatist and company sharer like Heywood put honest gatherers on a par with judicious audiences and fair-dealing playwrights.

The passage in *The Actors' Remonstrance or Complaint* quoted above continues with an example of one of the methods used by gatherers to defraud their employers:

> Nay, our very doorkeepers, men and women, most grievously complain that by this cessation they are robbed of the privilege of stealing from us with license: they cannot now as in King Agamemnon's days seem to scratch their heads where they itch not, and drop shillings and half crown pieces in at their collars.

One hundred years later the problem of preventing theft at the box still plagued the players, according to Judith Milhouse and Robert Hume.[49]

At the outset of this discussion of gatherers, I noted that they were an heterogeneous group. Not only does the evidence show a mixture of men and women, of hired men and sharers, but there are clear indications that a number of them owed their positions at least in part to the housekeepers of the theaters, rather than to the players who were responsible for the recruitment of the other hired men. Clearly Elizabeth Wheaton held her gatherer's place at the pleasure of the Condells as housekeepers at the Globe and Blackfriars. The dishonest John Russell had held the box at the recommendation of Edward Alleyn.

This anomalous situation presumably arises from the usual method of paying theater rents in the time. In all the cases known the players paid their rent not as a set sum delivered

---

[49] See their article "Box Office Reports for Five Operas Mounted by Handel in London, 1732-1734," *Harvard Library Bulletin* 26 (July 1978), 245-66.

to the owners of their playhouses, but as a percentage of the take at certain doors. Therefore the owners or housekeepers had as much interest in the collections of the gatherers as did the sharers themselves. The fact that in some theaters, like the Globe and Blackfriars and at certain periods the Fortune and the Red Bull, there was some overlap between players and the lay investors made no difference so far as gatherers were concerned. Those sharers, such as Greene and Condell and Shakespeare and John Heminges and John Shank, who were also housekeepers, had two cuts of the daily take, one as sharers and one as housekeepers. Several documents make clear references to this arrangement.

In the long wrangling about housekeepers' shares in the Red Bull theater one of the actions is in the Court of Requests. In reciting the early arrangements about the theater, Thomas Woodford says that he

. . . did by his indenture of lease . . . in the third year of the reign of your Majesty . . . made between the said Aaron Holland of the one part and Thomas Swinnerton of the other party demise and grant a seventh part of the said playhouse and galleries with a gatherers place thereto belonging or appertaining unto the said Thomas Swinnerton for divers years. . . .[50]

In a Chancery suit of 1623 a very clear statement about the arrangements for a gatherer's place is made in the bill of Thomas Woodford:

. . . To which eighteenth part there was then and still is incident and belonging by the usual custom a gatherer's place whereby in respect of certain orders made by and between the said company [of players and partners and] sharers or owners of the said house for the avoiding of all differences and controversies concerning their daily charge of gatherers there did arise and grow due unto the said eighteenth part three pence profit a day amounting to eight-

[50] Wallace, "Three London Theatres of Shakespeare's Time," p. 304.

een pence a week to be paid daily or at the end every week [to the said] Swinnerton or to such gatherers as he should nominate or appoint during . . . the time of their playing.[51]

In his answer to Woodford in this suit Aaron Holland questions Woodward's right to the eighteenth share, but he agrees that a gatherer's place was attached to it.

The same involvement of the housekeepers with the gatherers is found in the private theaters. In the draft for his patent with the supplementary papers prepared by Richard Heton, manager (apparently ambitious to be dictator) of the Salisbury Court playhouse and of Queen Henrietta's company in September 1639, the following explanatory note is added, apparently for the reassurance of the players:

> *The difference betwixt the first Articles and the last.*
> The housekeepers enjoy not any one benefit in the last which they had not in the first.
> And they paid only by the first.
> 1. All repairs of the house.
> 2. Half the gathering places. Half to the sweepers of the house, the stagekeepers, to the poor, and for carrying away the soil. . . .[52]

But the gatherers were not all simply appointees of the housekeepers, there were others who were attached to the company and not the housekeepers. One would guess that the housekeepers' appointees watched over the doors from which came the housekeepers' payments and that the company appointees presided over the doors from which came the money for the sharers. Some such division is implied in the statement about the "last articles" set out by Richard Heton.

For those gatherers who were hired men of the company and not representatives of the housekeepers it does not seem likely that gathering could have been a full-time job. What would a gatherer have done after the two or three hours it

[51] Hotson, *The Commonwealth and Restoration Stage*, pp. 84-85.
[52] Bentley, *The Jacobean and Caroline Stage*, II, 686-87.

might have taken him to collect admission fees? One would assume that he could be used in crowd scenes after the first or second acts, and there is a little evidence that he was. The members of crowds or small groups—often with no lines at all—are too unimportant to be named by book holders, but at one point in the plot of *Frederick and Basilia* the scribe has written "guard gatherers." And Greg writes that "Finally, the gatherers provide the Soldiers for sc. xviii"[53] The play was performed at Henslowe's Rose theater on 3 June 1597. I would assume that situations like this occurred not infrequently in later plays using "supers," but the evidence is disappointingly slight.

Another record shows that the employment of a gatherer was not necessarily exclusively collecting at the doors. It will be remembered that John Russell had been taken on as a gatherer through his friendship with Edward Alleyn. Again we refer to the letter about Russell. Bird's letter to Alleyn recounts his dishonesty with the box and declares that the members of the company have forbidden him ever to act as a gatherer again ". . . Yet, for your sake, he shall have his wages to be a necessary attendant on the stage, and if he will pleasure himself and us to mend our garments, when he hath leisure, we'll pay him for that too. . . ." An attendant on the stage might have been almost anything, but the company must have had experience with Russell as a tailor to entrust him with the repair of their garments. One would have thought this repair work the responsibility of the wardrobe keeper; perhaps Russell had assisted him before.

As already noted, any use of a gatherer on the stage must have been confined to the latter acts of the play, because his gathering activities would have kept him busy at the doors during the early acts. It is obvious, therefore, that the only conspicuous part for a gatherer, "Bolt, A Doorkeeper" in the Praeludium for Thomas Goffe's *The Careless Shepherdess* when it was performed at the Salisbury Court probably in 1638,

[53] Greg, ed., *Dramatic Documents from the Elizabethan Playhouses*, I, 125.

must have been prepared for an actor, not a practicing gatherer. Incidentally, the opening stage direction shows why the gatherers were sometimes called box-holders: "Bolt. *A Doorkeeper, sitting with a box on the side of the Stage.*"

STAGEKEEPERS

What little information we have appears to indicate that the stagekeepers were the most lowly of the hired men. Such duties as we hear about are those of janitors and miscellaneous walk-ons. Most explicit of the passages referring to them is the Induction to Ben Jonson's *Bartholomew Fair* performed by the Lady Elizabeth's men at the opening of Henslowe's Hope theater on 31 October 1614. It will be remembered that this house was a combination theater and bear garden and olfactory allusions in Jonson's Induction indicate that the bears were already in residence.

This induction is, in part, an example of one of Jonson's favorite devices, namely an anticipation of the attacks on his play by putting criticism of it in the mouths of obviously stupid or inconsiderable characters. Here the stupid character selected is the stagekeeper, and this choice indicates Jonson's observation of the popular estimation of stagekeepers.

The Induction on the Stage

Stage-Keeper. Gentlemen, have a little patience, they are e'en upon coming instantly. He that should begin the play, Master *Littlewit*, the *Proctor*, has a stitch new-fallen in his black silk stocking; 'twill be drawn up ere you can tell twenty. . . . But for the whole *Play*, will you have the truth on't? (I am looking, lest the *Poet* hear me, or his man, Master *Brome* behind the Arras) it is like to be a very conceited scurvy one, in plain English. When 't comes to the *Fair* once, you were e'en as good go to *Virginia* for anything there is of *Smithfield*. He has not hit the humors, he does not know 'hem. . . . But these Master-*Poets* they will ha' their own absurd courses; they will be informed of nothing! He has (*sirreverence*) kicked me three or four times about the Tiring-house, I thank him, for but offering to put in with my experience. I'll be judged by you *Gentlemen*, now, but for one conceit of mine! Would not a fine pump upon the Stage ha' done well, for a property now? And a *Punk* set under upon her head, with her stern upward and ha' been soused by my witty young masters o' the *Inns o' Court*? What think you o' this for a show now? He will not hear o' this! I am an ass! I! and yet I kept the stage in Master *Tarleton's* time, I thank my stars. . . .

    Book-holder: Scrivener. To him.

    Book. How now? What rare discourse are you fallen upon? Ha? Ha' you found any familiars here, that you are so free? What's the business?

    Sta. Nothing, but the understanding Gentlemen o' the ground here asked my judgment.

    Book. Your judgment, rascal? for what? Sweeping the stage? or gathering up the broken apples for the bears within? Away rogue. It's come to a fine degree in these *spectacles* when such a youth as you pretend to a judgment.

Not only do the ideas Jonson assigns this stagekeeper suggest his degree of intelligence, but the book holder expresses an equally low opinion of him. The stagekeeper must have been presented as an oldish man since he kept the stage in the time of the famous comedian Tarleton, who died in 1588 and whose great days were thirty to fifty years before the opening of *Bartholomew Fair*. The book keeper's term "youth" is therefore derogatory. His main function alluded to is sweeping the stage and clearing the auditorium of refuse for the bears.

Of course, it is quite probable that this role of the stagekeeper in the Introduction to *Bartholomew Fair* was taken by an actor impersonating the real stagekeeper at the Hope. But even so the lines must be intended to reflect the general duties and the accepted characteristics of this type of hired man.

Another duty of the stagekeeper is indicated in the postscript of a letter of Robert Daborne to Philip Henslowe. They had been corresponding about a play Daborne was writing too slowly while he appealed for more money. The letter was presumably written in August 1613. The postscript reads: "I pray sir let the boy give order this night to the stagekeeper to set up bills against Monday for *Eastward Ho* and on Wednesday the new play."[54] If the stagekeeper set up all the bills himself this was a fairly extensive daily job. How extensive is suggested by a joke John Taylor printed in his *Wit and Mirth*, 1629:

A Quiblet

Master Field the Player riding up Fleet street a great pace, a gentleman called him and asked him what play was played that day. He (being angry to be stayed upon so frivolous a demand) answered, that he might see what play was to be played upon every post. I cry you mercy (said the gentleman) I took you for a post, you rode so fast. [B6^v]

The joke is scarcely hilarious, but the "every post" implies quite a chore of bill-posting.

Other allusions to the work of the stagekeepers show them mostly in the parts of extras for crowd or battle scenes. I have seen nothing which would require much in the way of talent or experience.[55]

Late in the reign of King James the Company of the Revels presented the anonymous play, *The Two Noble Ladies*, at the Red Bull theater. Twice in the prompt manuscript (Egerton 1994) the book holder has made a note for himself that a stagekeeper is to come on, once as a guard and once as a soldier:

"guard Tay: Stage k:" (folio 228 [5]^b)
"Tay. Gib: Stage k:" (folio 233 [10]^a)

---

[54] Greg, ed., *Henslowe Papers*, p. 71.

[55] Leslie Hotson's article, "False Faces on Shakespeare's Stage," *Times Literary Supplement*, 16 May 1952, p. 336, is partly about stagekeepers, but it is a great disappointment. It is mostly conjecture. His only solid evidence comes from college plays, and it is surely obvious that the situation of the amateurs in college plays performed in private halls is vastly different from that in commercial theaters.

Evidently the John Russell, friend of Edward Alleyn who as we have seen was too dishonest to be a gatherer, was a stagekeeper, for William Bird wrote Alleyn in his complaint that though Russell was never to be allowed to hold the box again: "yet for your sake he shall have his wages, to be a necessary attendant on the stage."

In the prompt copy for Thomas Heywood's play, *The Captives* (Egerton 1994), which was licensed for performance by the Lady Elizabeth's men on 3 September 1624, the book keeper has jotted in two reminders of two appearances by stage-keepers: "Stage" (folio 61^b) where he appears as a country fellow and again on folio 70^a he has written "stagekeepers as a guard."

In certain types of situations at the inferior theaters the stagekeepers evidently did not bother to change from their blue smocks. In the arrogant prologue to his *Hannibal and Scipio* performed by Queen Henrietta's men at the Phoenix in 1635, Thomas Nabbes boasts of his play:

> 'Tis free
> As ever play was from scurrility.
> Nor need you ladies fear the horrid sight
> And the more horrid noises of target fight
> By the blue-coated Stage-keepers. . . .

The usual stage-sweeping duties of the stagekeepers are referred to in one of the commonwealth newsbooks among the Thomason Tracts (E 745 4) quoted by Howard H. Schless in a letter to the *Times Literary Supplement*.[56] He quotes from a rather jocose piece in *Mercurius Fumigosus*, for 17 June 1654:

> The same day a clear stage
> And from her no favor

Two masculine Women *Fencers*, being to fight a Duel, had chosen them two feminine men for their Seconds; the *stage-keeper* sweeping of the stage, one of the *Women Fencers* un-

[56] 6 June 1952, p. 377.

tiling the house of a Trencher; and throwing it at the other Woman Fencer's head, hit the *Stage Keeper* such a blow on his upper lip, that ever since he runs *open-mouth'd* at all Gamesters that come. . . .

An unusual statement about the stagekeepers and their payment is part of the documents called Heton's Papers of 1639 published from an unnoted source in *Shakespeare Society Papers*. Heton was manager and apparently part-owner of the Salisbury Court theater.[57] His statement about gatherers seems to indicate that in this theater housekeepers and fellows were not assigned the receipts from different doors as at other theaters. Unfortunately he gives nothing specific about what the duties of the stagekeepers were.

> *The difference between the first articles and the last.*
> The housekeepers enjoy not any one benefit in the last which they had not in the first.
> And they paid only by the first.
> 1. All repairs of the house.
> 2. Half the gathering places. Half to the sweepers of the house, the stagekeepers, to the poor, and for carrying away the soil.
> *By the last articles*
> We first allow them a room or two more than they formerly had.
> All that was allowed by the former articles and half the poet's wages which is 10^s a week.

The rest of Heton's document has no bearing that I can see on stagekeepers. Nor do I see why the housekeepers should have paid any part of the stagekeepers' wages; all the other chores mentioned are connected with the upkeep of the building. Perhaps this proposal to pay half the wages of the stagekeepers was a mere bargaining point; it cannot have cost very much.

[57] See Bentley, *The Jacobean and Caroline Stage*, II, 684-87 and VI, 103-107. Heton's statement about the wages of the poet (Richard Brome) is correct.

WAGES

As we have noticed, the hired men of London companies did not hold shares but were paid weekly wages by the company. How much?

To this question there is no answer that will hold for all companies throughout the period in spite of the fact that various books and articles assert that the standard wages of hired men were such and such. Probably the most common of these grossly oversimplified generalizations derives from Stephen Gosson's statement in *The Schoole of Abuse*, 1579: "Overlashing in apparel is so common a fault, that the very hirelings of some of our players, which stand at reversion of 6s by the week, iet under gentlemen's noses in suits of silk . . ." [6]. It should be kept in mind that Gosson was trying to show players to be proud and overweening. I suppose it is possible that in 1579 some hired men regularly received six shillings a week, but I am inclined to doubt it. And at any rate the facts given below show that not many of them did and few received regularly what they were promised.

The available data shows that payments to hired men varied with the company, the date, the success of the season, and the honesty of the sharers or manager. Wages, like most other payments, were affected by the Jacobean inflation. Some hired men are recorded as agreeing to wages of five shillings a week, some to six, some to eight and some to ten. Furthermore, we have reason to believe that not all the hired men in a given company at a given time received the same weekly wage.

Normally the pay came from the sharers of the company. In their petition to the Lord Chamberlain, Benfield, Pollard, and Swanston, sharers of the King's company in 1635, say that ". . . the said actors defray all charges of the house whatsoever (vizt) wages to hired men and boys, music, lights, &c. . . ."[58]

The man one would expect to have recorded most about

such wages is Philip Henslowe. The entries about wages for hired men in Henslowe's Diary are complicated by the fact Henslowe is handling the agreements for the sharers of his companies, but he appears also to be binding certain hired men to himself.[59] These payments show a good deal of inequality in the remuneration of different hired men. On 11 October 1602 Henslowe recorded that he had "Paid unto Underell at the appointment of the company for wages which they owed him the 11 of October 1602 the sum of . . . 10 shillings." In this entry it is clear enough that a hired man of the Admiral's company was being paid by Henslowe who charged the payment to the company, but there is no indication of how many days were covered by the payment.

In a fragment of the Diary now in the British Museum there is a note in the hand of Edward Alleyn:

Md that this 8th of December 1597 my father Philip Henslowe hired as a covenant servant William Kendall for 2 years after the statute of Westminster with 2 single pence, A to give him for his said service every week of his playing in London 10 shillings and in the country 5 shillings; for the which he covenanteth for the space of those 2 years to be ready at all times to play in the house of the said Philip and in no other during the said term.

Witness myself the writer
of this E Alleyn

This agreement with William Kendall is clearly different in character from the agreement with Underell, in which Henslowe was, as usual, acting for the company and charging his payment to their account. The Kendall agreement is a personal contract between Henslowe and Kendall and there is no indication that the payments were to be charged to the company. Later there were various charges brought by players against Henslowe that he contracted hired men to himself with

[59] See the complaint of the Lady Elizabeth's men about 1615. Greg, ed., *Henslowe Papers*, pp. 86ff.

an agreement never to leave his theater and that such agreements were intended to prevent the company from ever taking advantage of a better arrangement with another playhouse. The agreement with Kendall does show, however, that there was a sharp difference between the wages paid hired men when the company was playing in London and when it was playing on tour.

Earlier in the same year another agreement seems to be of the same general character with a notable difference in wage and a further difference that it was sanctioned by principal sharers in the Admiral's company:

> Memorandum that the 27 of July 1597 I hired Thomas Hearne with 2 pence for to serve me 2 years in the quality of playing for five shillings a week for one year and 6 shillings eight pence for the other year which he hath covenanted himself to serve me and not to depart from my company till this 2 years be ended. Witness to this
> John Singer
> James Donson [Tunstall]
> Thomas Towne

Another agreement entered in the Diary about the wages of a hired man appears to be still different in that the man is bound neither to Henslowe nor to the company, but to a leading sharer in the company:

> Thomas Downton the 25 of January 1599 did hire as his convenant servant [blank in the original] for 2 years to begin at Shrove Tuesday next & he to give him 8 shillings a week as long as they play and after they lie still one fortnight then to give him half wages. Witness P. H. & Edward Browne & Charles Massey.[60]

These various agreements make it clear enough that in the Lord Admiral's company there was no uniform payment for all hired men. Not only did the pay differ from man to man

[60] Foakes and Rickert, eds., *Henslowe's Diary*, pp. 217, 268-69, 238-39, 45.

but it might be altered with varying situations of the company. One contract says full pay in London, half pay on the road; the Thomas Downton contract does not mention half pay on the road, but it does stipulate half pay when "they lie still" for more than two weeks, i.e., when they were inactive because of plague, Lent, royal mourning, or any other form of suppression. Anyone familiar with the history of the theater in the reigns of Elizabeth, James, and Charles knows that these periods of dark theaters were quite frequent, sometimes lasting for months at a time.

This evidence from Henslowe's records shows the rather straitened circumstances of hired men in the last few years of Elizabeth, but they show only what was promised, not what was received. How often and how regularly did these hired men get the pay they had expected? The theater business is always precarious. Audiences are kept away by bad plays, bad weather, bad performances, war scares, riots, rival attractions, epidemics short of full plague visitations, and other hazards. If the company suffered, one can be sure the hired men suffered first. Other records show how much they suffered.

The most detailed statements about payments to hired men by the sharers in a London company come from the witnesses in the Chancery suit of *Ellis Worth and John Blaney v. Susan Baskervile and William Brown* in 1623. Susan, the relict of Thomas Greene (d. 1612), former manager of Queen Anne's company at the Red Bull, and her son William Browne were trying to collect from the remnants of the company money they claimed the players had owed to Thomas Greene and William Browne. A number of witnesses including both hired men and sharers like Thomas Heywood were called to testify about the financial affairs of the company, but relevant here are the statements of hired men about their pay.

Roger Clarke, dwelling in Golding Lane . . . aged 24, testified that he knew all the parties to the suit, and further testified "That he this deponent hath been for the space of these two years or thereabouts an hired servant in the company of players at the Red Bull and saith that when they hired him they agreed to give unto him 6 shillings a week so long as he should continue their hired servant and they did so set it down in their book and he saith that when good store of company came to the plays that the gettings would bear it, he this deponent was paid his 6 shillings a week, but when company failed he was paid after the rate of their gettings which sometimes fell not out for this deponent's part two shillings six pence a week, nor sometimes twelve pence a week neither had he any more pay than the gettings would bear although they agreed with this deponent to give him six shillings a week, and this deponent saith that the said company and all other companies of players in and about London whatsoever they agree to give unto any that they hire to be their servants or men they usually pay them no more than it will fall out to their shares, as company do come to plays, and if company do come in so fast and so many as that the getting will bear it then the said servants as freedmen [?] have the full of that was agreed they should have, or else not. . . ."

Another witness called to testify in this suit was "John King of the parish of St. Sepulchre London, gentleman, aged 48 years or thereabouts." King testified

That for the space of these 30 years past and upwards he hath been a hired servant to the company of sharers of the players of the Red Bull, and saith that when this deponent came first to be entertained in the said house and company the then sharers did agree with him this deponent to give him wages certain by the week, but yet withal they, the said sharers, told this deponent that if at any time it should happen the getting of the said company to be but small and to decrease that then he should not have his whole wages agreed to be paid unto him but to have his part of the loss thereof as well as the said company and to have a part proportionally only to their gettings, which course hath been ever since held and used amongst the said company. And he further saith that he is sure that they nor any of them the said Sharers do ever pass their promise otherwise than as aforesaid. And he saith that if it were otherwise and were a [duty?] and that the whole wages agreed upon ought always to be paid to the said hired men howsoever it happen, then might he this deponent might [sic] recover of the company above £100 for wages agreed upon which hath not been paid this deponent by reason that sometimes the getting of the said company were small. . . .

Still another hired man testified in this suit. He was "Richard Baxter of St. James's Clerkenwell . . . of the age of 30 years or thereabouts." Baxter testified

That at the time when he this defendant came to be entertained of the company of players at the Red Bull in or near Clerkenwell he [?] as an hired man to the company, the same company did offer and agree with him this deponent to give him ten shillings a week certain wages. But this deponent saith that divers times it fell out that the gettings of the company was so small as that at some times they did pay unto the hired men or servants no wages and some times half wages and some times less. And this deponent further saith that at such times as his said wages was not paid or abridged he did reckon the same up from to [sic] time to time hoping at some time or other he had received it of the company, but yet he saith he never could receive the same for he saith that at the time when he this deponent was entertained by the company none of the said company in particular did promise or agree to pay unto him this deponent the 10 shillings a week but only proposed [?] such an offer to him this deponent which he accepted of and in this manner he saith is all the promise that they of the said company or any of them do make unto any that they entertain. . . .[61]

These records show that in both the Admiral's company in Elizabeth's time and in Queen Anne's company in James's reign the wages promised varied from man to man and from

[61] London, Public Record Office C 24/500/103.

five shillings to ten a week. Moreover one Admiral's hired man agreed to have his wages cut 50 percent when the troupe was on the road, and another agreed to a reduced wage for his first year, and a third to a 50 percent cut when the company had to "lie still." Even with such agreed reductions no Henslowe record shows whether these hired men were always paid what they were promised. Given the fluctuating theater conditions in the 1590s and the three explicit statements of Queen Anne's hired men a couple of decades later, one doubts whether their pay was as regular as the agreements specified.

In King James's reign the hired men of Queen Anne's company were also promised wages varying from six to ten shillings per week, but all three agree that they seldom received their full promised wages, and Roger Clark says that no London company regularly paid the full promised wage and that the hired men did not expect it.

Such was the situation of hired men in the London companies of the period. They were not all paid the same wages in the same company. The wages they were promised varied from five shillings to ten a week, and in at least one instance a man was promised an increase the second year. According to the testimony of three hired men in the Chancery suit of *Worth and Blaney v. Baskervile and Browne* even these promised wages were often paid only in part or not at all. Of course not every company in London was as badly off as Queen Anne's men in 1623; some were probably worse off; no doubt the hired men of the prosperous King's company were better off. But there was no uniformity in wages promised and certainly no uniformity in wages paid. As so often one comes back to the constant precariousness of the theater. That men like John King stayed with such a hazardous occupation for thirty years seems as irrational in 1623 as similar conduct by modern players seems today.

CHAPTER V

Apprentices

THE CONVENTION of the Shakespearean theater most difficult for moderns to accept is that of the boy players. These
children and adolescents were assigned all female roles[1] in the
productions of the adult companies and most of the roles of
any sort in the performances of the boy companies. Since
comparatively few moderns have ever seen professionally *trained*
juvenile actors performing any roles except those corresponding to their own age and sex, many are baffled by the imagi-
native feat of picturing an adolescent boy enthralling a so-
phisticated audience with his performance of Rosalind, Lady
Macbeth, Webster's Duchess, or Ford's Annabella. Yet those
subjects of the early Stuart kings who had opportunities to

---

[1] This assertion that the boy apprentices were assigned *all* female roles in
the plays produced by the troupes of Elizabethan, Jacobean, and Caroline

see both boys and women in female roles were not impressed by the superiority of the actresses. Thomas Coryat, who published in 1611 a widely read book about his travels, said that in the theaters of Venice he had seen women on the stage. It was not, however, the superiority but the adequacy of the actresses that struck him:

> . . . I saw women act, a thing that I never saw before . . . and they performed it with as good a grace, action, gesture, and whatsoever convenient for a Player, as ever I saw any masculine Actor.[2]

Even more explicit in his comparison, and a great deal more experienced in the theater, was John Downes, book keeper and prompter in the Restoration companies of Davenant and of Betterton. Downes says that he was with Davenant at Lincoln's Inn Fields in 1662,

---

London has been questioned now and then by some Shakespearean scholar who thinks an adult player more likely for a certain role such as Lady Macbeth, Old Margaret in *Richard III*, or the witches in *Macbeth*. So far as I know the evidence offered for such assignments has been the individual scholar's conception of the requirements of such a role and his assumption of the inadequacy of any boy to carry it off.

The only evidence I have found of adults in female roles are the assignments of the veteran comedian John Shank to the role of "Petella, their waiting woman. Their servant John Shank" in the 1652 edition of Fletcher's *Wild Goose Chase*, and "A Kitching Maid by M. Anthony F [T]urner" in the 1631 quarto cast for the revival of Heywood's *Fair Maid of the West* Part I by Queen Henrietta's men. (See Appendix, p. 275.)

Petella is given no lines in the text; the Kitchen Maid appears in only one scene (III, 1) and has five lines. The assignment of the Kitchen Maid to Turner is an enigma; he is also down for the part of Bashaw Alcade in Part Two, presumably acted at court at the same time. Could he have played the Kitchen Maid in a much earlier performance by the Lady Elizabeth's company to which he had been attached? (G. E. Bentley, *The Jacobean and Caroline Stage*, 7 vols. Oxford, 1941-1968, II, 607-608.) Since Petella in *The Wild Goose Chase* has no speeches at all, Shank must have gagged his lines. I am not impressed by T. W. Baldwin's suggestion (*The Organization and Personnel of the Shakespearean Company*, Princeton, 1927, p. 176) that he was on to supervise the apprentices, but I have no better one.

[2] *Coryat's Crudities*, London, 1611, p. 247.

And as Book-keeper and Prompter, continu'd so, till Oc-
tober 1706. . . . Writing out all the Parts in each Play; and
Attending every Morning the Actors Rehearsals, and their
Performances in the Afternoons. . . .

And he wrote of Edward Kynaston, the great actor whom he
had prompted in many a performance:

> Mr. Kynaston Acted *Arthiope*, in the Unfortunate Lovers;
> The Princess in the *Mad* Lover; *Aglaura*; *Ismenia*, in the
> Maid in the Mill; and several other Women's Parts; he being
> then very Young made a Compleat Female Stage Beauty,
> performing his Parts so well, especially *Arthiope* and *Aglaura*,
> being Parts greatly moving Compassion and Pity; that it
> has since been Disputable among the Judicious, whether
> any Woman that succeeded him so Sensibly touch'd the
> Audience as he.[3]

Dramatists as well as theater functionaries reported the effective impersonations of some of the boy actors. Even such
an acid social and dramatic critic as Ben Jonson testified. Best
known is his epitaph on the boy player Salmon Pavy who had
achieved a reputation—"the stage's jewel"—before he died at
the age of thirteen in 1602.[4] More explicit evidence of Jonson's
satisfaction with the impersonations of the boy actors is written into a passage in his *The Devil Is an Ass*. One of his characters recites a feat achieved by Richard Robinson, a boy actor in the King's company, the troupe for which the play was
written:

> *Merecraft*. . . . But where's this lady?
> If we could get a witty boy now, Ingine:
> That were an excellent crack. I could instruct him.
> To the true height. For anything takes this dottrell.

[3] *Roscius Anglicanus*, London, 1708, p. C2.
[4] "cxx Epitaph on S. P. a child of Q. El. Chappel," *The Workes of Beniamin Jonson*, London, 1616. The boy's Christian name was Solomon or Salmon, not Salathiel as given in nearly all nineteenth- and twentieth-century reprints of the epitaph. See *Times Literary Supplement*, 30 May 1942, p. 276.

Ingine. Why, Sir, your best will be one o' the players!

Merecraft. No, there's no trusting them. They'll talk on't,
And tell their Poets.

Ingine. What if they do? The jest
Will brook the stage. But, there be some of 'em
Are very honest lads. There's Dick Robinson,
A very pretty fellow, and comes often
To a gentleman's chamber, a friend of mine. We had
The merriest supper of it there one night.
The gentleman's landlady invited him
To a Gossip's feast. Now he, sir, brought Dick Robinson,
Dressed like a lawyer's wife amongst 'em all;
(I lent him clothes) but to see him behave it,
And lay the law, and carve, and drink unto 'em,
And then talk bawdy, and send frolics! Oh!
It would have burst your buttons, or not left you
A seam.

Merecraft. They say he's an ingenious youth.

Ingine. Oh, sir! And dresses himself the best! Beyond
Forty o' your very Ladies! Did you ne'er see him?

Merecraft. No, I do seldom see those toys. But think you
That we may have him?

Ingine. Sir, the young gentleman
I tell you of can command him. Shall I attempt it?

[II,8]

Jonson's exploitation in this play, as in his *Bartholomew Fair*
and *Cynthia's Revels*, of the interest of his audience in the real-
life personalities of some of the players appearing on the stage
before them is a curious device for him. But more to the point
here is the evidence in this passage that the iconoclastic Jonson assumed his audience would acknowledge the complete
credibility of the female impersonations of a well-trained boy
actor such as Richard Robinson.

The tradition of boys appearing in public performances was
an old one in Shakespeare's time: by 1590 all English towns-
men had long been accustomed to their appearance in public

presentations. The municipal pageantry for local celebrations—visits of monarchs, inaugurations of mayors, religious festivals, coronations, royal weddings, and the like—had involved impersonations and frequently dialogue and singing by juvenile performers since at least the thirteenth century.[5] So that when the commercialization of the drama by the professional acting troupes developed in the sixteenth century there was no novelty in the appearance of boys with men in the travelling troupes in the provinces or in the more settled and prestigious companies in the London theaters.

Since these boys were all minors, they were seldom explicitly involved in those financial transactions and the subsequent litigation from which such a large part of our knowledge of the players and the theaters of the time has been derived. This fact helps to account for the smaller proportion of the boy players than of the adults now known. Occasionally totally unknown boys appear in unique records, as in the list of "Boys" in the record of the visit of Lady Elizabeth's company to Coventry in 1615 (see below, pp. 141-42) and the cast for Jordan's *Money Is an Ass*,[6] or the record of the burial of a boy actor of Queen Elizabeth's company in 1591. The parish registers of St. Peter and St. Paul in Aldeburgh carry the entry: "Humphrie Swaine, a Youth, and servant to one of her Majesty's players, was buried the same day (*7 June*) 1591."[7]

Furthermore the period of notoriety for a successful boy player was likely to be three to eight years, whereas adults like Joseph Taylor, Richard Perkins, Christopher Beeston, Richard Tarleton, Robert Benfield, John Heminges, John Lowin, Robert Armin, John Shank, Andrew Cane, and Will Kempe were all before the public for twenty to forty years, and consequently there was time for many more facts, anec-

[5] See H. N. Hillebrand, *The Child Actors*, University of Illinois Studies in Language and Literature 11, Champaign, 1926, pp. 9-39.

[6] See Bentley, *The Jacobean and Caroline Stage*, IV, 685-87.

[7] J. C. Coldeway, "Playing Companies at Aldeburgh 1566-1635," *Malone Society Collections* 9 1977 (1971), 22.

dotes, and comments about them to accumulate. Nevertheless a fair amount of information can be gleaned about the usual conditions under which a boy actor worked in London between 1590 and 1642.[8]

These children and adolescents of the theater, like most middle-class boys of their age group in English cities and towns of the sixteenth and seventeenth centuries, were apprenticed to experienced masters to learn their trade. The majority of such London apprentices were training to become good grocers or shoemakers, merchant-tailors, goldsmiths, haberdashers or fishmongers, printers or drapers, and the terms of their apprenticeships were regulated by the organized guilds to which their masters belonged. Thus the grocers regulated the conduct of their members:

> Ordinance at the meeting of 9 May 1595 of the Court of Assistants of the Grocers that no brother take an apprentice less than 8 or 9 years old or for less than eight years unless such apprentice be 21 years of age at least when he enters into his apprenticeship, so that none shall be made free of the company under 24 at the least, under pain of £3.6.8 to be paid for each offence.[9]

Something similar could probably be found in the records of most of the major London guilds. The apprentice system provided the training for future craftsmen and merchants; it provided part of the work force in a printer's shop or a grocer's establishment; and the fee paid by the father or guardian of the new apprentice[10] was a perquisite for the new master.

----

[8] I am confining my attention almost exclusively to the adult companies for several reasons. Most of the available material on the boy companies has been ably set forth by Hillebrand in *The Child Actors*, nos. 1 and 2. For another reason, the well-known boy companies like the Children of St. Paul's and the Children of the Chapel were only semi-professional. How many of them were primarily singers and how many nonmusical children illegally impressed, as indicated in the Clifton-Robinson suit, we have no clear evidence.

[9] Grocers Company, Court of Assistance, July 1591-July 1616, Grocers Company Book, Guildhall Library, London.

[10] When Shakespeare's colleague and friend Henry Condell apprenticed his

It is to be expected that the customary and long-established system of child labor and novice education would be followed by the dramatic companies, and in a general way it seems to have been. But the profession of player was never so well-integrated into the established economic system as that of grocers, goldsmiths, merchant-tailors, or drapers. Confusion has arisen from the assumption that the players were as strict and uniform as the great London companies which could punish irregularities in their own courts (as indicated in the Grocer's Ordinance of 9 May 1595). There was no legally sanctioned players' guild; though apprentices were taken, trained, and exploited by all theatrical companies, there is no evidence of a set age at which boys were taken and none for a uniform duration of their apprenticeship. The assumption that the players conformed strictly to the pattern of the craft guilds has led to a number or erroneous or dubious conclusions in T. W. Baldwin's exhaustive study of Shakespeare's troupe.[11] He contends that a boy actor was normally apprenticed at the age of ten years, that all apprentices served in feminine and juvenile roles for seven years, and that, if the apprentices remained with the company, they "graduated" or first took over major adult roles at the age of twenty-one. Basing his identifications on these assumptions, Baldwin casts most of the major roles in the plays of Shakespeare and of Beaumont and Fletcher, and sets the dates when many boys began to act and when they were "graduated" to adult roles.

Unhappily the evidence, mostly accumulated since Baldwin wrote, contradicts his assumptions in a good many specific instances. Many boy players were not apprenticed at the age

---

son William, aged fourteen, to Edward Pate, haberdasher, for a term of eight years on 9 June 1625, the elder Condell paid a fee of £20. E.A.B. Barnard, *New Links with Shakespeare*, Cambridge, 1930, pp. 37-38.

Similarly, Philip Henslowe in his record of loans and gifts to or in behalf of his nephew John Henslowe in 1596 included, "Laid out for him to Mr. Newman, dyer, when he took him to prentice, the sum of 40 shillings" (R. A. Foakes and R. T. Richert, eds., *Henslowe's Diary*, Cambridge, 1961, p. 230).

[11] Baldwin, *The Organization and Personnel of the Shakespearean Company*.

of ten, and many did not serve a seven-year apprenticeship. According to his own statement in his petition to the Lord Mayor's Court in August 1631, William Trigg, a leading actor of women's roles in the company of King Charles I, had been apprenticed to Shakespeare's friend, John Heminges, on 20 December 1626 for a term of twelve years for "la 'arte d' une Stageplayer."[12] John Wright testified in a Chancery suit in 1654 that he had been apprenticed to Andrew Cane (or de Caine or Keyne), the famous comedian of Prince Charles's (II) company, at the age of fifteen and had performed throughout his apprenticeship.[13] Stephen Hammerton, the unusually popular young actor of the thirties and forties, had "nine years then to come and to be expired" in his apprenticeship in 1629, according to the Bill of Complaint of William Blagrave, manager and part-owner of the King's Revels company.[14] In an indenture dated 14 November 1606, Alice Cooke apprenticed her son Abell to Thomas Kendall "to be one of the said Children of Her Majesty's Revels and to be practised and exercised in the said quality of playing . . . for and during the term of three years next ensuing."[15] The same term of apprenticeship is indicated in an agreement of 10 March 1607/08 between Martin Slater and the shareholders of the Whitefriars theater quoted in a King's Bench suit of 1609.

> Item, it is likwise . . . agreed . . . by and between the said parties that whereas by the general consent of all the whole company, all the children are bound to the said Martin Slater for the term of three years. He the said Martin Slater doth by these presents bind himself to the residue of the

[12] Mayor's Court Book, 7 Charles I, no. 53-M54, London Corporation Records.

[13] London, Public Record Office, C 24/785/55, quoted by C. J. Sisson, "The Red Bull Company," *Shakespeare Survey* 7 (1954), 67.

[14] London, Public Record Office, REQ-2-681 Court of Requests, quoted in G. E. Bentley, "The Salisbury Court Theatre and Its Boy Players," *Huntington Library Quarterly* 40 (1977), 140-41.

[15] King's Bench, *Coram Rege Rolls*, Michaelmas Term, 5 Jas. I m582, quoted in Hillebrand, *The Child Actors*, nos. 1-2, pp. 197-98.

company in the sum of forty pounds sterling that he shall not wrong or injure the residue of the said company in the parting with or putting away any one or more of the young men or lads to any person or persons, or otherwise without the special consent and full agreement of the residue of his fellow sharers, except the term of his or their apprenticeship be fully expired.[16]

Even in the major guilds of London the age of the newly indentured apprentice was not necessarily ten nor the term of his apprenticeship seven years. As already noticed William Condell, son of the actor Henry Condell, was fourteen when his father apprenticed him to an haberdasher for a term of eight years. Robert Armin, who eventually became principal comedian of the King's company and for whom Shakespeare prepared roles in the first half of the reign of King James, had first been apprenticed to a goldsmith. He bound himself to the goldsmith, "Iohn Louyson" in 1581 for eleven years. John Lowin, later one of the leaders of the King's company, also apprenticed himself to a goldsmith, Nicholas Rudyard, "for the terme of eight years beginning at Christmas in Anno 1593."[17] Lowin must have been approximately sixteen or seventeen years old at this time. Arthur Savill was apprenticed to the actor Andrew Cane for a term of eight years when he was fourteen years old.[18]

The only example I know of a stipulated seven-year term of apprenticeship for a young player is the statement of Edward Damport, made when his touring company was called before the authorities at Banbury on 2 May 1633:

. . . Has gone with this company up and down the country playing stage plays these two years last past. His father

[16] Transcribed by James Greenstreet, *New Shakespeare Transactions*, 1887-92, pt. 3, 276.

[17] Goldsmiths' Prentice Books, transcribed in *Malone Society Collections* 3 (1954), 141 and 167.

[18] See below, p. 126.

promised his master, Edward Whiting, that he should serve him seven years.[19]

But in spite of the variations in the age at which boy players were apprenticed and in the term for which they served, there is no doubt that the acting troupes used the apprentice system to train and hold their boy actors. In addition to the quoted references to the age of the boy and the term of his apprenticeship, there are a good many more in which these juvenile players are explicitly called apprentices. A number of these references indicate that in the adult companies like the Lord Chamberlain-King's company, the Admiral's men, Queen Anne's company, and Queen Henrietta's company, the boys were individually attached to specific fellows of the company, not to the organization as a body.

Most explicit is the statement of William Trigg, or Tregg, made in 1631 when he was nineteen or twenty years old, concerning the beginning of his own training. His petition to the Mayor's Court says that on 20 December 1626 he apprenticed himself to John Heminges, free of the Society of Grocers, to learn "la 'arte d' une Stageplayer."[20]

In his well-informed *Historia Histrionica*, James Wright records a good deal of information about the Restoration actors who had had their training before 1642. He characterizes the boys as "apprentices," sometimes giving the name of the sharer to whom the boy was bound. In the dialogue Lovewit prompts Truman to talk about the old times:

> . . . *Hart* and *Clun* were bred up boys at the *Blackfriars,* and acted women's parts. *Hart* was *Robinson's* boy or apprentice. He acted the Duchess in the tragedy of *The Cardinal,* which was the first part that gave him reputation. *Cartwright* and *Wintershall* belonged to the private house in *Salisbury Court; Burt* was a boy first under *Shank* at the

[19] *Calendar of State Papers, Domestic,* London, 1633-1634, p. 48.
[20] Mayor's Court Book, 7 Charles I, no. 53-M54, London Corporation Records.

Blackfriars, then under *Beeston* at the *Cockpit*, and *Mohun* and
Shatterell were in the same condition with him at the last
place. There *Burt* used to play the principal women's parts,
in particular *Clariana* in *Love's Cruelty*, and at the same time
Mohun acted *Bellmente*, which part he retained after the Restoration.[21]

The attachment of the boy actor to a particular leading sharer
is found much earlier in Henslowe's Diary in 1599 and 1600.
On 19 December 1597 Henslowe made an entry of a loan of
thirteen shillings he had made to William Bourne of the Admiral's men and noted that the witness to the transaction was
"Thomas Downton's bigger boy whom fetched it for him."
Apparently Downton had two apprentices at this time. From
later records in the Diary it is evident that one of these boys
was Thomas Parsons, but whether he was the bigger or the
smaller one is not clear.

> Delivered unto Thomas Downton's boy Thomas Parsons
> to buy divers things for the play of the Spencers the 16 of
> April 1599 the sum of £5.

> Lent unto Thomas Downton the 5 of June 1600 to buy a
> suit for his boy in the play of Cupid and Psyche the sum
> of £2.[22]

John Rice, one of the players listed by Heminges and Condell in the Shakespeare folio of 1623 as ". . . the Principal
Actors in all these Plays" was John Heminges' "boy" when
he performed before James I at the Merchant Taylors' dinner
for the King. Samuel Gilborne and James Sands were left
bequests as his former apprentices by Augustine Phillips in
his will of 4 May 1605. Phillips was quite explicit about the
legacy to this "my apprentice," James Sands; it was to be paid
to him "at the expiration of his term of years in his indenture

[21] James Wright, *Historia Histrionica*, London, 1699, p. B2.
[22] W. W. Greg, ed., *Henslowe's Diary*, 2 vols., London, 1904-1908, I, 73, 104, and 122.

of apprenticeship." Richard Burbage had as his apprentice, Nicholas Tooley, who in his will of 3 June 1623 speaks of "my late Master Richard Burbage" and my "late Master Richard Burbage deceased."

This attachment of a boy player to an established sharer rather than to the company as a whole seems to have been standard in the adult companies throughout the period. Indeed, in stage directions and in prompter's manuscripts it is not unusual to have the apprentice identified by his master's name, as Wright says "Robinson's boy or apprentice" rather than the boy's own name.

In the "Plot" for *Frederick and Basilea*, which was performed by the Admiral's men at the Rose in June 1597, an entrance direction in scene 9 reads: "To them Philipo Basilea E. Dutton his boye." In the fragmentary "Plot" for *Troilus and Cressida* as performed by the Admiral's men about 1599, there are two entrances for "m^r Jones his boy." In the "Plot" for *The Battle of Alcazar* acted by the Lord Admiral's Men about 1589 is the entrance direction "ij Pages to attend the moore m^r Allens boy, m^r Townes boy." The "Plot" for *The First Part of Tamar Cam* as acted by the Admiral's Men about 1602 has the entrance direction "To them Tarmia & her 2 sonns: Jack grigerie & Mr. Denygtens little boy" and at another point "Enter Pigmies: gils his boy & little will Barne."[23] Even in casts where several boys are named, one of them may be designated by his master's name, as in the cast for the manuscript play *The Soddered Citizen* performed by the King's men about 1630; though four of the boys are named, the performer of Miniona's servant is called simply "John: Shanks Boy."[24]

A few years later the same system of individual attachment prevailed in Prince Charles's (II) company according to an affidavit made by Henry Gradwell and William Hall, sharers in that troupe. In the Court of Requests suit of Susan Bas-

[23] W. W. Greg, *Dramatic Documents from the Elizabethan Playhouses*, 2 vols., Oxford, 1921, II, pls. III, V, VI^a, VII.

[24] J.H.P. Pafford and W. W. Greg, eds., *The Soddered Citizen*, Malone Society, London, 1936, p. 3.

kervile (mother and principal legatee of the player William Browne who died in 1634) against John Rhodes and his wife Anne, these two players testified that Susan Greene *alias* Baskervile had regularly received at the Red Bull playhouse ". . . seven shillings a week for an apprentice which was likewise the said Browne's."[25]

One wonders what was the sanction for these apprenticeships since there is not known to have been any officially recognized guild of players. Three records suggest that sometimes the boy was officially apprenticed to an actor who was a member of one of the London guilds but trained his apprentice to act in his company's plays rather than in the business of a grocer or a goldsmith. A number of London players and managers are known to have been free of city companies: Robert Armin, Andrew Cane, Robert Keysar, and John Lowin were Goldsmiths; John Heminges was a Grocer; John Shank was a Weaver; Thomas Downton was a Vintner; Thomas Taylor was a Pewterer; James Burbage was a Joiner.[26]

Apparently John Heminges used his privileges as a member of the Grocers Company in apprenticing the boy player, William Trigg, as noted above. It is also suggestive that Robert Armin, the comedian in Shakespeare's troupe, belatedly took up his freedom in the Goldsmith's Company in January 1603/04 after he had been a player for several years and then on 15 July 1608 took James Jones as his apprentice.[27] Similarly Andrew Cane, the comedian and at this time a leader in Prince Charles's (II) company[28] took the boy Arthur Savill, who played Quartille in *Holland's Leaguer*, as his apprentice in the Gold-

[25] Court of Requests, Miscellaneous Books, Affidavit Book, Hilary to Trinity Terms 10 and 11 Charles I, vol. 138, transcribed in the Wallace Papers, Huntington Library, San Marino, California.

[26] Edwin Nungezer, *A Dictionary of Actors and Other Persons Associated with the Public Representation of Plays in England before 1642*, New Haven, 1929; and Bentley, *The Jacobean and Caroline Stage*, II.

[27] See Jane Belfield, "Robert Armin, 'Citizen and Goldsmith of London,' " *Notes and Queries*, n.s. 27 (1980), 158-59.

[28] See G. E. Bentley, "The Troubles of a Caroline Acting Troupe: Prince Charles's Company," *Huntington Library Quarterly* 41 (1978), 217-49.

smith's Company. "I Arthur Savill the son of Cordall Savill of Clerkenwell in the County of Middlesex, gentleman, do put myself apprentice unto Andrew Cane of London Goldsmith for the term of eight years to begin at Midsummer last past."[29] The statement is dated 5 August 1931 and signed "Arthur Savile." Perhaps an extensive investigation of the Apprentice Books of a number of London guilds would reveal other examples of the use by London players of the city companies in which they had rights.

RELATIONS BETWEEN APPRENTICES AND SHARERS

The relationship between apprentice and master was presumably that of teacher and pupil. One extant record shows such a relationship fairly clearly. In 1607 the Merchant Taylors entertained King James, Queen Anne, and Prince Henry at dinner in their Hall. Ben Jonson was paid to write a speech of eighteen verses to welcome the royal guests, and the speech was delivered by the boy player John Rice. The expense accounts for the occasion show the master-apprentice relationship:

> To Mr. Hemminges for his direction of his boy that made the speech to His Majesty 40 shillings and 5 shillings given to John Rice the speaker.
> 45[s]

The subsequent entry in the accounts is another reminder of the importance of costume in all appearances of actors:

> To John Mr. Swinnerton's man for things for the boy that made the speech, viz. for garters, stockings, shoes, ribbons, and gloves. . . . 13 shillings[30]

The most extensive series of boy player attachments I have encountered is that asserted by John Shank, principal come-

[29] William Ingram, "Arthur Savill, Stage Player," *Theatre Notebook* 37 (1983), 21-22.

[30] The Merchant Taylors' Court Books, transcribed in *Malone Society Collections* 3 (1954), 172-73.

dian of the King's company from about 1615 until his death
in 1636. The veteran Shank, one of the chief share-holders in
both the Globe and the Blackfriars theaters, was involved in
the year 1633 in a dispute with his fellow sharers Robert Benfield, Thomas Pollard, and Eyllaerdt Swanston who were trying
to force him to sell to them some of his lucrative playhouse
shares. When the controversy was brought before the Lord
Chamberlain, the aggrieved Shank recited his faithful services
to the company:

> . . . the complainants [i.e., Benfield, Pollard, and Swan-
> ston] would violently take from your petitioner the said parts
> [i.e., his shares in the Globe and Blackfriars theaters] who
> hath still of his own purse supplied the company for the
> service of His Majesty with boys, as Thomas Pollard, John
> Thompson deceased (for whom he paid £40) your suppliant
> having paid for his part of £200 for other boys since his
> coming to the company, John Honiman, Thomas Hol-
> comb, and divers others and at this maintains three more
> for the said service.[31]

The statements of an angry old man (he died the next year,
still aggrieved, according to his will) reveal clearly enough his
feelings that his great services were not properly appreciated,
and that the three young upstarts were trying to push him
out of his just rewards. In such a mood not only would the
old man be prone to exaggeration but his statements about
the seven and more boy players are not so precise as one could
wish. He seems to say that both Thomas Pollard and John
Thompson were apprenticed to him—"hath still of his own
purse supplied the company for the services of His Majesty
with boys such as Thomas Pollard, John Thompson"—and
that Thompson's apprenticeship was bought from some other
master (who could have been an actor of another company or

[31] Lord Chamberlain's Warrant Books, transcribed in *Malone Society Collections* 2, pt. 3 (1931), 369.

a member of some guild).[32] Shank omits to say that the company probably paid him seven shillings a week or more for the services of his trainees, as William Browne, and later Browne's mother Susan Baskervile were being paid at about this time for the services of Browne's apprentice. Or as the Lord Admiral's men thirty-five years earlier were paying Henslowe three shillings a week for his boy James Bristow, whom Henslowe had bought from the player William Augustine for £8.[33]

Shank's further statement that he had "paid his part of £200" since his coming to the company (a period of approximately twenty years) for "John Honiman, Thomas Holcomb, and divers others" seems to apply to unnamed boys whose purchase price had been shared by all the patented members but who had not been especially attached to Shank.

The final assertion that "at this time maintains three more for the said service" is more ambiguous. "Maintains" should mean that these three boys lived with him and he housed and fed them. But Shank does not say that he "supplied them" as he says he did Pollard and Thompson, nor how much they cost him as he did for the expensive John Thompson. Furthermore, three boys seems a large number for one patented member in 1635 when there were about eleven other sharers in the organization. Certainly the three boys Shank "maintained" did not constitute the entire apprentice group in 1635. Some of the King's men's plays of the 1630s required more, even with doubling. One of the very few extant casts with assigned parts is that of Clavell's *The Soddered Citizen* of about 1630 which was never printed until the twentieth century, but the manuscript gives a very complete cast. It requires at least four apprentices. Women's roles are assigned to John Thompson, to "Will:Trigg" and to "John:Shank's Boy," and

---

[32] As Christopher Babham says he bought out the apprenticeship of the boy Stephen Hammerton from William Perry, a Draper. London, Public Record Office, REQ-681, quoted in Bentley, "The Salisbury Court Theatre and Its Boy Players," pp. 129-49.

[33] Greg, ed., *Henslowe's Diary*, I, 131, 134, and 203.

a juvenile role "Fewtricks, his boy" to Alexander Goffe.[34]
Furthermore, it would have been folly for a rich company like
the King's to have had no boys in reserve or in preliminary
training. To account for the number Shank "maintained" I
can only conjecture, rather lamely, that Shank was running a
boarding house for two or three apprentices of fellow sharers
who were unable to take a boy into their households—wid-
owers? bachelors? wittol cuckolds?

This personal attachment of boys in training to senior players of the company, and the residence of each boy in his master's household, could be expected to produce juvenile resentment, for the boy was involved in a student-teacher and a
father-son situation combined. No doubt such resentment often
did exist, but I have found little evidence of it. On the other
hand there are several extant examples of bonds of affection
produced not only between apprentice and master but sometimes between the boy and other members of his master's
household as well. The wills of several players testify to such
a happy relationship.

Augustine Phillips, who had been a leading member of the
Lord Chamberlain-King's company for a decade, died in May
1605. His will reveals ties of affection and trust with various
of his colleagues in the company, including seven sharers, "to
my fellows William Shakespeare, . . . Henry Condell . . .";
other sharers, John Heminges, Richard Burbage, and William
Sly are made executors in the event of the death or remarriage
of Phillips' wife Anne. Another member of the company, his
brother-in-law, Robert Goffe, was a witness to the will, and
£5 are left to be distributed among "the hired men" of the
company. But more to the point here are the legacies to two
of his apprentices:

> Item, I give to Samuel Gilborne, my late apprentice, the
> sum of forty shillings, and my mouse-colored velvet hose,

[34] See Pafford and Greg, eds., *The Soddered Citizen*, p. 3; and Bentley, *The Jacobean and Caroline Stage*, III, 162-65.

and a white taffeta doublet, a black taffeta suit, my purple cloak, sword, and dagger, and my bass viol.

Item, I give to James Sands, my apprentice, the sum of forty shillings, and a cittern, a bandore, and a lute to be paid and delivered unto him at the expiration of his term of years in his indenture of apprenticehood.[35]

Another member of the King's company, Thomas Pope, made his will on 13 February 1603/04 with a similar bequest: "Item, I give and bequeath to Robert Gough and John Edmans all my wearing apparel, and all my arms, to be equally divided between them."[36] Though Pope does not specifically identify Gough and Edmans as his apprentices, it is likely that they were, or had been. Both are fairly well known actors, both were the right age to have been his apprentices, both lived in Pope's parish, St. Saviour's Southwark, and it is notable that the legacies are similar to those which Augustine Phillips thought appropriate for *his* apprentice a year later.

An adult player who indicated a good deal of trust for the master of his apprentice days was Alexander Cooke, also a member of the King's company and known to have had roles in plays of Jonson, Shakespeare, and Beaumont and Fletcher. At the time he made his will in May 1614, Cooke had several small children whose baptisms are recorded in the registers of St. Saviour's Southwark. He was evidently worried about the future of these children. After ordering the payment of legacies to three of them, he continues:

. . . all which sums of money I do entreat my Master Hemings, Mr. Cundell, and Mr. Francis Caper (for God's cause) to take into their hands, and see it safely put into Grocers' Hall, for the use and bringing up of my poor orphans.[37]

[35] George Chalmers, *An Apology for the Believers in the Shakespeare Papers*, London, 1797, pp. 431-35.

[36] John Payne Collier, *Memoirs of the Principal Actors in the Plays of Shakespeare*, London, 1846, pp. 125-28.

[37] Chalmers, *An Apology for the Believers in the Shakespeare Papers*, pp. 447-49.

It may be further evidence of his trust in his former master that Cooke asked for the money to be deposited in the Hall of the Grocers, the company of which his master, Heminges, was a member.

A decade later another member of the King's company, Nicholas Tooley, made a will showing not only his affection for his deceased master, Richard Burbage, but continued close ties to various members of the Burbage family as well as to that other veteran leader of the Lord Chamberlain-King's company, Henry Condell. The will was dated 3 June 1623. Tooley specified:

Item, I do give unto Mrs. Burbage, the wife of my good friend Mr. Cuthbert Burbage in whose house I do now lodge, as a remembrance of my love in respect of her motherly care over me the sum of ten pounds over and besides such sums of moneys as I shall owe unto her at my decease. Item, I do give unto her daughter Elizabeth Burbage alias Maxey the sum of ten pounds to be paid over unto her own proper hands therewithal to buy her such things as she shall think most meet to wear in remembrance of me. And my will is that an acquitance under her only hand and seal shall be a sufficient discharge in law to my executors for payment thereof to all intents purposes and constructions and as fully as if her pretended husband should make and seal the same with her. Item, I give to Alice Walker, the sister of my late Master Richard Burbage deceased, the sum of ten pounds to be paid unto her own proper hands. . . . Item, I give unto Sara Burbage, the daughter of my late Master Richard Burbage, deceased that sum of twenty and nine pounds and thirteen shillings which is owing unto me by Richard Robinson to be recovered, detained, and disposed of by my executors hereunder named until her marriage or age of twenty and one years which shall first and next happen without any allowance to be made of use otherwise than as they in their discretion shall think meet to allow unto her. Item, I give unto Mrs. Condell the sum of ten pounds. . . . All the rest and residue of all and singular my goods chattels, leases, money debts and personal estate whatsoever and wheresoever (my debts legacies and funeral charges discharged) I do fully and wholly give and bequeath unto my aforenamed loving friends Cuthbert Burbage and Henry Condell to be equally divided between them part and part alike. And I do make, name, and constitute the said Cuthbert Burbage and Henry Condell the executors of this my last will and testament. . . .[38]

John Heminges, the veteran manager of the King's company and co-editor of the Shakespeare folio, evidently cherished his relationship with his former apprentice John Rice, whose actions he had directed when the boy made a speech before the King at Merchant Taylor's Hall in 1607. After several years as a sharer in the King's company Rice had left the stage. Heminges, in his will of 9 October 1630, left twenty shillings for a remembrance to "John Rice, Clerke of S^t. Saviours in Southwarke," and he indicated his confidence in the man by making "my loving friends M^r. Burbage and M^r. Rice" his overseers for his considerable estate.[39]

A different kind of example of affectionate relations between an apprentice and his master's family is found in a letter preserved among the Henslowe and Alleyn papers at Dulwich College. This undated letter, written in Edward Alleyn's hand, was dictated to him by his apprentice John Pyk (or Pig) when the company was on tour, perhaps in 1593. The jocular tone of the letter to Mrs. Alleyn and the domestic incidents alluded to suggest that the boy had been living in a happy family situation.

Mistress:
  Your honest, ancient, and loving servant Pig hath his humble commendations to you and to my good Master

---

[38] Prerogative Court of Canterbury, Byrd 83, transcribed in Bentley, *The Jacobean and Caroline Stage*, II, 649-50.

[39] James Boswell, ed., *The Plays and Poems of William Shakespeare . . . By the Late Edmund Malone*, London, 1821, III, 191-96.

Henslowe and Mistress and to my mistress' sister Bess for all her hard dealing with me I send her hearty commendations, hoping to be beholding to her again for the opening of the cupboard. And to my neighbor, Doll, for calling me up in a morning, and to my wife Sarah for making clean my shoes, and to that old gentleman, Monsieur Pearl, that even fought with me for the block in the chimney corner. And though you all look for the ready return of my proper person yet I swear to you by the faith of a fustian king never to return till Fortune us bring with a joyful meeting to lovely London.

I cease, your petty, pretty, pratling, parling pig.

By me John Pyk

Mistress, I pray you keep this that my master may see it, for I got one to write it, Mr. Downton, and my master knows not of it.

[addressed]

To his loving Mistress Alleyn on the Bankside over against the Clink.[40]

This evidence of the affection of certain apprentices for their masters and even for other members of the sharer's family are simply what has been preserved. I cannot believe for a moment that there were no resentful or rebellious apprentices in the London professional troupes. Some boys must have proved unteachable and some families uncongenial. Among the scores of sharers in London theatrical companies it is likely enough that there were players who were unsympathetic and even cruel. But the wills and letters cited are enough to demonstrate that the apprentices to the London players were not all the unhappy victims of child labor conditions.

[40] W. W. Greg, ed., *Henslowe Papers*, London, 1907, p. 41. That young Pyk (or Pig) was a favorite is suggested by another record in the Henslowe-Alleyn collection at Dulwich. In Philip Henslowe's inventory of the costumes of the Admiral's men in March 1598 there are eighty-odd items. The name of the actor for whom the costume was purchased is mentioned only five times: William Sly once, John Pyg four times. Foakes and Rickert, eds. *Henslowe's Diary*, pp. 317-23.

A different and rather obscure relationship is the ownership of a boy player and the receipt of the payments for him by a master who was not himself an actor. The clearest example of this is Philip Henslowe and his boy James Bristow. On 18 December 1597 Henslowe noted in his diary: "Bought my boy James Bristow of William Augusten [a player] the 18 of December 1597 for £8." Several times later he records payment to him by the company for this boy at the rate of three shillings per week. Evidently Henslowe himself was not training the boy as other players were; possibly this was just another of Henslowe's obscure sidelines.

RECRUITMENT

Unhappily the evidence concerning methods of recruiting these apprentices for the adult companies is too obscure to allow one to speak with assurance of any normal procedure. It has sometimes been assumed that most of the men who became sharers and hired men in the adult London troupes had had early training in the boy companies. This assumption has no doubt been encouraged by one of the few explicit references to London theatrical affairs that Shakespeare allowed himself to make in his plays. When questioning Rosencrantz about the boy company that has pushed the players visiting Elsinor out of their theater in town, Shakespeare makes Hamlet say:

> What, are they children? Who maintains 'em? How are they escoted? Will they pursue the quality no longer than they can sing? Will they not say afterwards, if they should grow themselves to common players—as it is most like, if their means are no better—their writers do them wrong, to make them exclaim against their own succession?
>
> [Folio text, II,2]

This statement might be taken to indicate that it was usual for the children of the boy companies to move on into troupes of adult players. Possibly such was the case, but however logical such a program may seem, we do not have the names of enough boy players who appear later in adult London troupes to allow generalizations. I can find only about thirty or thirty-five—like Nathan Field, Theophilus Bird, and Stephen Hammerton—who can be identified first as boy actors and later as members of adult troupes in the metropolis. This number seems very small when we recall that we have records of on toward 1,000 professional players in England in the years 1590-1642.

There are records of a few other methods of recruitment. One is playfully alluded to by Ben Jonson after he had had more than twenty years of experience with adult London companies, especially the Lord Chamberlain-King's men. In his *Masque of Christmas*, an entertainment which was presented at court in 1616, he alludes to a situation that cannot have been uncommon, else it would have missed its comic appeal. In the entertainment "Venus, *a deafe Tire-woman*" forces her way in so that she can see the performance of her son Cupid. To the spectators she boasts about the boy:

> Aye, forsooth, he'll say his part, I warrant him, as well as ere a Play boy of 'em all: I could ha' had money enough for him, and I would ha' been tempted, and ha' let him out by the week to the King's players. Master *Burbage* has been about and about with me; and so has old Mr. *Heminges* too; they ha' need of him. . . .

Of course this is fictional dialogue, but it was written by a man who knew a great deal about the London commercial theater situation, the company involved, and methods used. Burbage is known to have had apprentices and Heminges was the manager of the company in question. The dialogue would have lost most of its effect if the recruitment method asserted had been unheard of at the time.

A number of years later this same practice of boys being sought from their parents for apprenticeship in the theater is alluded to by William Prynne. Of course the attitude of Prynne is quite different from that of Ben Jonson's deaf tirewoman, but the Puritan propagandist could record facts whatever his bias. In *Histrio-Mastix. The Players' Scourge* or *Actors' Tragedy*, 1633, he laments:

> Pity it is to consider how many ingenuous witty, comely youths, devoted to God in baptism, to whom they owe themselves, their services; are oft times by their graceless parents, even wholly consecrated to the Stage (the Devil's Chapel as the Fathers phrase it) where they are trained up in the School of Vice, the Play-house (as if their natures were not prone enough to sin, unless they had the help of art to back them) to the vary excess of all effeminancy, to act those womanish, whorish parts which Pagans would even blush to personate. [Z2-Z2ᵛ pp. 171-72]

Still other recruitments are referred to by the players themselves. In the year 1635 the Sharers' Papers of Cuthbert and Winifred Burbage, brother and widow of Richard Burbage, recite certain facts in the history of the company:

> . . . The father of us Cuthbert and Richard Burbage was the first builder of Playhouses and was himself in his younger years a player . . . and to ourselves we joined those deserving men, Shakespeare, Heminges, Condell, Phillips and others, partners in the profits of that they call the house. . . .
>
> . . . Now for the Blackfriars, that is our inheritance, our father purchased it at extreme rates and made it into a playhouse with great charge and trouble, which after was leased out to one Evans that first set up the boys commonly called the Queen's Majesty's Children of the Chapel. In process of time, the boys growing up to be men which were Underwood, Field, Ostler, & were taken to strengthen the King's service and the more to strengthen the service, the boys daily wearing out, it was considered that house would be as fit for ourselves, and so purchased the lease remaining from Evans with our money and placed men players, which were Heminges, Condell, Shakespeare & . . . these new men [i.e., Benfield, Pollard, and Swanston who were petitioning to be given some of the Burbage shares in the two

houses] that were never bred from children in the King's service. . . .[41]

That the King's men were interested in acquiring the services of some of the boys of the Queen's Chapel when the Blackfriars was taken over is likely enough. However, at the time of this petition, 1635, the Burbages were recollecting events a quarter of a century in the past and the three men they name had been dead twenty-one, sixteen, and eleven years. Ostler, Field, and Underwood had indeed been boys in the Chapel company as is shown in the cast lists for Jonson's *Poetaster*, *Cynthia's Revels*, and *Epicoene* and they had all eventually become players in the King's company, but such biographical evidence as we have makes it doubtful that as boys these three came directly to King James's company in 1608 or 1609. It may be that the company took in several juveniles when they purchased the Blackfriars, but these three are the only former Chapel boys who are known eventually to have become sharers in the King's men.

So far as I know the only formal plan for acquiring boy actors for a major adult company is that revealed in a suit in the Court of Requests in the year 1632, *Christopher Babham v. Richard Gunnell*. Richard Gunnell was a well-known theatrical personality—player, theatrical manager, theater builder, and dramatist, or at least play doctor.[42] In 1629 he joined with William Blagrave, Deputy Master of the Revels, in building the Salisbury Court theater. Christopher Babham is a slightly known figure who was an investor in the Salisbury Court and its boy company. In his Bill of Complaint, 22 October 1632, Babham recites the arrangements at the beginning of the new enterprise:

That whereas one Richard Gunnell and William Blagrave, gentlemen, did join together as partners in share to erect and build a new stage playhouse in or near Dorset Court

[41] "Dramatic Records: The Lord Chamberlain's Office," *Malone Society Collections* 2, pt. 3 (1931), 370-71. For a discussion of the context, see Bentley, *The Jacobean and Caroline Stage*, I, 43-47.

[42] See Bentley, *The Jacobean and Caroline Stage*, II, 454-58.

137

in the parish of St. Bridget alias Brides, London, as also to train and bring up certain boys in the quality of playing with intent to be a supply of able actors to your Majesty's servants of Blackfriars when there should be occasion, and in the mean time for the solace of your Royal Majesty, when you should please to see them, as also for the recreation of your loving subjects. . . .

This assertion about a Restoration type of training school for young players is most surprising, and one might be inclined to doubt that the new troupe was formed for any such purpose, but Babham's opponent in the lawsuit confirms this statement in his reply to the charges. Gunnell's answer says:

. . . this defendant and William Blagrave gentleman did join together as partners in share to erect and build a new Stage playhouse . . . as also to train and bring up certain boys in the quality of playing not only with intent to be a supply of able actors to his Majesty's servants of the Black Friars when there should be occasion as by the said bill of complaint is suggested but the solace of his Royal Majesty when his Majesty should please to see them and also for the recreation of his Majesty's subjects.[43]

The existence of such a training school had been totally unsuspected, but these hostile antagonists agree that there had certainly been such an organization. A little more about the enterprise is revealed further along in the documents of the suit. Of course the principal bone of contention between the two parties was, as usual, monies paid or unpaid, but the charges and countercharges of plaintiff and defendant reveal a little more about this curious troupe of boys.

The new venture began at a bad time, for in 1630 there was a plague closing of thirty weeks[44] and the proprietors got very little return on their investment in theater building, costumes, fittings, plays, and the maintenance of the boys. Gunnell had

[43] Bentley, "The Salisbury Court Theatre and Its Boy Players," p. 137.
[44] See Bentley, *The Jacobean and Caroline Stage*, ii, 657-58.

to sell his holdings to Babham for £550. But Babham had the same problems as Gunnell had had before him, and did not make all his payments on time; he claims the properties were in worse condition than he had been led to believe. Hence the suit.

Babham in his explanation of the reasons for his delays in paying his installments recounts the number and the sad state of the boys after the plague had forced them to be idle for so many weeks:

> . . . the boys were delivered to your subject in far worse plight than he hoped, for amongst fourteen of them there was not found seven shirts, and but five sheets and a half to lodge them in, their apparel so ragged and so altogether unprovided of fitting necessaries that being in the time of pestilence it might have endangered your subject's life that was constrained to look over and provide a supply to their wants. Diverse of them were likewise sick, and one of them died occasioned by an ill diet, some of them being forced to steal, others to beg for want of sustenance. . . .

In his answer Gunnell, predictably, denies that the boys were in any such serious plight as Babham asserts, but he does agree that there were fourteen boys and adds that in order to avoid infection he had hired a house in Hackney to which he had moved his family and all fourteen boy players.

Both the agreement of the litigants and the large number of boys cited by each of them seem good evidence that the new enterprise was indeed intended to be in part some sort of training school. But the venture must have failed, for thirty weeks of plague-enforced idleness and all the initial expenses of a new company were surely too much for any new organization to withstand. And we know that in December of 1631 this new company of boys, apparently called the King's Revels company, though the name is never used in the lawsuits, was out of the Salisbury Court theater, and the new troupe of Prince Charles's (II) men was in. In the Signet Office Doquet Book is the entry dated December 1631: "A license unto Andrew Kayne and others by the name of servants of the Prince to exercise and practice all manner of plays in their new playhouse in Salusbury Court. . . ."[45] The presence of the new company in the Salisbury Court theater makes it evident that the training school was out, though there is a little somewhat contradictory evidence that the company of boys may have struggled on in the provinces.[46] Surely they could no longer have been seriously training boys for the King's company.

Was this Gunnell-Blagrave attempt to develop a training school for boy actors at the new Salisbury Court theater the first of its kind? That theater had influential connections, since both the Master of the Revels and the Deputy Master had a stake in it.[47] I suspect that this enterprise so helpfully outlined in the Court of Request suit of *Christopher Babham v. Richard Gunnell* was not without antecedent or successor, for in the theater-mad London of these years there was a constant demand for new boy players. The statement of Cuthbert Burbage in his petition to the Lord Chamberlain outlining the past of the King's company, "the boys daily wearing out" must have applied equally to all the scores of dramatic companies, London and provincial. Unhappily I can find no hard evidence of other such training companies, but I have come to suspect two fairly well known troupes, one earlier than the Blagrave-Gunnell venture and one later: the Lady Elizabeth's company and the King and Queen's Young company, or Beeston's Boys.

The Lady Elizabeth's company which was formed as an ordinary London troupe in 1611 evidently fell on hard times and in the next several years is found mostly in the provinces.

---

[45] Ibid., I, 302-303 for further evidence.

[46] See the account of the King's Revels company in ibid., I, 283-301. Of course, this chapter was written thirty or forty years before anyone but the Wallaces knew of *Babham v. Gunnell*; nevertheless, I blush to read my clumsy attempt to reconcile the contradictory evidence then available.

[47] See ibid., VI, 86-115.

Sir Edmund Chambers quotes from *Coventry Papers from Corporation MSS* published in the *Warwickshire Antiquarian Magazine*:

> One of the Company of the lady Elizabethe's players came to this Cittie the 27th of March and said to Thos: Barrowes Clothworker these words. vizt you are such people in this Toune so peevishe that you would have your throats cutt and that you were well served you would be fatched up with pursevaunts.
>
> Witness hereof   THOMAS BARROWES.
>
> The names of the players names named in the patent the lady Elizabethes players bearinge Date the xxxj[th] of May. Anno undecimo Jacobi [1613].
>
> John Townesend   } Sworn officers & none other named
> Josephe Moore   } in the patent.
> William Perry
> Robert Fintrye
> George Bosgrove
> Thomas Suell
> James Jones
> Charles Martyn   Boyes.
> Hughe Haughton
> James Kneller
> John Hunt
> Edward
> Raphe
> Walter Barrett
> 5 Horses in their Company.[48]

This entry in the Coventry records is quite unusual. The town clerk says explicitly that only Moore and Townsend were named in the patent. Both are known as Lady Elizabeth's men from a number of other records, largely provincial. Patents usually named six to twelve chartered members. Next, the

---

[48] E. K. Chambers, "Elizabethan Stage Gleanings," *Review of English Studies* 1 (1925), 182-83.

number of boys is excessive; twelve boys are more than any play would demand, and we are reminded of the fourteen boys Babham and Gunnell agree were in the training company of the King's Revels sixteen years later. This Lady Elizabeth's company does not seem to be the ordinary poor travelling troupe as they were supporting five horses. Of course, this evidence is quite inadequate to indicate that the troupe at Coventry was a training organization like the one Blagrave was organizing for the Salisbury Court in 1629, but I think it might be worth further investigation.

The other troupe about which I am tempted to speculate is the King and Queen's Young Company or Beeston's boys, 1637 to 1641 or '42. The Master of the Revels seems to have been involved in the organization of this company, as he had been in the Blagrave-Gunnell company. He says the troupe was formed at the King's command. It has been assumed that the resultant organization was an old-fashioned boy company.

But when the company offended the authorities, the Council called before it five men, all known adult actors, surely too many adults for an ordinary boy troupe. Furthermore when a ticket of privilege was issued for the Young company at the Cockpit on 10 August 1639, most—possibly all—of the players named were adults. Moreover when Christopher Beeston died he was succeeded by his son, William. William Beeston was sworn "his Majesty's Servant in Ordinary in the Quality and under the Title of Governor and Instructor of the King and Queen's young company of actors." Why Instructor?

In May 1640 William Beeston was jailed for presenting an unknown play with political allusions to the King's journey to the North. William Davenant was appointed six or seven weeks later to succeed young Beeston. Davenant's patent authorized him

> to take into his government and care the said company of players, to govern, order, and dispose of them for action

and presentments, and all their affairs in the said house as in his discretion shall seem best to conduce to his Majesty's service in that Quality. . . .[49]

This license to "govern" is unusual in patents for players and again suggests an abnormal company.

Then there is the odd statement written by the professional dramatist, Richard Brome, for the epilogue of his play *The Court Beggar* performed in 1639 or 1640 and printed in his *Five New Plays*, 1653.

> There's wit in that now. But this small Poet vents none but his own, and his by whose care and directions this stage is govern'd, who has for many years both in his father's days, and since directed poets to write and players to speak till he trained up these youths here to what they are now. I some of 'em from before they were able to say a grace of two lines long to have more parts in their pates than would fill so many Dry-fats. And to be serious with you, if after all this by the venomous practice of some who study nothing more than his destruction, he should fail us, both poets and players would be at loss in reputation.[50]

A further hint that the Beestons' enterprise at the Phoenix or Cockpit in Drury Lane had had some special instructional character is to be found in a Chancery suit, *Beeston v. Rolleston*, brought in 1651. The issue was the control of the Phoenix where there had been a certain amount of surreptitious playing since the Parliamentary prohibition, and to which Rolleston had secured the reversion from the ground landlord. In his bill in Chancery William Beeston says that after an agreement with Rolleston on 2 January 1650/51 he had

[49] See the *Malone Society Collections* 2, pt. 3 (1931), 395. For the context see Bentley, *The Jacobean and Caroline Stage*, I, 324-36.

[50] For the confusion about the environment and dating of this play and the allusions of this quotation, see Bentley, *The Jacobean and Caroline Stage*, III, 61-65.

entered upon the premises and laid out near two hundred pounds about the repairing and fitting the same for [his] occasions. And after that [he] took prentices and covenant servants to instruct them in the quality of acting and fitting them for the stage, for which the said premises were so repaired and amended, to his great charge and damage. . . .[51]

William Beeston's statement that he "took prentices and covenant servants to instruct them in the quality of acting and fitting them for the stage" seems to imply the continuation of the sort of enterprise Richard Brome had spoken of in the epilogue to *The Court Beggar* a decade before.

The sum of these several hints is certainly not conclusive proof that Beeston's Boys or the King and Queen's Young company was a training school for boy players as the troupe at the Salisbury Court theater had been planned to be. But the various documents appear to me to indicate at least that the organization of the Beestons at the Phoenix from 1637 to 1642 was something more than we had previously thought. The words "training," "instructor," and "governor" are used with abnormal frequency in these documents.

But even if there were additional training companies for boy actors besides the one organized by Blagrave and Gunnell in 1629, they were certainly insufficient to provide all the boy players needed for the numerous dramatic companies. The search for likely juveniles must have been unending. The number of boy players required must have been a good deal greater than those needed for the metropolitan troupes.

No doubt many of the boys went into the provincial troupes of whose personnel very little is known. We are prone to think that all professional players worked in the well-known London organizations. It is easy to forget how many road companies were touring the provinces in the years 1590-1642—far more than in London. Miss Alice B. Hamilton said recently that she had found notices of more than fifty different dra-

[51] Leslie Hotson, *The Commonwealth and Restoration Stage*, Cambridge, Mass., 1928, pp. 94-98.

matic companies in the records of Leicester alone during the sixteenth and seventeenth centuries.[52] Three quarters of a century ago in a rather superficial survey of touring companies in the provinces J. T. Murray found local records of the visits of more than 130 different acting troupes in 78 provincial towns from St. Ives to Aberdeen. Though many of these companies surely were short-lived, others evidently were not; they must have involved hundreds of players, and a good many of them must have come from London and not a few could have had juvenile training in London theatrical troupes. Not all boy actors can have been as talented as Nathan Field, Salmon Pavy, and Stephen Hammerton. If no London company had anything to offer the boy player after his voice had changed, the many provincial companies might offer employment, even if not a very good living.

All in all the fact is inescapable that hundreds of boy players must have been performing in London and in the provinces during the years 1590-1642, but the precise ways in which most of them came to their profession or later advanced from feminine to adult roles can at present be only conjectured from pitifully few examples.

WAGES

The remuneration for the boy players who were essential to every dramatic company of the period was food, lodging, training in the profession, and presumably clothes as indicated in *Babham v. Gunnell* above. I have found no record to suggest that any boy ever received cash from his company. He had been bought, in the instances we know, from his master in one of the regular guilds, or from his parents or guardians. The fees paid each week by the company for his services went to the master and not to the boy.[53] Thus Henslowe's

[52] *Records of Early English Drama*, Toronto, 1979, 1, 18.

[53] Apparently there were occasional exceptions to the retention of all payments by the master. When the Merchant Taylors' Company entertained the King, Queen, and Prince at dinner in June 1607, the boy actor of the King's

records show that the wages of the boy, James Bristow, whom he had bought from the player William Augusten for £8 on 18 December 1597, were three shillings per week in August 1600. They were paid by the company (greatly in arrears) to Henslowe because he owned the boy.[54]

By 1635 the rate of pay for apprentices like everything else had increased, as is shown in the papers of a suit in that year. William Browne, a sharer in the Red Bull company, died in November 1634. His mother and executrix Susan Greene-Browne-Baskervile brought an action against the company for money due her deceased son. In May 1635, two members of the company, Henry Gradwell and William Hall, testified that among other sums the company had paid Mrs. Baskervile was "seven shillings a week for an apprentice which was likewise the said Browne's."[55]

Spotty as the surviving information about recruiting, attachments, and wages of the boy players may be, it shows something of their position in the theatrical milieu of these years. Though the function of these apprentices was obviously important in the production of great plays like *As You Like It*, *A Woman Killed with Kindness*, and *The Maid's Tragedy*, they were completely subordinate and dependent in the organization of the London professional troupes.

---

company, John Rice, delivered a speech to the royal guests. The Merchant Taylors' records show that the boy's master, John Heminges, was paid forty shillings for coaching his apprentice in the speech, and the boy Rice himself was paid five shillings. One hopes that Heminges did not confiscate the five shillings (*Malone Society Collections* 3 [1954], 172).

[54] Foakes and Rickert, eds., *Henslowe's Diary*, pp. 118, 164, 167, 241.

[55] Court of Requests, Miscellaneous Books, Affidavit Book, Hilary to Trinity Terms 10 and 11 Charles I, vol. 138, transcribed in the Wallace Papers.

CHAPTER VI

Managers

THE COMPLEXITY of the affairs in which Elizabethan, Jacobean, and Caroline repertory companies were necessarily involved required that some one or two players be in charge, at least to the extent of authorizing the purchase of new costumes and costume materials; paying for new plays by freelance dramatists; getting scripts approved by the Master of the Revels, paying him for licenses for the theater and for occasional privileges, like playing during parts of Lent; paying the company's regular contributions to the poor of the parish, assessing fines against sharers or hired men for infringement of company regulations; calling rehearsals; collecting fees for court and private performances; supervising the preparation and distribution of playbills;[1] and perhaps for paying the hired

---

[1] The importance of playbills in the economy of the theatrical troupes of the time is indicated in the agreement between Thomas Greene and Martin

men. The extensive financial dealings of the Lord Chamberlain-King's company would have been chaos if all ten or twelve sharers had tried to perform these functions collectively.

On the other hand there is no reason to think that the earlier players' representatives whom I have, perhaps inaccurately, called "managers" usually had anything like the power over their companies later exercised by Davenant, Killigrew, or Garrick. Moreover, such power as these earlier "managers" did exercise appears to have varied a good deal from company to company and from the rather chaotic days of the 1590s to the more strictly organized times of the 1630s.

The familiar need for some sort of professional supervision even in amateur civic productions has been demonstrated by new evidence of their use discovered by Professor Coldewey. Early in the sixteenth century several towns near London—

Slater recited in *Greene v. Slater* in the Court of Common Pleas in 1607. Greene was presumably at this time manager of Queen Anne's company at the Red Bull; Slater, a sworn member of the company, had apparently been touring under the name of Queen Anne's company but with few, if any, of her patented members in his troupe. After the payment to him of £12 by Greene and the other named sharers in Queen Anne's company, Slater agreed that ". . . Although he be sworn one of Her Majesty's players yet in respect and consideration of the sum of £12 to him by them paid he the said Martin Slater shall forbear and be restrained from setting up any bills for playing or playing as in the name of Her Majesty's servants. . . ." And later in the document the point is repeated that neither Slater nor any other by his appointment will "set up or publish any plays or playbills . . . in the name of Her Majesty's players unless he the said Martin shall then have in his company to play with him five other of the said Her Majesty's servants . . ." (Court of Common Pleas, Mich 5 Jas I Roll 1789 MMCXIIII, as transcribed in the Wallace Papers, Huntington Library, San Marino, California).

The abuse in which Slater agrees not to indulge was apparently common. Some sharer in a London company would procure an exemplification of the company's patent, recruit a group of second-rate players, and tour the provinces posing as the authentic London company. Greene and his fellows bribe Slater to desist from this practice. However, the abuse in general continued, not only by Slater but by other London players. The Lord Chamberlain attempted to stop it in 1616 by an order sent to all provincial officials and naming several of the culprits, including Slater (see J. T. Murray, *English Dramatic Companies 1558-1642*, 2 vols., London, 1910, II, 343-44).

Chelmsford, Maldon, Heybridge and Lydd—repeatedly paid men from the metropolis, often called "property players," to supervise and to furnish materials for local dramatic productions. The payments were not small, and a few of the records show the services of the imported "property player" to have been extensive.[2]

In the professional touring troupes of the sixteenth century there seems always to have been a leading player and there are suggestions that he made arrangements and did a certain amount of directing, but the evidence is sparse and not very helpful.[3]

For the period after 1590 the man most often called a manager by modern writers is Philip Henslowe. But this is an error; he was not really a manager, though it seems that he was trying to become one when the Lady Elizabeth's men were tenants at his Hope theater in the years 1614-1615. Henslowe was essentially a theater owner and financier whose extant theatrical records are more extensive than those of any other man of his time. He certainly had many dealings with players, dramatists, tailors, fencers, upholsterers, Revels officials, carpenters, acrobats, and mercers. He laid out the money involved in transactions for the players, but he did so at the direction (usually recorded) of some sharer in the company. Like any financier or "angel" he had an influence on the actions of the companies playing at his theaters. His true function and the misconception that he was an early manager have been most thoroughly discussed by Bernard Beckerman.[4]

[2] See John C. Coldewey, "The Digby Plays and the Chelmsford Records," *Research Opportunities in Renaissance Drama* 17 (1975), 103-121; and his "That Enterprising Property Player: Semi-Professional Drama in Sixteenth-Century England," *Theatre Notebook* 31 (1977), 5-12.

[3] See David Bevington, *From "Mankind" to Marlowe*, Cambridge, Mass., 1962, *passim*; and the scenes with the travelling players in *Hamlet* and *Sir Thomas More*.

[4] "Philip Henslowe" in Joseph W. Donohue, ed., *The Theatrical Manager in Britain and America*, Princeton, 1972, pp. 19-62. Though Beckerman shows clearly that Henslowe was not a manager during the period of the Diary, he goes on to show, mostly from the later letters published in the *Henslowe Papers*

Who were the "managers" for the London professional troupes from 1590 to 1642? And what did they do? The answers to these questions must be less complete and definitive than one would wish, but there is quite a lot of scattered material bearing upon the subject.

The clearest and best defined function of "managers" in these years was dealing with officials—collecting fees for court performances, collecting cloth allowances for liveries for the royal companies, dealing with the Master of the Revels when the company had offended or wanted a new play licensed for performance. But there were others as we shall see.

A dozen or more of these "managers" or company representatives or leaders can be identified in eight or ten different companies during the fifty-two years of playing between 1590 and 1642. But in the first two decades, except for the entries in Henslowe's Diary, the evidence is so scattered and incomplete that one cannot build up a very useful picture of what these earlier managers did. It is likely, of course, that they carried out most of the chores which Heminges and Beeston are known to have undertaken later, but too little of the evidence is extant.

It is fairly clear that Edward Alleyn was performing managerial functions for the Admiral's and the Palsgrave's men in these early years and that he was followed by Edward Juby. It is also clear that Thomas Greene was doing the same for Queen Anne's men in the first decade of the reign of King James, and that the dramatist and clown, William Rowley, functioned as manager for the Duke of York-Prince Charles's company before he became one of the King's men. But the managers most frequently cited are John Heminges in his activities for the King's company, and Christopher Beeston successively for Queen Anne's men, the Lady Elizabeth's men,

---

(ed. W. W. Greg, London, 1907), that Henslowe appears to have been trying to develop real managerial powers over the companies at his theater, the Hope—first the Lady Elizabeth's men and then Prince Charles's—but he antagonized the companies, and there is no evidence that he established himself with the Master of the Revels or the Lord Chamberlain.

Queen Henrietta's company, and the King and Queen's Young company.

JOHN HEMINGES

The most fully documented of the managerial careers of the period is that of John Heminges, whose recorded activities on behalf of the Lord Chamberlain-King's company are numerous. From 1596 to 1630 he was always the sharer who received payment for plays performed before the court by the company. On occasions he was joined by another sharer: twice by Thomas Pope, once by George Bryan, once by Richard Cowley, and once by Augustine Phillips, but generally his name appears alone.

About fifty such payments to Heminges for court performances are recorded, reaching a total of well over £3,000.[5] If he was so consistently the receiver of payments by the Lord Treasurer's office, he probably received the payments for other restricted performances by the company at noblemen's houses, at the Inns of Court (like the performance of *The Comedy of Errors* at Gray's Inn in 1594 or *Twelfth Night* at the Middle Temple in 1602 or *Sir John Oldcastle* before the Lord Chamberlain and the Dutch Ambassador in 1600), or at entertainments for City companies.

Heminges was also the receiver of the cloth for the liveries of the fellows of the company—at least so far as the records show; most of the earlier records have been lost, but from 1619 to his death only Heminges is recorded as the recipient of the biennial allowances for the patented members of the company.[6] On various occasions Heminges, sometimes with another sharer, was used as the official representative of his

[5] David Cook and F. P. Wilson, "Dramatic Records in the Declared Accounts of the Treasurer of the Chamber, 1558-1642," *Malone Society Collections* 6 (1962), 29-81. This large sum is several times what it cost to build a new theater in Heminges' time.

[6] G. E. Bentley, *The Jacobean and Caroline Stage*, 7 vols., Oxford, 1941-1968, I, 90.

company. In 1615 when eight players representing the four London companies were called before the Privy Council to answer for playing during Lent, Heminges and Burbage were called to represent the King's men.[7]

Hemings' dealings with the Master of the Revels show him in another capacity as the representative of his company in whom, by implication, the Master had confidence. On 19 August 1623, Sir Henry Herbert noted that he had allowed

> For the King's players. An old play called *Winter's Tale*, formerly allowed of by Sir George Bucke and likewise by me on Mr. Heminges his word that there was nothing profane added or reformed, though the allowed book was missing; and therefore I returned it without a fee, this 19 of August 1623.

Hemings was also the man who paid fees to the Master of the Revels on behalf of the company. Sir Henry recorded on 20 March 1626/27 "From Mr. Heminges for this Lent allowance £2.0.0." Seven or eight years earlier Heminges had paid a fee to the Master for all four companies, "Of John Heminges in the name of the four companies for toleration in the holy days, 44*s.* January 29, 1618[/19]." Perhaps the most marked example of Hemings' standing with the Master is found in an Office Book entry of April 1627. Since there was no national copyright law, the publication of the Shakespeare Folio of 1623 had made the texts of these plays available to all acting troupes. On at least one occasion Heminges took care of this competition problem for the company. Sir Henry noted: "[Received] from Mr. Heminges in the company's name to forbid the playing of Shakespeare's plays to the Red Bull company, this 11 of April 1627—£5.0.0." A year before Hemings had handled some unknown situation for the King's men as shown in another entry of Herbert's on 7 July 1626: "[Received] from Mr. Heminges for a courtesy done him about

[7] E. K. Chambers, *The Elizabethan Stage*, 4 vols., Oxford, 1967, IV, 342. From the Minutes of the Privy Council.

their Black Friars house—£3.0.0."[8] Edmond Malone noted in Herbert's manuscript, from which he quoted extracts, that

> Heminges, however, it appears from Sir Henry Herbert's manuscript, took some concern in the management of the theatre, and used to present Sir Henry, as Master of the Revels, with his New Years' gift for three or four years afterwards. . . .[9]

Proper cultivation of the right officials was evidently one of a manager's contributions to the welfare of his company. We shall find Christopher Beeston making similar gestures.

The records of the Lord Chamberlain also show official assumptions that Heminges was the responsible agent in the affairs of the King's company and its members. When, in November 1628, a Henry Jenkins petitioned for permission to sue Richard Sharpe (a sharer in the company) for debt, the Lord Chamberlain replied, "I desire Mr. Heminges to satisfy the petitioner out of the first moneys accruing to Richard Sharpe either for his share or dividend, &c.[10] Another record from the office of the Lord Chamberlain presumably shows Heminges handling company affairs. On 14 December 1628 the Lord Chamberlain issued a warrant for the arrest "of Ambrose Beeland and Henry Wilson, Fiddlers, at the complaint of Mr. Heminges."[11] Since both these "Fiddlers" were musicians for the King's men it is likely that Heminges was acting for the company.

Certain other records suggest Heminges functioning for the company but are less explicit than the foregoing. There is an assertion in a Court of Request suit of 1619 that the company

[8] Joseph Quincy Adams, ed., *The Dramatic Records of Sir Henry Herbert, Master of the Revels, 1623-1673*, New Haven, 1917, pp. 25, 48, and 62n.

[9] Edmond Malone, *An Inquiry into the Authenticity of Certain Miscellaneous Papers and Legal Instruments . . .* , London, 1796, p. 251n.

[10] Lord Chamberlain's Petition Book, London, Public Record Office, 5/183, p. 43.

[11] Allardyce Nicoll and Eleanor Boswell, eds., "Dramatic Records, The Lord Chamberlain's Office," *Malone Society Collections* 2, pt. 3 (1931), 348.

had built a house for him on the grounds of the Globe. For a good many years before this, Heminges had lived in the parish of St. Mary Aldermanbury. At least twelve of his children were christened or buried there and he had held a number of parish offices. But after 1619 he appears no more in the records of that parish, except for the entry of his own burial. In the replication of John Witter dated 10 May 1619, to the reply of Heminges and Condell, Witter says:

> And the said defendant Heminges hath adjoining there unto [i.e., the Globe theater] . . . a fair house new builded to his own use for which he payeth but twenty shillings yearly in all at the most. . . .[12]

The building of this house for Heminges was presumably connected with his managerial duties for the company. His residence there would account for his appearance in the token books of St. Saviour's, Southwark, the parish of the Globe.[13]

Finally there are a couple of occasional verses alluding to Heminges as a well-known figure. Since he certainly had less fame as an actor than a number of his fellows, I can account for his mention only on the assumption that he was familiar as an agent or "manager" for the company. The less significant of the two is the ballad on the burning of the first Globe during a performance of *Henry VIII* in 1613. In the five verses Burbage, "the fool" (presumably Robert Armin) and "Henry Condy" are mentioned. The fifth stanza ends,

> Then with swollen eyes like drunken Flemings
> Distressed stood old stuttering Heminges.[14]

Though four sharers in the company are mentioned, Heminges seems to be given a special proprietary position. One

[12] C. W. Wallace, "Shakespeare and His London Associates," *University of Nebraska Studies* 10 (1910), 332.

[13] Bentley, *The Jacobean and Caroline Stage*, II, 467.

[14] First printed in *The Gentleman's Magazine* in 1816 and later published by J. O. Halliwell-Phillipps, *Outlines of the Life of Shakespeare*, 2 vols., London, 1907, I, 311. I do not fully trust the authenticity of these verses.

could wish to have more confidence in the contemporary origin of this ballad.

More significant is the epigram attributed to John Donne in a manuscript formerly in the library at Burley-on-the-Hill. Probably it was not written by Donne, but it is contemporary and the role given Heminges in the last couplet is quite fitting for the "manager" of the King's company.

> Epi: B: Jo:
> Tell me who can when a player dies
>   In which of his shapes again he shall rise?
> What need he stand at the Judgment throne
>   Who hath a heaven and a hell of his own?
> Then fear not Burbage, heaven's angry rod
>   When thy fellows are angels and old Heminges
>   is God.[15]

The choice of Burbage as a player in this epigram is easily accounted for, since he was the most famous London player alive at the time, but Heminges had little or no contemporary reputation as an impressive actor. If, however, he was manager of the King's company to which Burbage belonged, the reason for his selection by the poet for the position of final judgment is obvious. If the epigram had been written by any other lyric poet of the time, the selection of Heminges might have been fortuitous, but Ben Jonson certainly knew more about the inner workings of the dramatic companies of the time than most of his contemporary writers.

Since he was for so long a sharer in the Lord Chamberlain-King's company, more of the activities of John Heminges are recorded than of any of the others to whom I have attributed managership. So far as I can tell these activities were more or less typical of the office in the time.

[15] H.J.C. Grierson, ed., *The Poems of John Donne*, 2 vols., Oxford, 1912, I, 443. "Epi." stands for Epigram, not Epitaph. Hereford and Simpson reprint the epigram in the section of their volume called "Poems Ascribed to Jonson," *Ben Jonson*, 11 vols., Oxford, 1947, VIII, 439.

155

CHRISTOPHER BEESTON

Christopher Beeston, alias Hutchinson, left more records of his managerial activities than any other player of the period except John Heminges. His career differed in that he functioned for several different companies at different times, and in the fact that during most of his managerial years, i.e., 1612-1638, he was a theater owner, not just one of a group of housekeeping sharers like Heminges, Burbage, Shakespeare, and Condell.

Early in his career Beeston performed with the Lord Chamberlain's company; Ben Jonson listed him, along with Shakespeare, Condell, Burbage, Heminges, and six others as one of the comedians who created a role in *Every Man in His Humor* in 1598. But by 1602 he was one of the Earl of Worcester's men who became Queen Anne's players the next year; in their patent of 1609 he is named second to Thomas Greene, their leader at that time. In 1612 Thomas Greene died and in his will made Beeston one of the three overseers of the disposition of his considerable estate.[16] Beeston at this time succeeded Greene as leader of Queen Anne's company. The fact of his management is clearly stated by his fellows Ellis Worth, John Cumber, and John Blaney in their bill in Chancery against Susan Baskervile, widow of Thomas Greene. Susan had sued them for debts she claimed the company had owed her husband at the time of his death and which the company had made subsequent agreements to pay but had defaulted. The three players say in their Chancery Bill of 1623

And whereas your orators and the rest of their fellows at that time [i.e., Queen Anne's company] and long before and since did put the managing of their whole businesses and affairs belonging unto them jointly, as they were players, in trust unto Christopher Hutchinson alias Beeston, of

[16] F. G. Fleay, *A Chronicle History of the London Stage, 1559-1642*, London, 1890, pp. 192-94. From the transcript of James Greenstreet.

London, gentleman, who was then one of your orators' fellows. . . .[17]

Another lawsuit concerning the affairs of Beeston and Queen Anne's company, this time in the Court of Requests, shows Beeston buying and authorizing the buying of costume materials for the company. The suit, which was brought in 1619, concerns old debts which John Smith says that Beeston, along with his fellows Ellis Worth, Richard Perkins, and John Cumber, bought for the company. As usual, plaintiff and defendants deny most of each others' allegations, but the Bill and Answers, and the depositions of witnesses, make several statements that show some of Beeston's activities and frequently hint at his slipperiness. Smith says that he, between 27 June 1612 and 23 February 1616/17

> . . . at the earnest request and entreaty of one Christopher Beeston [did] deliver or cause to be delivered unto him the said Christopher Beeston and his assigns and at his request and by his direction unto and for the use of the company of players at the Red Bull . . . divers tinsel stuffs and other stuff for their use in playing. . . .

Three of Queen Anne's men who had been made parties to the suit, Ellis Worth, Richard Perkins, and John Cumber, chose to submit Answers separate from Beeston's. They say that with Beeston they were members of Queen Anne's company and had set forth divers plays and comedies at the Red Bull, and they continue that

> . . . for the better ordering and setting forth of which said plays and comedies there required divers officers and that every one of the said actors should take upon them some place and charge and for that the provision of the furniture and apparel was a place of greatest charge and trust and must of necessity fall upon a thriving man and one that was of ability and means, it was agreed by and between the said

[17] Ibid., p. 274.

company of actors in manner and form following: that is to say that the said Christopher Beeston in the Bill of Complaint named should defalk out of the collections and gatherings which were made continually whensoever any play was acted, a certain sum of money as a common stock towards the buying and defraying of the charges of the furniture and apparel aforesaid. And that the said Christopher Beeston should buy all the furniture, apparel, and other necessaries. . . . And that the said Christopher Beeston should with the said common stock so collected pay for the said commodities by him hereafter to be bought or otherwise that the said commodities should stand upon the sole and proper account and head of the said Beeston and that no other of the company should be troubled or employed in this business or should pay or stand charged or liable for any commodities so by the said Christopher Beeston to be bought but that the said Christopher Beeston should discharge and free the company and pay all such moneys as should arise by reason thereof . . . and upon this agreement the said Christopher Beeston did undertake this charge and trust and hath for the space of seven or eight years continually when there was any play deducted and defalked divers great sums of money out of the collections and gatherings aforesaid. . . .

Beeston's own Answer to the Bill of Complaint of John Smith, separate from those of Worth, Perkins, and Cumber, is mostly simple denials except for the statement that after Queen Anne's decease (March 1618/19) he had entered the service of Prince Charles.

On 5 May 1620 depositions of several witnesses were taken in the suit. One of them, William Freshwater, merchant tailor, aged seventy-two, gave testimony that verifies the observation that Beeston was buying costume materials for the company in 1612, the year of Thomas Greene's death. Freshwater says that about 1612 he bought materials and requested that

. . . If any the company or workmen belonging to the players at the Red Bull . . . did come of those stuffs he had
bought of the complainant or of any more or other stuff for
the use of the said company that he the complainant should
deliver them from time to time which he the said Beeston
the defendant then promised to see discharged and paid for.
. . .

Freshwater further testified that the orders for the stuffs were
made in Beeston's name, that Freshwater himself was a work-
man and had often gone to the Red Bull. He says that Smith
often refused to hand over the materials without some token
from Beeston. Another witness, Japhathe Weale, haberdasher, deposed that he had seen Beeston examine Smith's
account books in 1618 and acknowledge receipt of the materials. Still another witness, John King, identified here and in
a later suit as a hired man of the company, testified that he
knew it to be true that Smith would not deliver any materials
to any member of the company "except they brought a token
from the defendant, Beeston." King further testified that he
knew the company gave an allowance to Beeston to purchase
materials, ". . . and saieth that the said company did allow
him the said Beeston, one-half of the profit that came of the
galleries towards the satisfying of the complainant's debt which
he received weekly. . . ." King goes on that Smith delivered
materials to Beeston for eight or nine years, but that the company began to break up about three years before [i.e., 1617]
"and at the separation of the said company the said Beeston
did take and carry away all the apparel that was then amongst
the said company and converted them to his own use. . . ."[18]
    The various documents of this suit suggest that Christopher
Beeston was a rather slippery character, but the point of interest at the moment is that as manager and "a thriving man
and one that was of ability and means" he bought costume

[18] C. W. Wallace, "Three London Theatres of Shakespeare's Time," *University of Nebraska Studies* 9 (1909), 318, 321-22, 331, 332, 333-34.

materials for the company and was reimbursed by half the profits from the galleries, paid weekly.

The fact that Beeston "at the separating of the said company" in 1617 is alleged to have carried off the costumes is surely not unconnected with the fact that he was at that time building the Phoenix theater, often called the Cockpit in Drury Lane, a house that was his own property and at which he managed, sequentially, several companies of players until his death in October 1638.[19]

Near, or perhaps attached to, his new theater, Beeston appears to have had a residence, as Heminges had at the Globe. After the London apprentices raided and partially destroyed Beeston's new Phoenix on Shrove Tuesday 1616/17, several of them were charged in the Middlesex Special Session of Oyer and Terminer with defacing "the dwelling house of Christopher Beeston."[20]

Since the documents of the Chancery suit of the players against Susan Baskervile show clearly that buying materials for the company was part of Beeston's duties as manager or leader of Queen Anne's troupe, one would assume that he continued this practice with later companies that played in his own theater, when he was even more "a thriving man and one that was of ability and means." Whether other managers or leaders had the same responsibility of buying for their companies, the evidence is too meager to prove, but one would assume that they did.

Beeston's managerial activities after he was established in the Cockpit were as extensive as those of Heminges for a more distinguished and more publicized company, for Beeston was both landlord and manager. Some of the later evidence suggests that he ruled with a high hand over the companies playing at the Phoenix.

His activities for each company at his theater are attested by various records between 1611 and 1638. Like Heminges, Beeston was usually the man who received payment when his

---

[19] See Bentley, *The Jacobean and Caroline Stage*, VI, 47-77.
[20] Ibid., p. 56.

companies performed at court, but fewer payments were recorded. No troupe of the time had anything like the prestige of the King's company or played so often before royalty.

Beeston was also like Heminges in receiving the livery allowances for Queen Henrietta's company so long as they performed at his playhouse. But here his position is not so clear: the warrants for two of the allowances seem to be lost, one names no recipient, and once William Allen signed the receipt.

The managerial position of Christopher Beeston is indicated by the Master of the Revels in 1622. At the time Sir Henry took over his new office, he made a list of the London companies of players and their theaters. When Edmond Malone saw Herbert's manuscript in the eighteenth century, part of the leaf with these lists had already "mouldered away," but three entries remained, one of which was: "The chief of them at the Phoenix. Christopher Beeston, Joseph Moore. . . ."[21] Beeston's position is similarly recorded twelve years later when Queen Henrietta's company was performing at his theater. Thomas Crosfield, the Fellow of Queen's College, Oxford mentioned before, took notes on the facts about London dramatic troupes told him by one of the wardrobe keepers for a visiting London company. Part of his account reads: "2. The Queen's servants at the Phoenix in Drury Lane. Their master Mr. Beeston. . . ."[22]

Just as Heminges ordinarily represented the King's men in their dealings with the Master of the Revels, so Beeston acted for his companies at the Phoenix. His function and his standing with Sir Henry show up most clearly in two entries of the early thirties. The first concerns difficulties about a comedy of James Shirley, the company's attached dramatist at this time.

18 Nov. 1632. In the play of *The Ball*, written by Sherley, and acted by the Queen's players, there were divers personated so naturally, both of lords and others of the court,

[21] Adams, ed., *The Dramatic Records of Sir Henry Herbert*, pp. 62-63.
[22] Bentley, *The Jacobean and Caroline Stage*, ii, 688.

that I took it ill, and would have forbidden the play, but that Beeston promised many things which I found fault withal should be left out and that he would not suffer it to be done by the poet any more, who deserves to be punished; and the first that offends in this kind, of poets or players, shall be sure of public punishment.

Another entry of Herbert's only nine months later shows Beeston in a transaction reflecting relations with the Master not unlike those of John Heminges:

Received of Beeston for an old play called *Hymen's Holiday*, newly revived at their house, being a play given unto him for my use, this 15 Aug. 1633, £3.0.0.
Received of him for some alterations in it £1.0.0.[23]

Again like Heminges, Christopher Beeston took pains to cultivate the Master of the Revels for the benefit of his companies, and, no doubt, of himself as well. The exact date of this entry was not copied by Malone when he had the now lost manuscript in his hands but presumably it was about 1633. Herbert wrote: "Meeting with him [Beeston] at the old exchange, he gave my wife a pair of gloves, that cost him at least twenty shillings." Another record of Sir Henry's is perhaps less reliable since it was made after the Restoration when he was struggling to reassert his old authority as Master of the Revels and was probably overstating his case, but the item nonetheless does show Beeston's position. In December of 1660 Herbert made a series of notes for his arguments for the reinstatement of his old privileges: "To prove that Mr. Beeston paid me £60 per annum besides usual fees and allowances for Court plays."[24] Whether or not the large fee of £60 was exaggerated, the item is clear enough in its assertion of Beeston's position.

After Queen Henrietta's men left (or were forced out of) the Phoenix, Beeston's position as manager of the new com-

[23] Adams, ed., *The Dramatic Records of Sir Henry Herbert*, pp. 19 and 35.
[24] Ibid., pp. 67 and 101.

pany becomes even clearer. The new troupe was called the King and Queen's Young company or Their Majesties' Servants. In spite of its name and various references, it was not an old-fashioned boy company but involved several adults.[25] In origin the company was more official than most, for the Lord Chamberlain issued a warrant on 21 February 1636/37: "A Warrant to swear Mr. Christopher Beeston his Majesty's servant in the place of Governor of the new Company of the King and Queen's boys."[26] And three days later the Master of the Revels noted in his Office Book, "Mr. Beeston was commanded to make a company of boys, and begin to play at the Cockpit with them same day."[27]

Another testimony to his command at the Phoenix or Cockpit in Drury Lane is an order sent on 10 June 1637 to the Masters and Wardens of the Stationers' Company by the Lord Chamberlain. His Lordship observed that he had been told that certain London printers were proposing to print plays belonging to the players but which had been stolen or gotten from them by indirect means. He therefore ordered the Masters and Wardens that if any such plays were brought to Stationers Hall that the publishers be forbidden to print without

some certificate in writing under the hands of John Lowin and Joseph Taylor for the King's Servants [John Heminges had died in 1630] and of Christopher Beeston for the King's and Queen's Young company or of such other persons as shall from time to time have the direction of those companies. . . .[28]

Other documents demonstrating Christopher Beeston's activities as manager of the companies at the Phoenix from 1617 to his death in 1638 might be cited, but these are enough to

[25] See Bentley, *The Jacobean and Caroline Stage*, I, 324n.
[26] Nicoll and Boswell, eds., "Dramatic Records, The Lord Chamberlain's Office," p. 382.
[27] Adams, ed., *The Dramatic Records of Sir Henry Herbert*, p. 66.
[28] Nicoll and Boswell, eds., "Dramatic Records, The Lord Chamberlain's Office," pp. 384-85.

show what he did. His activities were obviously similar to those of John Heminges for the King's men at the Blackfriars and the Globe, except that as owner of the theater Beeston's powers seem greater than those of Heminges. The charges brought against Beeston by John Smith and by Queen Anne's men and his dealings with Queen Henrietta's company during the plague of 1636-37[29] also show that powerful as he was, he was not the generally trusted representative that Heminges was.

THOMAS GREENE

There is a reasonable amount of evidence that before Christopher Beeston took over as manager of Queen Anne's company at the Red Bull his predecessor in management was the comic actor, Thomas Greene, who was so successful in the part of Bubble in Cooke's play *The City Gallant* that the piece was published in 1614 as *Greene's Tu Quoque or The City Gallant*. For the second issue of this play an Epistle to the Reader was written by Thomas Heywood, Greene's fellow sharer and principal dramatist for the company.

> As for Master Green, all that I will speak of him (and that without flattery) is this (if I were worthy to censure), there was not an actor of his nature, in his time, of better ability in performance of what he undertook, more applaudent by the audience, of greater grace at the court, or of more general love in the city: and so with this brief character of his memory I commit him to his rest.

These qualities would be very useful in the manager of a company, especially the rather unexpected "greater grace at the court," and there is evidence that Greene was the manager, at least for the last eight or ten years before his death. His name heads the list of sharers in the draft patent for the company probably in 1603 or 1604. He is also named first in

[29] See Bentley, *The Jacobean and Caroline Stage*, I, 236-39.

the company's patent dated 15 April 1609 in the Patent Rolls. In a Chancery suit of 16 June 1623 his widow and executrix (Greene died in 1612) says that:

> . . . the said Thomas Greene deceased . . . was a fellow actor or player of and in the company of actors or players of the late queen's majesty, Queen Anne . . . and was one of the principal and chief persons of the said company, and a full adventurer, storer, and sharer of in and amongst them. . . .[30]

Half a dozen times early in the reign of James, Greene was the recipient of payments for plays given at court by Queen Anne's company. In the first few years of the reign John Duke was usually payee, but from 1608-1612, it was Thomas Greene.

Greene is also seen acting for the company in an agreement made with Martin Slater in 1607, partly transcribed above. The agreement provides that Slater will not set up any bills, or play in London or in the country as the Queen's company unless he has with him five of the sharers of Queen Anne's troupe. Though eight other members of the company are mentioned, the agreement is with Greene and the papers are docketed "*Thos. Greene v. Martin Slater.*"[31]

More conclusive evidence of his managership is the testimony given by Thomas Heywood, the dramatist and sharer in Queen Anne's company. In the Chancery suit of 1623 *Ellis Worth and John Blaney v. Susan Baskervile and William Browne*, Heywood was called as a witness. He testified:

> . . . there was no cause for the defendant Susan to pretend any debt to be due to her said husband Greene at his death by the said company for this deponent saith that the said Thomas Greene had in his life time for divers years the taking and receiving of the profits of the half galleries for

[30] James Greenstreet's transcription, *Transactions of the New Shakespeare Society*, 1880-86, pt. 3, ser. 1, p. 499.

[31] Transcript of an entry on Roll 1789 of the Court of Common Pleas, transcribed in the Wallace Papers.

the said company and whether he ever gave account thereof or no to the company this depondent saith he certainly knoweth not, but verily believeth that the said company was not any way indebted unto the said Thomas Greene at the time of his death, but that he was rather indebted to the said company. . . .[32]

This testimony of Thomas Heywood, who had been a fellow of the company for years, seems clear enough; it is corroborated by the testimony of his fellow, Richard Perkins, another well-known player whose performance in *The White Devil* had been praised by John Webster. Perkins said in his testimony as a witness in the same suit that he too thought that the company had owed nothing to Susan's husband since,

Thomas Greene had for certain years the receiving of the profits of the half galleries at the Red Bull for the company, and he saith that to his remembrance he did never know or hear that the said Greene did account to the said company at any time for the same. . . .

The agreement of these two prominent sharers seems to me to leave little doubt that Thomas Greene was acting as manager of Queen Anne's men before Christopher Beeston took over after his death. The arrangement to which both Heywood and Perkins refer, for Greene to take the profits of the half galleries, sounds like a sensible device for supplying the manager with funds for purchases and payments, but I know of no reference to such a specific plan in any other company. In fact I have seen no reference to show how other companies kept their managers supplied with funds.

OTHER MANAGERS

So far as we can tell now, John Heminges and Christopher Beeston were the longest lasting and the most fully recorded of the company managers of the period. There is ample evi-

[32] London, Public Record Office, C 24/500/103.

dence, however, that there were others; indeed, enough evidence to suggest that every company of the time probably had a manager. Perhaps a few examples of the managerial activities of certain of the players for other companies will show how common this type of organization was.

The most inclusive statement implying that each London company had a manager or chief is the one referred to before that Richard Kendall, one of the two wardrobe keepers at the Salisbury Court theater, made to Thomas Crosfield on 18 July 1634 when his company was playing at Oxford. Crosfield numbered the stories which Kendall told him. The one of principal interest here is "5. Of the several companies of players in London which are in number 5." Under this rubric Kendall listed the companies, obviously in order of importance.

> 1. The King's company at the
> private house of Blackfriars: The masters
> or chief whereof are ⎰ Mr. Tailor
> ⎱ Mr. Lowin.

These two prominent sharers in Shakespeare's old company succeeded to Heminges' duties; in fact in his last receipt of payment for court performances in 1630, their names were joined with his. After Heminges' death in that year, Lowin and Taylor always signed for the court payments, often joined by another old sharer, Eyllaerdt Swanston. Unlike Heminges, they were prominent actors as well as managers. When the Queen gave to the company the costumes that had been made for her spectacular performance of *The Faithful Shepherdess* in 1633/34, it was Taylor to whom she presented them. These two new managers also generally received the company livery allowances and dealt with Herbert for the company as Heminges had done.

The next item in Kendall's report of London theatrical affairs is: "2. The Queen's servants at the Phoenix in Drury Lane. Their master Mr. Beeston. . . ." Enough of Beeston's activities have already been recounted.

After the Queen's men under Beeston comes, "3. The Prince's Servants at the Red Bull in St. John street, the chief Mr. Cane a Goldsmith, Mr. Worth Mr. Smith £2,000." It is not clear what the £2,000 means, but we shall hear more later about Andrew Cane, or Keyne or de Caine. It is true that he was a member of the Goldsmith's Company and after the closing of the theaters seems to have returned to his old trade, but in 1634 he had been a player for at least twelve years.

After the report on Prince Charles's company in Thomas Crosfield's notes comes, "4. The Fortune in Golden Lane, the chief Mr. William Cartwright, Edward Armestead, John Buckle, John Kirke." William Cartwright was an old-timer in the theater, having appeared in Henslowe's Diary as early as 1598. He was a friend of Edward Alleyn, and his picture hangs in the gallery at Dulwich College. He is often confused with his son and namesake who continued as a prominent player into the Restoration. Kendall's assertion that William Cartwright was managing the company at the Fortune in 1634 is verified by an entry in the Office Book of the Master of the Revels showing that two years later William Cartwright Senior was performing one of the duties we have seen being discharged by Heminges and Beeston.

Received of old Cartwright for allowing the [Fortune] company to add scenes to an old play and to give it out for a new one, this 12th of May, 1636 . . . £1.0.0.[33]

The last and fullest account among Crosfield's notes is the one Kendall gave of his own troupe:

5. The Company of Salisbury Court at the further end of Fleet street against the Conduit: The chief wereof are 1. Mr. Gunnell a Papist. 2. Mr. John Young. 3. Edward Gibbs a fencer. 4. Timothy Reed. 5. Christopher Goad. 6. Sam. Thompson. 7. Mr Staffield [Stutville]. 8. John Robinson. 9. Curtis Greville. These are the chief wereof 7 are called

[33] Adams, ed., *The Dramatic Records of Sir Henry Herbert*, p. 37.

sharers, i.e., such as pay wages to the servants and equally share in the overplus: other servants there are as two Close keepers $\left\{\begin{array}{l}\text{Richard}\\\text{Kendall}\\\text{Anthony}\\\text{Dover}\end{array}\right.$ &c [34]

Before Gunnell became manager of the Salisbury Court theater he had had a career as a Palsgrave's and then as a Prince's man at the Fortune theater in which he had an interest. The first indication of his managerial functions known to me is a bond which six of the Palsgrave's men signed to him in 1624 agreeing to continue to play together at the Fortune and posting a forfeit.[35]

About a year later Gunnell is found dealing with the Master of the Revels much as Heminges and Beeston did. At times, it is not clear how regularly, theaters were allowed to offer miscellaneous entertainment during Lent when they were supposed to be closed. In Lent of 1624/25 Sir Henry Herbert recorded payments from Gunnell for such privileges: "From Mr. Gunnell, in the name of the dancers of the ropes for Lent this 15 March, 1624. £1.0.0." Four days later the Office Book records a further payment for Lenten entertainment. "From Mr. Gunnel to allow of a Masque for the dancers of the ropes this 19 March, 1624. £2.0.0.[36]

In 1629 Gunnell, in partnership with William Blagrave, Deputy Master of the Revels, built the Salisbury Court theater in which he managed a company intended as a training

[34] Frederick S. Boas, ed., *The Diary of Thomas Crosfield*, London, 1935, pp. 72-73, quoted in Bentley, *The Jacobean and Caroline Stage*, II, 688-89.

[35] A Chancery suit of 1654, *Andrew de Caine v. William Wintersall and Wife Margaret*, discovered by Leslie Hotson and transcribed in *The Commonwealth and Restoration Stage*, Cambridge, Mass., 1928, p. 52.

[36] The first entry is from Adams' collection, *The Dramatic Records of Sir Henry Herbert*, p. 48. The second Adams overlooked. It is taken from his source, Boswell's edition of Malone's *Plays and Poems of William Shakespeare*, London, 1821, III, 66.

school for boy actors for the King's men at Blackfriars.[37] This troupe was succeeded at Gunnell's Salisbury Court by Prince Charles's (II) company, the troupe that Richard Kendall lists. About three months after Kendall visited Thomas Crosfield, Richard Gunnell died.

The managers who succeeded Christopher Beeston at the Phoenix or Cockpit in Drury Lane are very explicitly named. Six or seven months after his father's death William Beeston was officially appointed. In the Lord Chamberlain's Warrant Books is the entry:

> A warrant to swear Mr. William Beeston His Majesty's servant in ordinary in the quality and under the title of Governor and Instructor of the King's and Queen's young company of actors. A certificate also for him.[38]

A couple of years later he and two other adult members of this company were jailed for acting a play without license, and the playwright William Davenant replaced him by the Lord Chamberlain's order. This was a very unusual procedure, for there is no indication that the company had anything to do with the appointment; Davenant was a dramatist and an aspiring courtier; there is no evidence that he was ever a player. The warrant of the Earl of Pembroke and Montgomery is also more elaborate than most such:

> Whereas in the playhouse or theatre commonly called the Cockpit in Drury Lane, there are a company of players or actors authorized by me (as Lord Chamberlain to His Majesty) to play or act under the title of the King's or Queen's Servants and that by reason of some disorders lately amongst them committed they are disabled in their service and quality. These are therefore to signify that by the same authority I do authorize and appoint William Davenant, gentle-

[37] G. E. Bentley, "The Salisbury Court Theatre and Its Boy Players," *Huntington Library Quarterly* 40 (1977), 129-49.

[38] Nicoll and Boswell, eds., "Dramatic Records: The Lord Chamberlain's Office," p. 389.

man, one of Her Majesty's servants, in me and my name to take into his government and care the said company of players to govern, order, and dispose of them for action and presentments, and all their affairs in the said house as in his discretion shall seem best to conduce to His Majesty's service in that quality. And I do hereby enjoin and command them all and every of them that are so authorized to play in the said house under the privilege of His or Her Majesty's servants; and everyone belonging as prentices or servants to those actors to play under the said privilege that they obey the said Mr. Davenant and follow his orders and directions as they will answer the contrary. Which power or privilege he is to continue and enjoy during that lease which Mrs. Elizabeth Beeston alias Hutchinson hath or doth hold in the said playhouse. Provided he be still accountable to me for his care and well ordering the said company. Given under my hand and seal this 27th of June 1640.

P. & M.[39]

This order seems to make Davenant more of a dictator than a manager; such powers must have been good training for his later Restoration career. But the duration of Davenant's governorship was short. In the following year there is an establishment list of the Servants of the Chamber. Under the section "Revels" appears, "Governor of the Cockpit Players, William Beeston."[40]

Managerial problems of another London troupe of about the same time are aired in a previously noted lawsuit in the Court of Requests brought by William Bankes against Andrew Cane (Keyne, de Caine) and Ellis Worth in February 1634/35. This suit and its implications have been discussed more thoroughly elsewhere[41] but one or two of its points concerning managership may be helpful here. Worth and Cane were

[39] Ibid., p. 395.
[40] Ibid., p. 326.
[41] G. E. Bentley, "The Troubles of a Caroline Acting Troupe: Prince Charles's Company," *Huntington Library Quarterly* 41 (1978), 217-49.

joint managers of Prince Charles's company at the Red Bull in St. John's Street, as Kendall had told Crosfield in July 1634. This suit concerns affairs of the company beginning two years before, when they were playing at the Salisbury Court before moving to the Red Bull. Banks, who had become a sharer in the company by paying £100.0.0 into the company treasury, calls Worth and Cane "Wardens" of the company, and at another point "Stewards" for the troupe. Worth and Cane deny that they were "Wardens," but they say nothing about "Stewards." In any case the suit makes it clear that they acted as managers and assessed sharers for moneys they had spent for costumes and furnishings, as Beeston had done for Queen Anne's men twenty years before. The suit shows that Banks was disciplined for irresponsible conduct, though it is not clear whether all the sharers or only Worth and Cane were responsible for his suspension.

Finally, something must be said about the managership of Richard Heton, a slightly known figure at the Salisbury Court theater in the last years of Caroline playing. Nothing certain is known of the earlier activities of this man who first appears officially when, like other managers, he collected fees for three court performances given by the Salisbury Court players in October 1635 and February 1635/36. The dates suggest that he may have succeeded Richard Gunnell who had been buried from the parish church of the Salisbury Court, St. Bride's Fleetstreet, on 7 October 1634.[42]

In the Court of Requests is a suit docketed *Heton v. Brome*, brought in February 1639/40 but dealing with events covering earlier years; it concerns Brome's contract as attached dramatist for Queen Henrietta's company at the Salisbury Court.[43]

[42] The manuscript registers of St. Bride's, Fleetstreet, now deposited in the Guildhall Library, London.

[43] The suit was discovered and transcribed by C. W. Wallace some seventy years ago, but never published by him except for a few hints and a sentence or so. It was printed from the Wallace Papers, now in the Huntington Library, by Ann Haaker, "The Plague, the Theater, and the Poet," *Renaissance Drama*, n.s. 1 (1968), 283-306.

Actually the suit is not so much concerned with the familiar activities of a company manager; its primary importance is its revelation of the obligations of an attached dramatist to the company for which he has contracted to write exclusively, as Brome had done.[44] Though the suit in the Court of Requests was brought in the name of the sharers in the company, Richard Heton's name heads the list, and the papers of the suit are docketed *Heton v. Brome*, an indication that Heton was manager of the company at the time the suit was brought.

Much more revealing of Heton and his activities as manager of Queen Henrietta's company in its last years at the Salisbury Court are certain curious documents discovered by Peter Cunningham and published by him more than a century ago without discussion or any hint as to their source.[45] The first of the Heton documents Cunningham found he headed "The following 'Instructions' are endorsed 'Mr. Heton's Papers.' " They reveal the astonishing powers Richard Heton was hoping to exercise over the company some time after an event of March 1639 which Heton alludes to in his justification of his proposals. The document reads in part:

That the patent for electing Her Majesty's company of comedians be granted only to myself [in contrast to all known company patents for adult companies of the reigns of James and early in the reign of Charles, which were granted to the sharers of the company] that I may always have a company in readiness at Salisbury Court for Her Majesty's service, and that if all or any of the company go away from Salisbury Court to play at any other playhouse already built or hereafter to be built, they from thenceforth to cease to be Her Majesty's servants, and only the company remain-

---

[44] For a full discussion of this relationship, see G. E. Bentley, *The Profession of Dramatist in Shakespeare's Time*, Princeton, 1971, especially Chapter IV, "The Dramatist and the Acting Company" and Chapter VI, "The Dramatists' Contractual Obligations."

[45] *Shakespeare Society Papers* 4 (1849) 95-100. His documents are reprinted in full in Bentley, *The Jacobean and Caroline Stage*, II, 684-87.

ing there to have that honor and title. Myself to be sole governor of the company. The company to enter into articles with me to continue there for seven years upon the same conditions they have had for a year and half last past, and such as refuse, to be removed and others placed in their rooms; for if they should continue at liberty as they now are and have power to take Her Majesty's service along with them, they would make use of our house but until they could provide another upon better terms and then leave us as in one year and half of their being here they have many times threatened when they might not exact any new impositions upon the housekeepers at their pleasure. . . .

The second document is endorsed, "Heton's draft of his patent." This draft patent generally conforms to the standard formal patents which are extant for previous companies except for the lines that read:

. . . Now know ye that we [that is, the King, in whose name all patents were issued] of our especial grace, certain knowledge and mere motion, have licensed and authorize and by these our letters patent do license and authorize our said servant Richard Heton or his assigns from time to time and at all times hereafter to select, order, direct, set up, and govern a company of comedians in the said private house in Dorset House yard for the service of our dear consort the Queen and there to exercise their quality of playing. . . .

The third section of the Heton Papers as published by Peter Cunningham seems to be more or less a series of jottings or reminders, part of which only reinforce or elaborate those claims for dictatorial powers in the first two documents. The first is headed "My Intention for the rest."

That such of the company as will not be ordered and governed by me as of their governor, or shall not by the Master of His Majesty's Revels and myself be thought fit comedians for Her Majesty's service, I may have power to discharge from the company, and with the advice of the Master of the Revels to put new ones in their places. . . .

There is no clear evidence that Heton achieved these powers but it is difficult to imagine a man like Heminges even aspiring to them in his dealings with the King's men.

Finally there is a series of notes which Cunningham introduces as "The short memorandum subjoined was found with the preceding documents" endorsed, "Instructions Touching Salisbury Court Playhouse, 14 September, 1639." These memoranda concern not Heton's powers and privileges as manager of Queen Henrietta's company, but a new set of arrangements, payments, and privileges between the company and the housekeepers of the theater. Though interesting they are not strictly relevant here. Two of them are, however, partly verifiable from other sources and thus tend to lend credence to Cunningham's mysterious documents.

In comparing the advantages to the players in the new contract of the company with the housekeepers as compared with the last, Heton says that in the new they get everything they had before plus "Half the Poets wages which is 10 shillings a week." We know from the summary of Richard Brome's contract as attached poet for the theater that he received twenty shillings a week.[46] Another verifiable sum is the one Heton cited in his next item of advantage to the players, "Half the licensing of every new play which half is also 20 shillings." Sir Henry Herbert's Office Book shows that for the last several years he had indeed been charging the companies £2.0.0 for the licensing of each new play.

These powers that Richard Heton was trying to establish are much more like those which had been granted to William Davenant when he took over from William Beeston than they are like those we have seen John Heminges exercising for the King's company. Indeed, they suggest the authority of Restoration managers more than that of the Elizabethan, Jaco-

---

[46] See the *Heton v. Brome* suit in Haaker, "The Plague, the Theater, and the Poet."

bean, and early Caroline company leaders and agents. There is no evidence I have seen which indicates that this shift of power from the sharers to the manager was taking place at the Globe and Blackfriars as it was at the Phoenix and Salisbury Court. Indeed, the system evolved in the reign of Elizabeth and formalized by Shakespeare, Burbage, Heminges, Condell and the others seems to have changed very little, though the company grew in size, wealth, and prestige, during the half century of its existence.

The foregoing potpourri of examples makes it clear enough, I think, that normally each troupe of players during the period selected someone, most often a senior sharer, to handle the company's official and financial affairs. Obviously the powers of these managers varied widely from company to company, and for several troupes they increased as the Civil Wars approached. The evidence shows that the differences between the Caroline dramatic organizations and the Restoration ones was rather less than has been commonly supposed.

CHAPTER VII

London Companies on Tour

THE HISTORY of English players on tour is much too extensive and too complex to be fully discussed in its entirety in any single chapter or even any single volume. During the period 1590-1642 there were scores of companies on the road at different times, not only in the British Isles, but on the Continent as well.[1]

The majority of these touring troupes were not London companies, but peripatetic provincial organizations. Therefore most of the town and great house records concern troupes of players that seldom or never played in the London theaters. Nevertheless, so far as one can tell, the conditions they met on their tours were essentially the same as those encountered by the Lord Admiral's men. This chapter is intended primar-

[1] See J. T. Murray, *English Dramatic Companies 1558-1642*, 2 vols., London, 1910, II; and A. Cohn, *Shakespeare in Germany in the Sixteenth and Seventeenth*

ily to show what conditions were common, not the particular tours of the London troupes. Fuller, but still incomplete and inadequate notes on the tours of particular major companies, are to be found in the second volume of *The Elizabethan Stage* and the first volume of *The Jacobean and Caroline Stage.*[2]

In spite of the fact that so many of the records do concern provincial organizations, the metropolitan players did go on the road often enough. In earlier years this touring had been taken for granted. In a signed letter of the Earl of Leicester's players to their patron in 1572 asking for a license, the custom is stated clearly. The license is to be used, ". . . to certify that we are your household servants when we shall have occasion to travel amongst our friends as we do usually once a year, and as other noblemen's players do and have done in times past. . . ."[3]

The London companies also toured in plague times, or during London inhibitions, or when some other situation made business in town particularly bad. Such was the situation of

---

Centuries, London, 1865. In the many years since these two books were published numerous articles and monographs have recorded visits of English players unknown to these major scholars, and more records are appearing yearly as the archives of more and more British and Continental towns are thoroughly searched for dramatic records.

Murray's book is the most compendious on the subject, but it is none too satisfactory. A large part of the records he notes are taken from nineteenth-century town histories and not from the original documents, and he missed a number of records. For instance, Giles Dawson ("Records of Plays and Players in Kent," *Malone Society Collections* 7 [1965]) worked on the manuscript records of thirteen towns in Kent alone and found notations of 2,000 payments to visiting entertainers between 1450 and 1642, many not to be found in Murray in any form. It is certain that the examination (which is constantly going on) of original town documents and great house muniment rooms in other counties in England will unearth many more payments to touring entertainers.

[2] E. K. Chambers, *The Elizabethan Stage*, 4 vols., Oxford, 1923; G. E. Bentley, *The Jacobean and Caroline Stage*, 7 vols., Oxford, 1941-1968.

[3] *Malone Society Collections* 1 (1911), 348-49. From the manuscripts of the Marquis of Bath at Longleat.

the travelling players in *Hamlet*. Hence some discussion of touring is essential for an understanding of the professional life of a London player in Shakespeare's time.

For the major London companies, touring was nearly always an unpleasant and comparatively unprofitable expedient to compensate for London misfortunes, and as the metropolitan companies became more prosperous they resorted to the road less frequently than they had in the reign of Elizabeth and in the early years of James. But though these troupes made fewer road trips in the later years, they knew that touring could never be entirely abandoned. This fact is illustrated by Richard Heton's draft patent as late as 1638 or 1639. His proposals show not only that he knew Queen Henrietta's company might have to travel, but he also noted some of the customary settings for provincial performances.

There is no evidence that Heton's proposed patent was ever issued officially but his proposals are illuminating:

> . . . And the said comedies, tragedies, histories, pastorals, masques, interludes, morals, stage plays, and such like to show act and exercise to their best profit and commodity as well within their aforesaid playhouse in Dorset House yard, as in any city, university, town, or borough of our said realms and dominions, there to sojourn and abide, if at any time they with their company and associates (whom our said servant Richard Heton shall think fit to select) shall have occasion (by reason of sickness in London or otherwise) to travel, to exercise publicly to their best profit, commodity, and advantage their aforesaid comedies tragedies &c. at all time or times (the time of divine service only excepted) before or after supper within any town halls, guildhalls, moothalls, schoolhouses, or any other convenient places whatsoever. And the same comedies, tragedies, &c. with the times they are to be acted, to proclaim in such places as aforesaid with drums, trumpets, and by public bills, if they think fit, notwithstanding any statute, act,

proclamation, provision, restraint or matter whatsoever to the contrary.[4]

Richard Heton was an arrogant man, and he was proposing for himself and his company more rights and privileges than any is known to have secured. Note particularly the "notwithstanding" clause at the close. Many towns specifically forbade several of the privileges he is proposing. Nevertheless, his proposals show what other troupes would have found desirable, and most of which they did, now and then, succeed in getting. But the norm, as we shall see, fell far short of Heton's demands.

The provincial records of the visits of London companies are usually inadequate, seldom naming any plays or more than one of the players present; frequently the name of the visiting company is omitted. Even the fuller records can be misleading, for the account of a visit by the Lady Elizabeth's company, for instance, may refer to a secondary provincial troupe using an exemplification of the London license, or even be a wholly fraudulent document. The provincial records were set down as accounts of moneys paid out; the clerks show on interest in theatrical history.

Shakespeare expresses the usual attitude toward metropolitan companies on tour when he makes Hamlet ask Rosencrantz about the troupe newly arrived at Elsinore:

What players are they?

Ros. Even those you were wont to take such delight in, the tragedians of the city.

Ham. How chances it they travel? Their residence, both in reputation and profit, was better both ways.

About the same time Ben Jonson was also articulating the standard observation about touring players. In scene four of

---

[4] The document was found by Peter Cunningham and published in the *Shakespeare Society Papers* 4 (1849), 95-100, without any indication as to where he found it. There is a convenient complete transcription in Bentley, *The Jacobean and Caroline Stage*, II, 685-86.

the third act of *Poetaster*, the player, Histrio, is being told how fine a playwright Crispinus is. Tucca says:

> If he pen for thee once, thou shalt not need to travel, with thy pumps full of gravel any more, after a blind jade and a hamper; and stalk upon boards and barrel heads, to an old cracked trumpet. [167-70]

The same attitude toward metropolitan companies on the road is voiced thirty years later by Donald Lupton in his *London and the Country Carbonadoed and Quartered into Several Characters*, 1632. In his Character twenty "Play-houses" he writes:

> Sometimes they [the players] fly into the country; but 'tis a suspicion that they are either poor or want clothes, or else company, or a new play; or do as some wandering sermonists, make one sermon travel and serve twenty churches.
> [G1ᵛ]

These sneers at touring companies are justifiable for the most part, and especially as applied to the scores of provincial companies. Yet only Heton has mentioned the most frequent cause that drove major London troupes to take to the road, namely the plague. This virulent and usually fatal disease was really endemic in London until the Great Fire destroyed most of the rats in 1666. But there were several years in Shakespeare's era when the death rate was appallingly high: 1593, 1603, 1610, 1625, 1636-37. In these years many of the richer Londoners fled the city, all the theaters were closed, bearbaiting was suppressed, and fairs were cancelled.

The Lord Mayor and Council of London always knew that crowds spread the disease, and in the earlier days there were constant petitions to the Privy Council to close the playhouses. But some time in the nineties there seems to have been an agreement that when the parish clerks reported a total of thirty or more plague deaths per week in the combined parishes of London, then the theaters would be closed. This number is recorded in the draft license for Queen Anne's company of about 1604.

. . . And the said Comedies, Tragedies, Histories, Interludes, Morals, Pastorals, Stage plays and such like to show
and exercise publicly when the infection of the plague shall
decrease to the number of thirty weekly within our city of
London and the liberties thereof. . . .[5]

This regulation explains the point in the passage in Middleton's *Your Five Gallants*, probably acted in 1607 and published
in 1608,

'tis e'en as uncertain as playing, now up now down, for if
the Bill rise to above thirty, here's no place for players.
. . .[6]

But not long after, the danger limit was raised to forty. A
character in Lodowick Barry's *Ram Alley* acted about 1608 and
published in 1611, says, "I dwindle . . . as a new player at a
plague bill certified forty. . . ." And this number is verified
in the patent for the King's company issued in 1619.

It is easy to see how great was the terror of the citizens
which led to such restrictions when it is noted that in the
single week ending 4 August 1625, for instance, 3,659 Londoners died of the plague. Hundreds of infected houses were
marked with the sign "Lord have mercy upon us." And many
bodies were dumped unceremoniously and uncoffined into open
pits.[7] No Londoner in Elizabethan, Jacobean, or Caroline audiences would have had any trouble understanding the pre-
dicament of Friar John recounted in the second scene of the
last act of *Romeo and Juliet*:

Going to find a barefoot brother out,
One of our order, to associate me
Here in this city visiting the sick,
And finding him, the searchers of the town,
Suspecting that we both were in a house

---

[5] *Malone Society Collections* 1, pt. 3 (1910), 266.
[6] 1608 quarto F2ᵛ.
[7] See F. P. Wilson, *The Plague in Shakespeare's London*, Oxford, 1927, *passim*.

Where the infectious pestilence did reign,
Seal'd up the doors, and would not let us forth,
So that my speed to Mantua was stay'd.

Such catastrophes drove all metropolitan companies out of London and into the provinces to avoid starvation. Every London player expected to go on the road sooner or later, and of course the provincial companies were nearly always travelling. The reception they met varied with the town and the prejudices of the authorities in charge at the moment.

Hundreds of entries in the records of towns all over England attest the varying receptions of the touring troupes. Often they were not allowed to perform at all, though they were generally given a gratuity in deference to their master. In the accounts of the Chamberlain at Leicester in 1594-95 is the entry: "Item. Given to the Lord Morley's players who were not suffered to play . . . 5s."[8] In the Southampton records is the item dated 18 October [1592]: ". . . to the Earl of Worcester's players for that they should not play . . . £1.0.0" (398).

The discomforts of touring as noted by Jonson in *Poetaster* are less serious than the hazards mentioned by the players of Lord Strange in a petition to the Privy Council of uncertain date (1591-1594):

> . . . For as much (right honorable) our company is great and thereby our charges intolerable in travelling the country, and the continuance thereof will be a mean to bring us to division and separation whereby we shall not only be undone but also unready to serve her majesty when it shall please her highness to command us. . . .[9]

These complaints in the petition are obviously from the sharers of the company, but the hired men had equally good rea-

[8] Murray, *English Dramatic Companies*, II, 306. Hereafter when only page numbers are given for provincial records, a reference to this volume is to be understood.

[9] R. A. Foakes and R. T. Rickert, *Henslowe's Diary*, Cambridge, 1961, pp. 283-84.

sons to dread touring. Henslowe's contract with the hired man, William Kendall, in 1597 specified that ". . . He to give him for his said service every week of his playing in London 10 shillings and in the country 5s. . . ."[10] Even worse was the touring situation of Robert Houghton, who testified in his examination in 1633 at Banbury that he

> Came to this company the Thursday before Easter last and played his part in stage plays at Sir William Spencer's [and] at Keinton two or three days this week. Received nothing but meat and drink from them.[11]

NUMBER OF PLAYERS IN COMPANIES ON TOUR

It is reasonable to expect that companies on tour would consist of fewer players than they had when settled in London, and various documents indicate that this was the case. When the Master of the Revels on 9 April 1624 licensed the touring company led by William Perry, he specified a group "not exceeding the number of twenty." The Master of the Revels made a similar stipulation when he licensed on 28 November 1634 a touring group led by William Daniel. The license was copied by the clerk when the company visited Norwich 3 September 1635.

> A Patent under the hand and seal of Sir Henry Herbert Master of the Revels bearing date the 28th of November 1634 made to . . . and the rest of their company not exceeding the number of fifteen persons.[12]

Among the thousands of records of provincial visits one would hope to have found quite a few that noted how many men and boys made up the roster of the visitors. But, as noted before, the town records are financial accounts and the clerks were interested in the amount of money put out; numbers or names are set down, as a rule, only when the visit led to a

[10] Ibid., pp. 268-69.
[11] *Calendar of State Papers, Domestic*, London, 1633-34, p. 49.
[12] Murray, *English Dramatic Companies*, II, 273 and 357.

disturbance or a crime. Most of the records of numbers come from great house account books, possibly because the numbers suggested the cost of bedding and feeding.

The earliest of the accounts to give numbers is fictional, but set down by a man with extensive theatrical experience. In his *News from Hell*, 1606, Thomas Dekker wrote a list of expenses for Charon in his ferrying business:

> Item. Lent to a company of country players, being nine in number, one sharer and the rest journeymen that with strolling were brought to death's door 13d. upon their stock of apparel, to pay for their boat hire because they would try if they could be suffered to play in the Devil's name.
> . . .   [H-H^v]

A similar, though indefinite number is implied for a touring group of Queen Anne's men. In a lawsuit of 1607 there is quoted an agreement between Thomas Greene, manager of Queen Anne's company at the Red Bull, and Martin Slater, leader of a touring group. It is agreed that Slater

> shall forbear and refrain from setting up any bills for playing as in the name of Her Majesty's servants unless he the said Martin has gotten into his company to play five others of Her Majesty's players. . . .[13]

Of course the five would be sharers in the company; with Slater they would make six, but hired men and boys would be required as well and Slater's touring Queen Anne's troupe would presumably consist of ten to twelve.

Lord Derby's men who visited Chatsworth in 1611 consisted of "xiiij Players" and were paid £3 on the 5th of June for playing two plays, one after dinner and one after supper.[14] The next year when Derby's men visited the Earl of Cum-

---

[13] Transcript of an entry on Roll 1789 of the Court of Common Pleas, transcribed in the Wallace Papers in the Huntington Library, San Marino, California.

[14] Lawrence Stone, "Companies of Players Entertained by the Earl of Cumberland and Lord Clifford, 1607-39," *Malone Society Collections* 5 (1960), 21.

berland's establishment at Londesborough they carried thirteen players and played four plays. They were paid £4 on 26 March 1612. Later in the same year the Lady Elizabeth's company with sixteen players also came to Londesborough and on the nineteenth of July were paid forty shillings for performing one play "after supper." In 1619 the same castle was visited by fifteen players "who belonged to the late Queen," i.e., Queen Anne who had died four months before. On the 14th of July they were paid thirteen shillings, four pence though they did not play.

One of the more explicit records in these accounts from the books of the Earl of Cumberland and Lord Clifford is the one accompanying the payment of £5 on 11 February 1619/20.

> Item. Given this day in reward to a company of players in number fourteen by his Lordship's appointment, the same being the King's players, the sum of five pounds, which players stayed here at Londesborough from Tuesday till Friday and played 5 plays. So paid them which was my Lord's reward . . . £5[15]

A larger number of players was carried by the Lady Elizabeth's company when they visited Plymouth in 1618/19, no day or month given.

> Item. Given to the Lady Elizabeth's players being 20 persons which had the King's hand for playing as well by night as by day . . . £3.6.

In 1636, when the long plague of 1636-37 was only in its second month, the number of players in the provincial company of John Costine is given at Manchester in 3 July.

> To John Costine, a player with 10 in his company to avoid the town & not to play these dangerous times . . . 00.06.08[16]

There are about a half a dozen other records of provincial visits in which the clerk sets down the number of players in

---

[15] Ibid., pp. 21, 23, 24.
[16] Murray, *English Dramatic Companies*, ii, 385 and 331.

the touring company, all of them within the limits of the numbers cited here, though some are records of London companies and others of companies not known to have had London seasons. All these numbers indicate a reduction in the size of the London troupes when they took to the road. For comparison we can note that the only full rosters for a London company are those from the combined patent list and hired men list of the King's company in 1624 and 1625; these two lists total thirty-five names without the boys.[17] Accordingly the average touring troupe would appear to have been less than half the size of the London King's company at the time of the death of King James.

Several caveats about these figures should be noted. 1) The date of the King's lists is later than most of the provincial notices; 2) the King's company was more prosperous than any other and therefore probably larger; 3) the provincial notices that record the number of players is far less than 1 percent of the total provincial notices reported. There is a further caveat to be noted in two other provincial notices that are abnormal. The first is the list of twenty-eight names of players set down in the Mayor's Court Books at Norwich on 10 March 1634/35. No company is named and the actors were denied permission to play. I think this is a list of players of two different companies that were in Norwich at the same time.[18] The other abnormal list is one reported by Sir Edmund Chambers[19] from an article in the *Warwickshire Antiquarian Magazine*. The entry notes the misdemeanor of "One of the Company of the Lady Elizabethe's players" who came to town on 27 March 1615. Though the entry says it lists the names in the patent of 31 May 1613, it records fourteen names but states that John Townsend and Joseph Moore were "Sworn officers none other named in the patent." The list, therefore, must record those present at Coventry in 1615. This entry has a further distinction in that the twelve names following Townsend and Moore

[17] See Bentley, *The Jacobean and Caroline Stage*, I, 15-18 and 80-81.
[18] Ibid., I, 283-89.
[19] "Coventry Papers from Corporation MSS.," *Warwickshire Antiquarian Magazine*, pt. 7 (1873), 406, in *Review of English Studies* 1 (1925), 182-84.

are bracketed and labeled "Boyes" and that the entry closes with the statement "5 Horses in their Company." Though the total number of players is similar to the number given in other provincial records, the number of named boys is unique. I am also baffled by the notation of five horses, a notation that suggests more affluence than one associates with companies on tour.

Such evidence as we have, then, suggests that the complement of a London company on the road was not more than half their metropolitan roster. How many of these men were players and how many musicians and other stage functionaries, the evidence does not show. I would guess that most of them were players, some of them performing chores they would disdain in London.

REPERTORIES OF TOURING COMPANIES

When the London companies found it necessary to take to the road they presumably reduced their repertories as well as their personnel. It would have been foolhardy to cart all their manuscripts about the country, and many plays that had been produced on the stage of the Globe or Rose or Fortune would have been more difficult to mount in the temporary playing places in provincial towns. Though the records from Chatsworth and Londesborough quoted above show touring companies performing two, four, and five plays, only one account I know of states just how many plays a London troupe was carrying. When the Salisbury Court players visited Oxford in July 1634, one of the company told Thomas Crosfield, a Fellow of Queen's, that "They came furnished with 14 plays."[20] What part of the repertory of this troupe fourteen plays was cannot be ascertained, but it was less than one-fifth of those owned by Queen Henrietta's men at this time and about one-twelfth those owned by the King's men.[21]

[20] F. S. Boas, *The Diary of Thomas Crosfield*, London, 1935, p. 73.
[21] Bentley, *The Jacobean and Caroline Stage*, I, 250-59 and 108-134.

Procedures on Town Visits

When a touring company reached a selected town they first went to the local authorities to get permission to play. Scores of the provincial notices gathered by Professor Murray indicate this procedure by beginning "This day. . . ." Thus at Norwich on 7 June 1617 the clerk made the entry "This day Henry Sebeck showed forth to this court a patent . . ." or a year later "This day John Townsend brought a license. . . ."[22]

The custom was a good deal older than these two notices, as is shown in an account published by R. Willis, who says he was seventy-five years old when his book was printed in 1639.

> Upon a Stage-play which I saw
> when I was a child
>
> In the city of *Gloucester* the manner is (as I think it is in other like corporations) that when players of interludes come to town, they first attend the Mayor to inform him what nobleman's servants they are, and so to get license for their public playing. . . .[23]

This permission to play in the town was sometimes granted, though when denied the players were often given a "reward" presumably out of respect for their patron. Sometimes the reasons for denial were given and sometimes not. The statement in the Mayors' Court Books at Norwich on 28 June 1622 gives no reason:

> The company of players of the late Queen Anne came this day and desired to have leave to play according to a patent under the King's privy signet dated ultimo Octobris Anno xv°. And they are forbidden so to do. And there is allowed to them as a gratuity xl[s].

[22] Murray, *English Dramatic Companies*, II, 344.
[23] *Mount Tabor or Private Exercises of a Penitent Sinner . . . Also Certain Occasional Observations*, London, 1639, p. 110.

Sometimes permission was refused without reason and in words that suggest hostility. Such is an entry in the Receivers' Account Book at Plymouth in 1616 or 1617: "Item given to two companies of players which were not suffered to play, to rid them out of town xxxˢ."[24] The hostility occasionally produced even more severe restrictions. On 20 September 1594 the Chamberlain's accounts at King's Lynn note:

> Also at this day it is agreed, by Master Mayor, Master Newelect, and the common council that there shall not hereafter be any plays suffered to be played in this hall called Trinity hall nor the hall called St. George's hall.

Twenty years later on 14 October 1616 the Mayor and Aldermen of King's Lynn went much further in their hostility to players:

> At this day it was agreed that a letter shall be written by Master Mayor and the Aldermen to the Lord Chancellor of England, and the town's High Steward to entreat that he will be a means that all the companies of players which yearly resort to this town may not be suffered here to use playing, notwithstanding their grants and patents made unto them.[25]

But though hostility was sometimes involved in the refusal of permission to play, there were often sound reasons for denying permission; probably the most common was fear of plague infection. At Worcester in 1631 the King's company was dismissed for this reason. "Given to the King's players by Mr. Mayor's direction to prevent their playing in this city for fear of infection . . . 13s. 4d."[26] In the Chamberlain's Accounts at Gloucester the plague is specifically mentioned (as in many other entries in other towns). The entry is not precisely dated but falls in the year between 29 September 1636

---

[24] Murray, *English Dramatic Companies*, II, 346 and 384.
[25] David Galloway and John Wason, "Records of Plays and Players in Norfolk and Suffolk, 1330-1642," *Malone Society Collections* 11 (1981), 70.
[26] Murray, *English Dramatic Companies*, II, 410.

and 29 September 1637: "Item paid unto William Daniel one of the King's Revels because he should not play being in the contagious time by order of the Justices . . . £1.6.8"[27] Earlier during the terrible plague of 1603 the Chamberlain's accounts of King's Lynn carry under date of 22 July the entry:

> xx[s] allowed to Mr. Mayor for ii companies of players. Paid out of the hall here to Mr. Mayor that he bestowed of the Earl of Huntington and the Lord Evers their players to keep them from playing here this dangerous time.[28]

Other infectious diseases are occasionally mentioned as the reason for the prohibition. In the Gravesend Corporation Minutes for the year 1635-36 is the entry:

> November 25. Paid to the players, for not playing in the town by the appointment of Mr. Mayor and the Court by reason of the Small Pox . . . 00.05.00[29]

Now and then a very unusual reason for denying playing permission is recorded: at Canterbury in the year 1602-03 there is the entry in the Chamberlain's accounts:

> Item paid to Thomas Downton, one of the Lord Admiral's players for a gift bestowed upon him and his company being so appointed by Mr. Mayor and the Aldermen because it was thought fit they should not play at all in regard that our late Queen was then either sick or dead as they supposed.   xxx[s][30]

Such reasons for refusing a company permission to play are understandable enough in any time, but in a number of towns there was administrative distrust of theatrical performances for more particular Elizabethan and Jacobean reasons. The Mayor and his officers were responsible for maintaining their

[27] Ibid., II, 285.
[28] Galloway and Wason, "Records of Plays and Players in Norfolk and Suffolk," p. 69.
[29] Dawson, "Records of Plays and Players in Kent," p. 81.
[30] Ibid., p. 18.

own dignity and keeping the peace in their town. A few of the local records state this problem clearly enough, as in the Chester records under date of 20 October 1615:

> Moreover at the same Assembly consideration was had of the common bruit & scandal which this city hath of late incurred & sustained by admitting of stage players to act their obscene and unlawful plays or tragedies in the common hall of this city thereby converting the same being appointed & ordained for the judicial hearing & determining of criminal offences, and for the solemn meetings & concourse of this house into a stage for players & a receptacle for idle persons; & considering likewise the many disorders which by reason of plays acted in the night do often times happen & fall out to the discredit of the government of this city & to the great disturbance of quiet & well-disposed people & being further informed that men's servants & apprentices neglecting their master's business do resort to inn houses to behold such plays & there many times wastefully spend their master's goods. For avoiding of all which inconveniences it is ordered that from henceforth no stage players upon any pretence or color whatsoever shall be admitted or licensed to set up any stage in the said common hall or to act any tragedy or comedy or any other play, by what name soever they shall term it, in the said hall or any other place within this city or the liberties thereof in the night time or after vi of the clock in the evening.[31]

The Chester fathers were severe in their condemnations, but less explicit records from other towns show a similar uneasiness. In the Burgmote Books at Canterbury is the statement under date of 12 August 1634:

> Also at this Court it is ordered that Master Mayor shall be allowed & paid to him by Master Chamberlain 20 shillings which he gave to certain players which came to this city to

[31] Murray, *English Dramatic Companies*, ii, 235.

play having commission in that behalf, to the end to avoid disorders and night walking which might come thereby.[32]

It is not difficult to understand the worries of the Court in a provincial town with no street lights of any kind and only a set of often ignorant citizens for amateur policing.

An example of what the town authorities at Canterbury were fearing is to be found in the records of a hearing at Ludlow in November 1627.

1627. Nov. 22. The information of Richard Errington, of the city of London, pewterer, aged fifty years or thereabout, deposeth and sayeth that upon yesterday, about ten or eleven of the clock at night, this deponent, being one of the company of His Majesty's players who then were acting in the said house, & this deponent taking money at the door, he saw certain persons in number five or six, whom this deponent doubting to have been drinking, thinking that they would have offered to this deponent wrong, this deponent took his money out the box and put it in his hand. Then the said persons began to brabble among themselves & thereupon one other of the players came unto the door & demanded what the cause of the noise was. Thereupon one of the persons whom this deponent hearing his name since to be Powell, drew a rapier & ran at this deponent, and this deponent putting off the thrust, closed in with him & took hold of his arm. Whereupon one of the sergeants, William Baker, being called to search of the said house to keep the peace, the foresaid persons fell upon the said Baker & most beastly abused him. And this deponent caused one of his servants, who had a link lighted in his hands, to go forth of the door to give light unto the sergeant & to know who abused him. But one of the said company, whose name as this deponent is since informed is Henry Wilding, forced

32 Ibid., II, 234.

the said servant back again, & gave him sound blows, asking him, "Keep indoors; what is this to thee?"[33]

This testimony is corroborated by the man who brought out the link, John Hill. Such affrays were associated, not without reason, with the visits of players and one can understand how the simplest solution might seem to be to keep the players out of town.

PROVINCIAL PLAYING PLACES

The town hall was doubtless one of the most convenient playing places for the players when they were on the road, but there was often opposition to such use of an official and more or less ceremonial hall. Galloway and Wasson found a record of 17 June 1614 of legal action to be taken at Ipswich if the players got to perform in the moot hall:

> It is agreed at this assembly that it shall not be lawful from henceforth for the Bailiff of this town for the time being or any of them to give any allowance to any players that shall resort to this town to play nor give leave to any such players to play in the moot hall at any time. And if the Bailiffs of this town or any of them should do contrary to this agreement that then the said bailiffs or such of them that shall hereafter give any such allowance or leave to play in the moot hall shall forfeit for every such offence every of them xx[s][34]

But of course towns differed and administrations differed. While some administrations were clearly hostile others were not simply permissive but cordial. Naturally the hope of the touring company was that first they would be allowed to pre-

---

[33] Ibid., II, 326. A very full record of a more bloody affray was recorded in Norwich in 1583. It occurred when Queen Elizabeth's company was playing in the yard of the Red Lion in St. Stephen's in June of that year. See David Galloway's transcription in *The Elizabethan Theatre* 7 (1980), 103-110.

[34] "Records of Plays and Players in Norfolk and Suffolk," p. 184.

sent a play for the Mayor. R. Willis, whose account of his childhood attendance at a play in Gloucester is quoted above, testifies to this custom, probably early in Elizabeth's reign:

> . . . and if the Mayor likes the actors or would show respect to their lord and master, he appoints them to play their first play before himself and the Aldermen and Common Council of the city; and that is called the Mayor's play, where everyone that will comes in without money, the Mayor giving the players a reward he thinks fit to show respect unto them. At such a play my father took me with him and made me stand between his legs as he sat upon one of the benches where we saw and heard very well. . . .

A record of the reward given for the Mayor's play was found by Giles Dawson in the Chamberlain's records of Canterbury for the year 1599-1600: "To the Lord Admiral's players in reward for a play which they played before Mr. Mayor and many of his friends in the Court hall and so ordered by Mr. Mayor and the Aldermen under their hands . . . 40s"[35]

Sometimes the courtesies shown the players went beyond the Mayor's play and a cash reward. At Ludlow there are two entries in the accounts of July 1590:

> Item, to the Queen's Majesty's players   10s. Item, unto them a quart of white wine and sugar at their departing 12d.[36]

At Canterbury in the year 1608-1609 the company of Queen Anne was shown a similar courtesy:

> Item given to Queen's Majesty's players by Mr. Mayor and the Aldermen's consent   20s. Mr. Mayor and the company with him being at the play by them made at the Checker and also spent then in beer and biscuits   8[d]   20s 8d.[37]

---

[35] Dawson, "Records of Plays and Players in Kent," p. 18.

[36] Murray, *English Dramatic Companies*, II, 325.

[37] Dawson, "Records of Plays and Players in Kent," p. 19.

Thus when the touring players were fortunate they performed their first play in a town before the Mayor and preferably in the town hall, though sometimes elsewhere, as at Canterbury where Queen Anne's men acted before the mayor and aldermen at the Checkers Inn. The players, of course, hoped to be granted permission to present regular commercial performances elsewhere in the town after they had entertained the mayor and his guests. Often they did, but only a few of the town accounts tell where. The Checker Inn at Canterbury, to which the mayor took his guests, was presumably also used for commercial performances. Two other accounts show inns, the obvious places, being used by the players as theaters for popular audiences. At Norwich on 7 June 1583 the Mayor's Court Books record that after ten of the Earl of Worcester's company had been refused permission to play but given a reward of 26s 8d "for their Lord and master his sake" the players nevertheless "did play in their host his house."

Several years later, also at Norwich, the clerk noted on 17 June 1601, that:

> Whereas my Lord of Hertford's players were suitors to have leave to play at the sign of the White Horse in Tomeland, but for this day it is ordered that no players or plays be made or used in the said house either now or hereafter.[38]

This same inn was used in 1624 by the Lady Elizabeth's players in defiance of a prohibition. The report of their action was entered in the Mayor's Court Books at Norwich on 26 April 1624:

> This day Wakefield, having brought to Master Mayor a note which he found fastened upon the gate of the house of Thomas Marcon, being the sign of the White Horse near Tomeland in Norwich wherein was written these words, 'Here within this place at one of the clock shall be acted an

[38] Murray, *English Dramatic Companies*, II, 336 and 338. Earlier Queen Elizabeth's company had performed at the Red Lion Inn. See n. 33 above.

excellent new comedy called *The Spanish Contract* by the Princess' Servants. Vivat Rex.'[39]

The players got into a good deal of trouble for their defiance of the mayor's order, and the leaders of the troupe named in their papers, John Townsend, Alexander Foster, Joseph Moore, and Francis Wambus were called to task and Wambus was committed. Such troubles were not too uncommon. The unique feature of this record is the copy of the playbill. It is the only copy known from the time, though records of the existence of playbills are common enough.

The most explicit information about the use of an inn by a company of touring players comes from the frequently mentioned diary of Thomas Crosfield. In his notes, which he took on his conversations with a member of the Salisbury Court company of players in July 1634, are set down a number of facts about this touring company and the circumstances of their playing in Oxford. The last few lines of Crosfield's report of his conversation read:

> They came furnished with 14 plays. And lodged at the King's Arms where Franklin hath about 3 pounds a day while they stay. i.e., for every play 4 nobles besides the benefit of seats.

Franklin was the owner of the King's Arms, and other entries in the diary show that he customarily had plays at the King's Arms, at least at the time of the Act at the University.[40] How typical the financial arrangement was one cannot say, since it is the only one known. But the arrangement had something in common with the rent agreements at various London theaters, and one might guess that something of the sort prevailed in other provincial inns used by London companies on tour. One might also guess that the landlord placed his "seats" in the galleries around his inn yard, at least that would accord with some of the rent agreements in London.

[39] Murray, *English Dramatic Companies*, II, 348.
[40] Boas, *Diary of Thomas Crosfield*, pp. 73 and xxv-xxvi.

It is not surprising to find inns used as playing places in the provinces since many of the London inns had been so used. Before 1590 London companies had performed in town at the Bell Inn, the Bel Savage, the Bull, the Cross Keys, and at the Red Lion. After 1590 there were still performances at the Cross Keys, the Bull, and the Boar's Head. With so much London experience of the suitability of inns as playhouses the touring companies would naturally seek inns as playing places for their performances when they were on the road.

But inns and the town hall were not the only provincial theaters. It is much more surprising to find records of churches being used for play performances in the provinces, yet two accounts have survived which show that one company had intended to perform in a church and another actually did so.

In the records of the town of Syston, near Leicester, is the item: "1602. Paid to Lord Morden's players because they should not play in the church . . . 12d." A decade earlier Lord Beauchamp's players had actually used the church, though not with permission. On 10 June 1590 in the Mayors' Court Books at Norwich is the entry:

> This day John Mufford, one of the Lord Beauchamp's players being forbidden by Mr. Mayor to play within the liberties of this city and in respect thereof gave them among them xxˢ and yet notwithstanding they did set up bills to provoke men to come to their play and did play in XXe church. Therefore the said John Mufford is committed to prison.[41]

Unusual local records about a playing place are found in the churchwardens' accounts for Sherborne in the County of Dorset.[42] Here several entries show the players paying rent to local officials rather than receiving gratuities. There are half

[41] Murray, *English Dramatic Companies*, II, 402 and 336.

[42] A. D. Mills, "A Corpus Christi Play and Other Dramatic Activities in Sixteenth-Century Sherborne, Dorset," *Malone Society Collections* 9 1977 (1971), 13-15.

a dozen such entries between 1589 and 1603, such as one in 1598: "of the Queen's Majesty's players for the use of the church house . . . 2/"; and another in 1603: "of certain players for the use of the church house . . . 4/6." Other items in these accounts show the church house being rented to amateurs.

Another provincial playing place, though not mentioned in town records, is cited in other documents as a familiar temporary theater. In Heton's proposed patent for Queen Henrietta's company, he specifies that the company, when on tour, be allowed to play "at all time or times (the time of divine service only excepted) before or after supper within any town halls, guildhalls, moothalls, schoolhouses, or any other convenient places whatsoever. . . ." Heton might be suspected of asking unprecedented privileges, but schoolhouses are mentioned also in the official players' pass issued by the Lord Chamberlain for the King's company in May 1636:

> . . . His Majesty is graciously pleased that they shall as well before his Majesty's setting forth on his main progress as in all that time & after till they shall have occasion to return homewards, have all freedom & liberty to repair unto all towns corporate, mercat[ory] towns & other where they shall think fit & there in their Common Halls, moot halls, schoolhouses or other convenient rooms act plays comedies & interludes without any let hinderance or molestation whatsoever (behaving themselves civilly). Wherein it is his Majesty's pleasure and he doth expect that in all places where they come they be treated & entertained with such due respect & courtesy as may become his Majesty's loyal & loving subjects towards his servants. . . .[43]

One would think that the schoolhouses in most provincial towns would not afford a hall large enough to accommodate a profitable audience, but it is notable that both these records include them though they do not mention the more suitable

[43] From the Lord Chamberlain's Warrant Books, *Malone Society Collections* 2, pt. 3 (1931), 378-79.

inns. Presumably these documents, intended for the town authorities, mention only those halls over which the town fathers had control.

The most surprising, indeed unique, playing place for the touring troupes is recorded at Bristol. Kathleen M. D. Barker had found in records at Bristol and elsewhere references to a theater in Wine street used sometimes by travelling players.[44] The most illuminating of the several records comes from the will of Nicholas Wolffe, Cutler, dated 2 June 1614. Wolffe stipulates that the annuities he has provided are to be paid forever,

> . . . provided always . . . that all the annuities and yearly rents before mentioned and limited to be paid out of my said playhouse shall continue due and payable so long only as the same playhouse shall continue as a playhouse that such players as do resort to the said city or inhabit within the same do usually play there and may be permitted and suffered quietly to play there and no longer.

Among provincial towns only Bristol, so far as presently discovered records reveal, had such a theater in the period 1590-1642. Presumably it was a boon to players on the road, and one would expect further allusions to it to turn up. That Wolffe had experienced or feared municipal interference with his playhouse is implied in his words "may be permitted and suffered quietly."

ROUTES AND DURATION OF PROVINCIAL TOURS

There is very little reliable evidence of the route a London company took when it had to travel. Not only are the transcriptions of local records grossly incomplete, but such records as have been printed usually ignore the title of the com-

[44] Kathleen Barker, "An Early Seventeenth-Century Provincial Playhouse," *Theatre Notebook* 29 (1975), 81-84. See also Mark C. Pilkinton, "The Playhouse in Wine Street, Bristol," *Theatre Notebook* 37 (1983), 14-21 for additional records.

pany, and when a company name is mentioned it is sometimes inaccurate. Now and then the King's name on the license is taken for the name of the company; sometimes the London company named is not really the London troupe. The prevalence of such touring subsidiaries is indicated in an order sent out by the Lord Chamberlain in 1617. This document was brought to Norwich by Joseph Moore of the Lady Elizabeth's company. The Lord Chamberlain's order read in part:

> Whereas Thomas Swinnerton and Martin Slaughter being two of the Queen's Majesty's company of players, having separated themselves from their said company, have each of them taken forth a several exemplification or duplicate of his Majesty's letters patent granted to the whole company and by virtue thereof they severally in two companies with vagabonds and suchlike idle persons have and do use and exercise the quality of playing in diverse places of this realm to the great abuse and wrong of his Majesty's subjects. . . . And whereas William Perry having likewise gotten a warrant whereby he and a certain company of idle persons with him do travel and play under the name and title of the Children of his Majesty's Revels. . . . And whereas also Gilbert Reason one of the Prince his Highness players having likewise separated himself from his company hath also taken forth another exemplification or duplicate of the patent granted to that company and lives in the same kind and abuse. And likewise one Charles Marshal, Humphry Jeffes, and William Parr: three of Prince Palatine's company of players having also taken forth an exemplification or duplicate of the patent granted to the said company and by virtue thereof live after the like kind and abuse. . . .[45]

Obviously the local authorities could not tell for sure whether the company visiting them was the true London troupe or not, so that any two records of visits of Queen Anne's company do not necessarily refer to the same group.

[45] Murray, *English Dramatic Companies*, II, 343-44.

Such situations make it impossible to trace with any assurance the route of any London company on the road. The most reliable evidence I can find about the tour of a London company comes from a series of letters between Edward Alleyn on tour and his family in London. There are six letters which run from May to September in the year of the severe plague of 1593.[46] Alleyn, though a Lord Admiral's man, was on tour with Lord Strange's company. The principal subject of the letters is fear of the plague, precautions to be taken against it, and friends who have been victims.

Alleyn's first letter in the series is dated "from Chelmsford the 2 of May 1593." The second letter is written to Alleyn by Philip Henslowe "from London the 5 of July 1593," in which he says, ". . . I pray you likewise do my commendations unto all the rest of your fellows and I pray God to send you all that good health that we have as yet at London. . . ."

The third letter is written by Alleyn from Bristol to his wife in London on 1 August. He says

> . . . if you send any more letters, send to me by the carriers of Shrewsbury or to West Chester or to York to be kept till my Lord Strange's players come. And thus sweetheart with my hearty commendations I cease from Bristol this Wednesday after St James his day being ready to begin the play of Harry of Cornwall. . . . We shall not come home till All Hallows Tide. . . .

The fourth letter is written by Henslowe to Alleyn, apparently in August 1593 with news about the family of another touring player, ". . . Robert Brown's wife in Shoreditch and all her children and household be dead and her doors shut up. . . ."

The fifth letter from Henslowe to Alleyn, dated 14 August 1593, comments on an event of the tour:

> . . . very glad to hear of your good health which we pray God to continue long to his will and pleasure for we heard

<hr>

[46] Foakes and Rickert, eds., *Henslowe's Diary*, pp. 274-81.

that you were very sick at Bath and that one of your fellows were fain to play your part for you which was no little grief unto us to hear, but thanks be to God for amendment for we feared it much because we had no letter from you when the other wives had letters sent. . . . & I pray you son commend me heartily to all the rest of your fellows in general for I grow poor for lack of them. . . .

The final letter in the series was written on 28 September from Henslowe to Alleyn:

. . . It hath pleased the Lord to visit me round about and almost all my neighbors dead of the plague, and not my house free for my two wenches have had the plague, and yet thanks be to God liveth and are well. . . . and as for my lord a Pembroke's which you desire to know where they be they are all at home and have been this five or six weeks for they cannot save their charges with travel as I hear and were fain to pawn their apparel for their charge. . . .

These letters show that Lord Strange's men had started their tour before May the 2nd, and Alleyn says in his letter of August 1st that "we shall not be home till All Hallows Tide." Thus the tour was expected to last for at least six months. Since 1593 was a bad plague year, the tour may have lasted longer than most, but the plagues of 1603, 1610, 1625, and 1636-37 were at least as bad.

Since the earliest letter is sent from Chelmsford, near London, that stop may have been an early one. The other letters show that from Bath and Bristol the company expected to go on to Shrewsbury, West Chester, and York, covering a large area. Presumably Strange's men were having more success than Henslowe reported for Pembroke's company.

The lines quoted are eloquent of the fear of the plague by all the correspondents; the passages deleted as irrelevant for the tour are largely concerned with plague fears and plague precautions.

SUMMARY

Incomplete and inaccurate as these town records are, they do show the astonishing multiplicity of theatrical productions in England during the reigns of Elizabeth, James, and Charles. Murray alone lists more than one hundred companies on tour and Stone and Dawson add several others. The London companies played under the same conditions as the others though they seem to have commanded somewhat more respect from local authorities.

The extent and duration of the tours of the Londoners cannot be ascertained except in the case of Lord Strange's company in 1593. But in the periods of long plague closing when the theaters were often closed for months[47] the companies must have toured until they lost too much money as Pembroke's men did in 1593.[48]

One would guess that such bankruptcy from touring was not unusual, but the only other example I know is the suggestion of impending bankruptcy in the petition of Lord Strange's men quoted above.

On arriving at a town the first act of the touring players was to call on the local authorities to get permission to play, first, if possible, before the mayor and his guests in the town hall, later before the general populace for entrance fees. Often permission to play at all was denied, for a variety of reasons, or no reason, though usually some cash gift was made to the prohibited players.

---

[47] See Bentley, *The Jacobean and Caroline Stage*, II, 652-72.

[48] I know of only one recorded exception to the plague touring rule. During the visitation of 1636-37 an apparently unique grant was made to the King's company:

The King having commanded servants the players to assemble their company and keep themselves together near the Court, gives them an allowance of £20 per week, which is to be paid to John Lowin and Joseph Taylor, on behalf of their company; such allowance to commence from the first of November last, to continue during his Majesty's pleasure, and to be taken as of his princely bounty. [*Calendar of State Papers, Domestic*, London, 1636-37, p. 228.]

When a London company concluded that it would be forced to tour, one of the first steps would have been to select the personnel of the travelling group and the repertory to be carried. The number of touring players seems to have varied from ten to twenty, but I have found no evidence as to the principle of selection. One would guess that sharers had first choice, since their professional income would have been reduced to nothing while the theaters were closed. Some boys and hired men presumably were included, but certainly not all of them. The repertory taken would have been a selection from the plays owned; the only number of plays known to have been taken was fourteen, but this number may have been larger than most since the company was playing at Oxford.

Such were the conditions encountered by the London dramatic companies when they decided they had to take to the road to escape London prohibitions. There is little evidence that the local authorities received the travellers with enthusiasm, except perhaps in some of the great houses and castles. But though indications of hostility can be found, the records do not show it to have been so pervasive as Puritan comments imply. General hostility is not compatible with the great numbers of provincial visits recorded. Travel in sixteenth- and seventeenth-century England was not comfortable even for royalty, and for the metropolitan players it can scarcely have been profitable. But touring was an inescapable part of the life of London players.

CHAPTER VIII

Casting

THE CASTING of plays by the professional companies of London in the years 1590-1642 was a simpler process than it usually is in the twentieth century. In the first place, all these troupes were repertory companies, hence the available players were fixed as to numbers and familiar as to talents and limitations. In the second place a high proportion of the plays produced were prepared by a dramatist with the specific company in mind, so that he could develop at least his principal characters with some consideration for the talents of the fellows of the company. This phenomenon of the custom-made play of course characterized the work of all attached dramatists while they were committed to write for their particular companies[1]—dramatists like Heywood, Fletcher, Massinger,

---

[1] See G. E. Bentley, *The Profession of Dramatist in Shakespeare's Time*, Princeton, 1971, pp. 30-37.

Shakespeare, Shirley, and Brome. In Elizabeth's time this knowledge of the producing company also guided many of the horde of playwrights paid by Philip Henslowe to write plays for the Admiral's and for Worcester's men. The many recorded instances in which Henslowe made down payments or installment payments to various playwrights show that the writer knew as he worked what company was expected to produce his play.[2]

These facts made anything in the nature of tryouts unnecessary and made it unlikely that a play written for the company would include major roles unsuited to the abilities of permanent members of that troupe. There is one sort of exception to this rule pointed out in Heywood's popular play *The Rape of Lucrece*. At the end of the 1608 edition is a Note to the Reader: ". . . we have inserted these few songs, which were added by the stranger that lately acted *Valerius* his part, in the form following." Two songs follow. Essentially the same note appears in the editions of 1609, 1614, 1630, 1638. There is a rather unconvincing attempt to identify this stranger in Allan Holaday's edition of the play.[3] So far as one can tell from the available evidence, however, this use of a player from outside the company was unusual.

But not all plays produced by London troupes had been written for them. More difficult casting problems could arise when a piece originally written for some other company had to be staged. In 1603 or 1604 the King's men (possibly when they were still the Lord Chamberlain's company) appropriated Marston's *Malcontent*, written shortly before for a boy company. In this instance Shakespeare's company made rather extensive changes in the text, as can be seen by a comparison of the first two quartos with the third. The new version is one-third again as long; it has an induction in which Sly, Bur-

---

[2] See, for example, partial payments made in 1597, 1598, and 1599 to Chettle, Haughton, Dekker, Jonson, Drayton, and Hathaway. R. A. Foakes and R. T. Rickert, eds., *Henslowe's Diary*, Cambridge, 1961, pp. 63, 64, 65, 73, 85, 88, 89, 99, and 123.

[3] *Illinois Studies in Language and Literature*, vol. 34, no. 3 (1950), pp. 16-19.

bage, Lowin, Sinklo, and Condell take part under their own names, and they reveal the fact that Burbage is to take the role of Malvole. Perhaps the most significant change is the addition of a comic character to the play, Passarello. This addition is not an insignificant one, for Passarello's role, with the other lines added to support him, runs to 257 lines, almost as many as the Fool has in the nearly contemporary *King Lear*. George Hunter has made the brilliant suggestion that the company had these lines added in order to exhibit Robert Armin, the new comedian of the troupe.[4]

Similar, though surely much less drastic, changes must have been required when William Cartwright's *The Royal Slave*, written to be performed by the undergraduates at Christ Church, Oxford, was, by order of the King, presented by the King's company at court on 12 January 1636/37.[5]

These plays were single examples, but casting problems must have been encountered when sizable chunks of the repertory of one company were transferred to another. Such a large transfer took place when Christopher Beeston added a good part of the repertory of the Lady Elizabeth's company to that of Queen Henrietta's men.[6]

Still another cause for casting adjustments arose when a London troupe revived a play which, though written for them, had been first cast thirty years or more before. Examples are *Othello, the Moor of Venice* presented by the King's men at court on 6 December 1636 and *Every Man in His Humour* shown before the King on 17 February 1630/31. All the original actors in each play were either dead, retired, or too old for their original roles at the time of the Caroline performances before royalty.

A few plays have printed statements in the quartos about

---

[4] John Marston, *The Malcontent*, ed. George K. Hunter, London, 1975, pp. xlvii-xlix.

[5] See G. E. Bentley, *The Jacobean and Caroline Stage*, 7 vols., Oxford, 1941-1968, III, 134-41.

[6] Ibid., I, 218-22 and 250-59.

casting changes. One of the most explicit is to be found in the 1633 edition, the first, of Marlowe's *Jew of Malta*. This play had been frequently acted in Henslowe's theaters in the early 1590s, and of course Edward Alleyn had become famous in the leading role. For the 1633 performance Thomas Heywood wrote a dedication and two prologues and two epilogues, presumably at the request of the manager of Queen Henrietta's company, his friend Christopher Beeston. One prologue is explicit about the casting of a revival.

The Prologue to the Stage at
the Cockpit

We know not how our play may pass this stage,
(Marlowe) But by the best of poets* in that age
The Malta Jew had being, and was made;
(Alleyn) And he then by the best of actors* played.
In *Hero and Leander* one did gain
A lasting memory; in *Tamburlaine*,
This Jew, with others many, th' other won
The attribute of peerless, being a man
Whom we may rank with (doing no one wrong)
Proteus for shapes and Roscius for a tongue,
So could he speak, so vary. Nor is't hate
(Perkins) To merit in him* who doth personate
Our Jew this day, nor is it his ambition
To exceed, or equal, being of condition
More modest; this is all that he intends
(And that too at the urgence of some friends):
To prove his best, and if none here gainsay it,
The part he hath studied, and intends to play it.

Richard Perkins was the leading actor in Queen Henrietta's and an old friend of Heywood's.

The recasting necessitated by the passage of time is similarly recorded in the prologue which the King's men commissioned for their revival of *Bussy d'Ambois*. These lines appear in the 1641 (third) quarto of the play.

> . . . FIELD is gone,
> Whose action first did give it name, and one
> Who came the nearest to him, is denied
> By his gray beard to show the height and pride
> Of D'AMBOIS' youth and bravery; yet to hold
> Our title still a-foot, and not grow cold
> By giving it o'er, a third man with his best
> Of care and pains defends our interest;
> As RICHARD he was liked, nor do we fear
> In personating D'AMBOIS he'll appear
> To faint, or go less, so your free consent,
> As heretofore, give him encouragement.

Apparently this "third man" was Eyllaerdt Swanston, for Edmund Gayton says in his *Pleasant Notes upon Don Quixote*, 1654,

> . . . for he was instantly metamorphosed into the statliest, gravest, and commanding soul, that ever eye beheld. *Taylor* acting *Arbaces* or *Swanston D'Amboys* were shadows to him.
>
> [E1, p. 25]

A very few plays are printed in editions that record numerous cast changes in a revival. The 1623 quarto of Webster's *Duchess of Malfi* prints a cast for the performance of the play by the King's company. Such printed casts are extremely rare, and this one is rarer still because it records certain changes in the casting since the first performance, probably nine or ten years before, by the same troupe. This cast names fifteen different members of the organization, but six of them occur in pairs and numbered:

> Ferdinand, 1 *R. Burbidge*, 2 *I. Taylor*.
> Cardinall, 1 *H. Cundaile*. 2 *R. Robinson*
> Antonio, 1 *W. Ostler*. 2 *R. Benfield*.

Since Burbage died in 1619 and Ostler in 1614, and since Condell had ceased to act, the players numbered 2 must have replaced those numbered 1 in a revival between 1619 and 1623.

These general conditions of casting can be supplemented

and extended by a consideration of the comparatively few remaining printed casts and manuscript prompt copies and "Plots." It must be borne in mind that such lists have been preserved for only a tiny fraction of the plays of the period known at least by title, about 1,500,[7] that several of them are mere lists of players with no assignment of roles, and that several of the lists or casts are of dubious authority or are irrelevant for the London professional companies.

There are several types of such lists or casts: "Plots," folio lists, quarto lists, casts in manuscript, casts of questionable authority, and casts of amateurs.

Earliest and most irregular are the seven "Plots" prepared for plays—six of them lost—produced in the last dozen years of Elizabeth's reign. The basic work on these peculiar and difficult documents has been done by Sir Walter Greg in his *Dramatic Documents*. He defines and then explains:

> Theatrical Plots are documents giving the skeleton outline of plays, scene by scene, for use in the theatre, a small group of which has survived from the last twelve years or so of Elizabeth's reign. . . . It is clear to us now that there was nothing exceptional about the plays for which Plots were required. Although we are without external information on the point we may suppose that these were prepared for the guidance of actors and others in the playhouse, to remind those concerned when and in what character they were to appear, what properties were required, and what noises were to be made behind the scenes. The necessity for some such guide would be evident in a repertory theatre, and we may feel assured that the Plot was exhibited in a place convenient for ready reference during performance. There seems, indeed, every probability that documents similar in general character to those we possess were usual, if not universal, in Elizabethan playhouses. . . .[8]

[7] See Bentley, *The Profession of Dramatist in Shakespeare's Time*, p. 199.

[8] W. W. Greg, ed., *Dramatic Documents from the Elizabethan Playhouses*, 2 vols., Oxford, 1931, I, 2 and 3-4.

There are seven of these Plots extant, most of them mutilated, and one or two in fragments so small as to be almost useless except to indicate that they had been similar in character to the others. They have all been so fully and expertly analyzed by Sir Walter Greg that detailed treatment here would be supererogation; I simply summarize parts of Greg's work.

The Plot for *The Dead Man's Fortune* seems to have been prepared for the Admiral's men about 1590. The second Plot, that for *2 Seven Deadly Sins*, appears to have been prepared for a revival by Lord Strange's men also about 1590. The third Plot is for *Frederick and Basilea*, a play performed as new by the Admiral's men at the Rose 3 June 1597. The fourth is the Plot for *Fortune's Tennis*, a mere collection of fragments but preserving enough names to make clear that it was prepared for performance by the Admiral's men, conjecturally about 1597-98. The fifth Plot is another fragment, but a larger one, for the production of *Troilus and Cressida* by the Admiral's men probably in 1599. The sixth Plot, that for *The Battle of Alcazar*, was prepared for a revival by the Admiral's men, probably late in 1598 or early in 1599. Sir Walter says of it, "This Plot, in spite of its mutilated condition, really affords the key to the whole series, since it is the only one for which there is extant a text of the play enabling us to examine its construction in some detail."[9] The seventh Plot was prepared for a revival of the first part of *Tamar Cam* by the Admiral's men in 1602. The original manuscript has disappeared and Sir Walter has had to work from a transcript of the original made by George Stevens and printed in 1803.

In his *Dramatic Documents* Greg has written a section on "General Characteristics" of these Plots. He says:

> In its most fundamental aspect a Plot consists of the record of the successive entrances of the characters of a play, with some record expressed or implied, and varying much in completeness, of the corresponding exits. This is essential, but almost all examples exhibit in varying degrees two other

[9] Ibid., I, 145.

features: namely some record of properties and other requirements of the stage, and some record of the actors assigned for the individual parts.[10]

Since only one Plot, that for *The Battle of Alcazar*, was prepared for a play which is still extant, one can only guess the importance of roles in most of these Plots from the number of scenes in which the character appears and sometimes from a general knowledge of the story.

Nevertheless these Plots do offer grounds for a few observations. The superior status of the sharers is attested by the common but not invariable use of "Mr." with their names. Sharers are generally assigned what appear to be the major roles, though Richard Allen was given the role of Frederick and the prologue and the epilogue in *Frederick and Basilea*.

Somewhat surprising is the large number of performers identified in the fullest of the Plots: twenty-four are named in *The Battle of Alcazar* and twenty-nine in *Tamar Cam I*. A number of these players are unknown or only slightly known from other records and several may have been gatherers or attendants. In the Plot for *Frederick and Basilea* unnamed "Attendants" and "Gatherers" are assigned minor roles.

Perhaps most conspicuous is the amount of doubling in several of these Plots. Many players have an extra role or two, and in *Frederick and Basilea* Thomas Hunt has five, and "black Dick" has five. In *The Battle of Alcazar* the majority of the actors named have more than one role, and Mr. Charles has three, W. Kendall has four, and George Somerset has five. In *Tamar Cam I* Towne has three, "Mr. Sam" three, Dick Jubie seven, W. Cartwright five, and Thomas Marbeck at least eight.

The second class of casts or player lists is that found in the seventeenth-century collected editions of the plays of Jonson, Shakespeare, and Beaumont and Fletcher, specifically in the Jonson folio of 1616, the Shakespeare folio of 1623, and the second Beaumont and Fletcher folio of 1679. For the purpose of identifying roles the least helpful of these is the list pub-

[10] Ibid., I, 73.

lished by John Heminges and Henry Condell in their collection of the plays of Shakespeare. It is headed "The Names of
the Principall Actors in all these Playes." The twenty-six names
which follow are simply Heminges' and Condell's acknowl-
edgment of the contributions of their fellows who had brought
Shakespeare's plays to life on the stage. All of them had been
sharers in the company at one time or another, but the plays
they performed in, or the dates of the contributions, do not
appear. Some of these players, like Augustine Phillips, died
about the middle of Shakespeare's career, or like Will Kempe
left the company at about that time. Others, like John Lowin,
Robert Armin, and John Shank had not joined the company
until half the plays had been produced. Others, like Nathan
Field, were babes in arms when Shakespeare wrote his earliest
plays; still others, like Joseph Taylor, could have performed
only in revivals since he did not join the King's company until
after Shakespeare's death in 1616. No doubt they all did perform in the plays of the company's chief dramatist, but at
various times, and in one or two instances only in revivals.
All of these men eventually became sharers in the company,
and this fact is apparently the basis of Heminges' and Condell's selection of names for their list. The First Folio is very
much a company document, edited and dedicated by the
manager of the company and his longtime associate. They
have listed only twenty-six names; obviously many more players
would have been required to stage the thirty-six plays printed
in the folio. Clearly most, if not all, the hired men and boys
required for productions at The Theatre, the Globe, and
Blackfriars have been omitted. The list is not inclusive, but is
a roll of the principal members of the Lord Chamberlain-King's
whom Heminges and Condell chose to honor.

More helpful than the Shakespeare folio single list of the
"Principall Actors in all these Playes" are the groups of players whose names Ben Jonson printed with each of the nine
plays included in his "Works" in 1616. Unlike Heminges and
Condell, he attached each list to a particular play and gave
the date of production. Jonson, the most meticulous and per-

haps the most arrogant dramatist of his time, is also the first
English playwright to acknowledge the cooperation of the
players by naming some of them with every play. Appended
to each comedy or tragedy is a list of players like that which
accompanies the piece that was given pride of place, *Every
Man in His Humor*:

This Comœdie was first
Acted, in the yeere
1598.
By the then L. Chamberlayne
his Seruants.
The principall Comœdians were.

Will. Shakespeare.	Ric. Bvrbadge.
Avg. Philips.	Joh. Hemings.
Hen. Condel.	Tho. Pope.
Will. Slye.	Chr. Beeston.
Will. Kempe.	Joh. Dvke.

With the allowance of the Master of Revells.

Each of the six following comedies and two tragedies has a
similar list. Three of the comedies, produced by boy companies, have lists of six or eight boys each. The other plays were
all produced by the Lord Chamberlain-King's company and
each is accompanied by a list of six, eight, or ten players.
This company is sufficiently well known for us to tell roughly
what Jonson's principle was in naming players. Most of these
players—in the case of *Every Man out of His Humor* all of
them—were sharers in the company at the time the play was
produced. In the *Every Man in* list the first eight were sharers;
Beeston and Duke were only hired men, and as such were
properly placed last in the list. Jonson ignored the apprentices
required for the roles of Dame Kitely, Mrs. Bridget, and Tib.
Though there is no indication which parts in the play were
taken by Beeston and Duke, it is likely that they played minor
characters, perhaps doubling two or three.

For *Every Man out of His Humor*, acted the following year
by the same company, Jonson listed only six players; all six

were sharers. For the company's performance of *Sejanus* in 1603, eight players are named, six of whom were sharers at the time. The other two, John Lowin and Alexander Cooke, became sharers later, but in 1603 they were apparently only hired men. There are no clues to their roles.

For *Volpone*, acted two years later in 1605, Jonson named only six performers, including Lowin and Cooke again, but by 1605 they may have become sharers. For *The Alchemist* of 1610 the playwright listed ten King's men, eight of whom were sharers. The other two, John Underwood and William Eccleston, were apparently still hired men in 1610, though they both became sharers later. The *Catiline* list of 1611 is the same as that of *The Alchemist* of the previous year, except that the boy Richard Robinson appears instead of the sharer Robert Armin. Obviously there was no comic role for Armin in this tragedy. It is interesting that Jonson chose to name the boy Robinson, since he had excluded all performers of women's roles from his other lists for this company. Was Robinson notably effective? Jonson singled him out for special praise as a female impersonator in the text of *The Devil Is an Ass* performed by the company five years later.

According to this catalogue, then, Jonson thought that when he collected for posterity those plays he deemed worthy of him[11] he also thought it worthwhile to let posterity know the names of the players who created these roles on the stage, but not *which* roles, nor *all* the performers. About 80 percent of those named were sharers; only one boy was named and six hired men, two of them twice. All these hired men were evidently promising actors, for all of them later became sharers in this or in other companies. The lists also indicate that major roles in Jonson's plays were seldom, if ever, taken by hired

---

[11] It should be remembered that Jonson was being selective. Several of his dramatic compositions, written before *Catiline* and *The Alchemist*, were omitted: *A Tale of a Tub*, *The Case is Altered*, *Richard Crookback*, *Hot Anger Soon Cooled*, *Robert II*, *King of Scots*, *The Page of Plymouth*, *The Isle of Dogs*, and probably others, since he told Drummond of Hawthornden in 1618/19 that half of his comedies were not in print.

men, though some of the hired men named were evidently talented enough to be made, at a later date, sharers in the King's company.

The third folio with lists of players is the Beaumont and Fletcher second folio of 1679. Since at the date of publication Beaumont had been dead for sixty-three years and Fletcher for fifty-four, it is unlikely that either had anything to do with the lists.

In the first Beaumont and Fletcher folio of 1647, none of the thirty-four plays and a masque had been accompanied by any list of players, though the dedication was signed by the ten patented members or sharers of the King's company still available five years after the closing of the theaters. The second folio adds eighteeen plays not printed in the folio of 1647 because they had previously appeared in quartos, making a total of fifty-two plays and a masque. Twenty-five of these plays are accompanied by short lists of players, presumably those of the first performance. All but two of the twenty-five lists are attached to plays belonging to the King's company. Most of these lists name eight actors, but one names four, two name five, three name six, and two name seven. Never are roles assigned.

These lists in the second Beaumont and Fletcher folio are not very helpful. In the first place their authenticity is questionable; no one knows who made them or when, whereas the Shakespeare list was made by John Heminges and Henry Condell, two of the most knowledgeable theater men of their time, and both had acted in the plays of their friend Shakespeare. The Jonson lists were made by one of the most experienced and certainly the most meticulous playwright in London. The lists in these two folios may not tell us all we want to know, but what they do tell can be relied upon.

Not only is the authenticity of the 1679 lists uncertain, but none is dated; some seem to be for revivals, so that sometimes one cannot tell whether a given player in a list was a hired man or a sharer at the time represented by the list. It appears that most of those named were sharers at the time, and there are more names of apprentices than in the Shakespeare and Jonson lists—as one might expect considering the greater prominence of women's roles in the Beaumont and Fletcher plays.

These plays were so frequently revived that their owners, the King's company, withheld most of them from publication for many years, and therefore (in the usual absence of reliable external evidence) the date of first performance for most of them can be only guessed. Indeed, for most of the plays with actor lists the dates currently assigned for first performances depend upon the biographical facts in the careers of the players named, on the shaky assumption that these lists represent first productions. This assumption is a dubious one, since we do not know when or by whom these casts were set down. Several of the men named are known to have been first hired men and later sharers. Their status at the time the list was made is therefore probably unascertainable.

So much for the information about roles and status to be derived from these folio lists of nearly two hundred names (involving a good many duplications). They look very promising at first glance, but further investigation proves them disappointing. More can be learned from the casts or lists in a few quarto editions of Jacobean and Caroline plays.

Before the Restoration of Charles II, quarto editions of English plays very rarely printed casts or even lists of the players. There are only fifteen or sixteen such quartos among the 800 or more plays printed before 1660.[12] They all come from the second half of the period, and for some reason more than half of them were published in the years 1629, 1630,

---

[12] There are a few quartos that name one or two actors, usually on the title page or in a prologue or preface. These men were, as one would expect, leading players like Edward Alleyn, Will Kempe, Richard Perkins, or Thomas Greene, whose names might be relied upon to attract attention and therefore to sell books. Of course no player ever achieved such distinction while he was still a hired man. Now and then a player gets mentioned in the dialogue, as when Jonson flatters Burbage and Nathan Field in *Bartholomew Fair* or Richard Robinson in *The Devil Is an Ass*.

1631, and 1632. It should be no surprise that the majority of these printed casts and lists come from the productions of King Charles's company or Queen Henrietta's. These helpful quartos are:

Middleton, *The Inner-Temple Masque*, 1619, Prince Charles I
Webster, *The Duchess of Malfi*, 1623, King's
Massinger, *The Roman Actor*, 1626, King's
Ford, *The Lovers' Melancholy*, 1629, King's
Carlell, *The Deserving Favorite*, 1629, King's
Shirley, *The Wedding*, 1629, Queen Henrietta's
Massinger, *The Renegado*, 1630, Queen Henrietta's
Massinger, *The Picture*, 1630, King's
Heywood, *The Fair Maid of the West*, I, 1631, Queen Henrietta's
Heywood, *The Fair Maid of the West*, II, 1631, Queen Henrietta's
Marmion, *Holland's Leaguer*, 1632, Prince Charles II
Nabbes, *Hannibal and Scipio*, 1637, Queen Henrietta's
Richards, *Tragedy of Messalina*, 1640, King's Revels
Fletcher, *The Wild Goose Chase*, 1652, King's
Davenport, *King John and Matilda*, 1655, Queen Henrietta's
Jordan, *Money is an Ass*, 1668, King's Revels

In addition to these casts in printed quartos there are four others for plays first acted in the reigns of James or Charles but not printed until the nineteenth and twentieth centuries. They are:

Fletcher and Massinger, *Sir John Van Olden Barnavelt*, BM. MS. Add. 18653, acted 1619, King's
Clavell, *The Soddered Citizen*, privately owned, acted c. 1630?, King's
Massinger, *Believe as You List*, BM. MS. Egerton 2828, acted 1631, King's
Wilson, *The Swisser*, BM. MS. Add. 36759, acted 1631, King's

The Swisser and *The Soddered Citizen* manuscripts have formal casts prefixed to the texts of the plays. The *Sir John Van Olden Barnavelt* and the *Believe as You List* manuscripts are prompt copies. For the latter an unusually full, though not complete, cast can be pieced out from the prompter's notes.[13] These quarto and manuscript lists of performers are set out in full with some analysis in the Appendix.

Nearly all these casts or lists are fuller than any in the three folios, and all but two or three assign most of the major roles in the play. Unfortunately these plays which we can cast with some assurance constitute less than 2.5 percent of the plays surviving from our period, to say nothing of the hundreds of lost plays. And about half of them were produced by the King's men, the wealthiest and largest troupe, presumably better equipped to cast their plays effectively than organizations like the Palsgrave's company, Queen Anne's company, or the Duke of York's company, to say nothing of the minor troupes of Queen Elizabeth's reign. We cannot be certain, of course, that the practices revealed by the casts of the King's company and of Queen Henrietta's company are equally characteristic of their competitors at the Red Bull, the Fortune, or the Hope; nor is there any assurance that the casting of these plays, produced in the years 1619 to 1642, is an accurate reflection of the normal distribution of roles in the years 1590-1618. Players, however, are notoriously conservative in their methods, and it is rather likely that production customs of the earlier period did not differ radically from those of the later. One has to remember, of course, that troupes like King Charles's company and Queen Henrietta's men had a good deal more money and other resources than the troupes of the nineties like the Lord Admiral's men or Lord Strange's.

---

[13] Since this study is concerned with professionals, I am eliminating from consideration the several casts for amateur productions, most of them Oxford or Cambridge college plays like *Zelotypus, Melanthe, Ignoramus, Loiola, The Rival Friends,* or *Valetudinarian,* or school plays like *Apollo Shroving,* performed by schoolboys at Hadleigh in Suffolk, or amateur country house productions like those of Mildmay Fane, Earl of Westmorland.

CASTING GENERALIZATIONS

From these printed and manuscript casts and lists a few general conclusions may be drawn.

1) The overriding importance of the sharers in each company is unmistakable. The list of "Principall Actors" in the Shakespeare folio names sharers only; the condensed casts given by Ben Jonson in his "Works" of 1616 name sharers forty-one times, hired men ten times, an apprentice once; the actor lists in the second Beaumont and Fletcher folio, though of uncertain authority and doubtful date, appear to give the same predominance of sharers, but the lists of this folio of 1679 record more names of apprentices than do the Shakespeare and Jonson collections.

In the casts of the printed quartos and formal manuscripts the dominance of sharers is again shown. The major adult roles are given to sharers: at least 123 of all roles cast, though roughly one-third of all the parts in these plays have no performers assigned.

2) The names of the sharers listed in these casts exhibit another phenomenon: no extant cast assigns roles to *all* the players known to have been sharers at the date of first performance of the play.[14] For the King's company the casts of the 1630s average about seven fellows, whereas their royal patent of 24 June 1625 had named thirteen and their livery list of 6 May 1629, fourteen. By 1631 Heminges and Condell were dead, and several of the plays had no major comic role for John Shank, but even so there were always at least three or four sharers not assigned. What did they do? Minor unassigned roles with doubling problems are a possibility, but surely not a very extensive one, since the company was paying twenty-one hired men according to the list of those protected on 26 December 1624.[15] Did the unnamed sharers have some sort of supervising functions?

3) These same quarto and formal manuscript casts name

---

[14] *The Battle of Alcazar* seems to be an exception to this generalization.
[15] See Bentley, *The Jacobean and Caroline Stage*, I, 15-16.

hired men about fifty-two times and apprentices about sixty-five times. The hired men and apprentice counts are somewhat less assured than those of the sharers because of the uncertain status of the named performer in a few instances, and the uncertain identity in some instances when only nicknames are used. These rough figures suggest that the apprentices were more conspicuous on the stage than the hired men were; and this in spite of the fact that such records as we have indicate that the major companies enrolled a good many more hired men than apprentices. The conclusion, as suggested in Chapter IV, seems to be that hired men contributed more to the London troupes as stagekeepers, prompters, wardrobe keepers, gatherers, musicians, and walk-ons than they did as identifiable performers.

A further indication that apprentices were generally more conspicuous on stage than hired men is to be seen in the assignment of leading roles. Richard Allen, who played Frederick and presented the prologue and the epilogue in *Frederick and Basilea*, is the only hired man I can find playing a lead, but even in this play "Dick (Dutton's Boy)" appears as Basilea in eleven scenes.

Shakespeare's plays, though not cast, show prominent roles written for the apprentices in the company. Boys have the lead in *The Merchant of Venice, As You Like It, All's Well that Ends Well*, and *Cymbeline*. Often Shakespeare planned the second role for a boy, as in *The Comedy of Errors, Romeo and Juliet, Henry VI, Part I, Twelfth Night, The Merry Wives of Windsor, Measure for Measure, Macbeth, Antony and Cleopatra*. In twelve of the plays of Shakespeare the third role was prepared for a boy.[16]

As one might have expected, leading roles are given to boy actors in many of the plays of Beaumont and Fletcher. The longest role in the play was prepared for a boy player in *The*

[16] The line counts are conveniently set out in T. W. Baldwin's *The Organization and Personnel of the Shakespearean Company*, Princeton, 1927, between pp. 226 and 227.

Knight of Malta, The Humorous Lieutenant, The Laws of Candy, The Pilgrim, and *A Wife for a Month.* The second longest role went to an apprentice in *The Captain, A Very Woman, The Lovers' Progress, Thierry and Theodoret, The Pilgrim, The Double Marriage,* and *Love's Pilgrimage.* Even in plays whose lines have not been counted one calls to mind the prominence of roles for the boys in *The Duchess of Malfi, The Fair Maid of the West, The Roaring Girl, 'Tis Pity She's a Whore,* and *The Northern Lass.*

4) A certain amount of typecasting is suggested by these folio, quarto, and formal manuscript lists. Most obvious is the specialization of the comedians. Their general popularity during the reigns of Elizabeth, James, and Charles is attested in the multiplicity of popular allusions to them—more than to other players except for the stars like Alleyn, Burbage, and possibly Joseph Taylor, and to the managers like Heminges and Beeston. See the allusions to Tarleton, Kempe, Thomas Greene, William Rowley, Armyn, Shank, William Robbins, and Timothy Reade.[17] The customary casting of these men in comic roles is indicated not only by the many allusions to them and by their assignments such as Greene to Bubble in *Greene's Tu Quoque;* Rowley to Plumporridge in *The Inner Temple Masque,* the fat clown in *All's Lost by Lust,*[18] the Fat Bishop in *A Game at Chess;* Shank to Hilario in *The Picture,* Hodge in *The Soddered Citizen,* Sir Roger in *The Scornful Lady;* and William Robbins to Carazie in *The Renegado,* Rawbone in *The Wedding,* and Clem in *The Fair Maid of the West.*

Equally indicative of the specialization of the comedians is the omission of the names of such popular players from the casts of plays without prominent comic roles. We have already noted the absence of Robert Armin's name from the Jonson folio list of players for the tragedy of *Catiline,* though

---

[17] Consult under their names in Edwin Nungezer, *A Dictionary of Actors and Other Persons Associated with the Public Representation of Plays in England before 1642,* New Haven, 1929; and Bentley, *The Jacobean and Caroline Stage,* II.

[18] Though there is no cast for this play, Rowley's performance is recorded in the dramatis personnae as "*Iaques,* a simple clownish Gentleman, his sonne, personated by the Poet."

he was listed as a player in the almost contemporary *Alchemist*. Though John Shank had a reputation as a comedian and was a prominent fellow of the King's company and a part-owner of their two theaters, his name does not appear in the casts or lists for their plays omitting his specialty, *Sir John van Olden Barnavelt*, *The Deserving Favorite*, *The Swisser*, or *Believe as You List*. One odd appearance of John Shank's name is in the full cast for *The Wild Goose Chase* where he is assigned the role of "PETELLA their waiting-woman Their Servant Mr. Shanck." But there are no lines for Petella in the play. I can only conjecture that Shank gagged his lines, but this is a feeble guess since there seems to be little scope for Petella in this comedy.

A similar practice is indicated in the casts for Queen Henrietta's company. Their principal comedian, William Robbins, is listed as playing the comic roles of Carazie in *The Renegado*, Rawbone in *The Wedding*, and Clem in *The Fair Maid of the West*; but in *King John and Matilda* and *Hannibal and Scipio* which are without important comic roles his name does not appear.

Typecasting for comedians is also suggested but not demonstrated by the change in type of comic roles which Shakespeare wrote for the Lord Chamberlain's company while the buffoon and dancer, Will Kempe, was a fellow of the troupe— Costard, Dromio, Launce, Bottom, Shallow, Dogberry—to the new type of singing court fool which he wrote after Kempe's departure and his replacement by Robert Armin—Touchstone, Feste, the Fool in *King Lear*. Professor Ringler's ingenious argument that Armin played Edgar in *King Lear* and that the Fool was played by a boy[19] is interesting but not convincing. Such casting would seem to me to violate not only the normal practices of the professional players but the whole tradition of the Court Fool which is emphasized in the tragedy by the coxcomb and by the frequent references to it.

[19] "Shakespeare and His Actors: Some Remarks on *King Lear*," *Proceedings of the Comparative Literature Symposium*, vol. 12, ed. Wendell M. Aycock, Lubbock, Texas, 1981, pp. 183-94.

There are further suggestions of at least periodic typecasting in the frequently noted appearance in three of Shakespeare's comedies of the late nineties of paired heroines of contrasted stature and contrasted temperaments—Helena and Hermia, Beatrice and Hero, Celia and Rosalind. Since there are no clues yet discovered to the identities of the boys for whom the roles were written, or even any assurance that two particular boys were playing together for several years, this suggestion must be taken as speculative though attractive.

Somewhat similar is Baldwin Maxwell's contention that the "hungry knave" characters in the Beaumont and Fletcher folio plays were written for John Shank. The roles are Corporal Judas in *Bonduca*, Geta in *The Prophetess*, Mallfort in *The Lover's Progress*, Lazarello in *Love's Cure*, Onus in *The Queen of Corinth*, and Penurio in *Women Pleased*. The excessive leanness of each of these characters is pointedly remarked upon in the text of the play.[20] All seem to have been written while Shank was a fellow.

These examples from the plays of Shakespeare and of Fletcher are not quite the same as the others in that they suggest an attached dramatist or poet-in-ordinary writing roles for particular players in his company, not the company's regular assignment of roles according to the specialties of its fellows and apprentices.[21]

Another sort of evidence of typecasting, at least for one man for a short period, is to be seen in a series of contemporary allusions to Stephen Hammerton during the last few years before the closing of the theaters. The most comprehensive of these allusions is the one made by Wright in his *Historia Histrionica*.

[20] Baldwin Maxwell, "The Hungry Knave in the Beaumont and Fletcher Plays," *Philological Quarterly* 5 (1926), 299-305.

[21] The classic attempt to cast all the Shakespearean plays and a number of others performed by the Lord Chamberlain-King's company is that of Baldwin, *The Organization and Personnel of the Shakespearean Company*. While there are many valuable suggestions in this book, a good many of Baldwin's conclusions seem to me to go far beyond his evidence.

. . . at the same time *Amyntor* was Play'd by *Stephen Hammerton* (who was at first a most noted and beautiful Woman Actor, but afterwards he acted with equal Grace and Applause, a Young Lover's Part). . . .[22]

The statement about the apprenticeship of Hammerton is verified, at least so far as the dates are concerned, by statements in a suit in the Court of Requests in 1632.[23] Hammerton's apprenticeship would have expired in or about 1638 shortly before the references to him in the young lovers' roles.

Hammerton as a juvenile lead, almost a matinée idol, is attested by a few epilogue allusions in plays of the King's men after the "noted and beautiful Woman Actor" had become an adult. In the epilogue to Shirley's *The Doubtful Heir* the Captain questions the gentlemen in the audience about the play they have just seen:

> . . . now, pray tell
> How did the action please ye? was it well?
> How did king Stephen do, and tother Prince?

Since the king in the play is named Ferdinand, Stephen must mean the actor, Stephen Hammerton.

The same sort of implication about this actor is to be found in the epilogue to John Suckling's comedy for the King's men, *The Goblins*. The speaker inquires about the reception of the play:

> *The women—Oh, if* Stephen *should be kill'd!*
> *Or miss the lady, how the plot is spill'd.*

Since there is no Stephen in the play, Hammerton must have played Orsabrin.

Of the same sort, though even more flattering to young Hammerton, are two passages in the epilogue for Thomas Killigrew's *The Parson's Wedding*, a Blackfriars play of about

---

[22] See Bentley, *The Jacobean and Caroline Stage*, II, Appendix, p. 693.
[23] See G. E. Bentley, "The Salisbury Court Theatre and Its Boy Players," *Huntington Library Quarterly* 40 (1977), 129-49.

1640.[24] At the end of the play, the Captain, about to speak the epilogue, puts off Lady Love-all with, "Think on't, *Stephen* is as handsome, when the Play is done, as Mr. Wild was in the Scene." And a little later the Captain concludes the play with

> What say you, Gentlemen, will you lend your hands to join them; the Match you see is made; if you refuse, *Stephen* misses the Wench, and then you cannot justly blame the Poet. For you know they say, that alone is enough to spoil the Play.

Even several years after the closing of the theaters the popularity of Stephen Hammerton in romantic roles was still remembered. In his verses for the Beaumont and Fletcher folio of 1647 Henry Harington wrote:

> *Ladies cannot say*
> *Though* Stephen *miscarri'd that so did the play.*

These miscellaneous examples do show that at various periods in its history the King's company, at least, assigned certain roles to particular players who had developed specialties. It appears to me notable that most of the roles cited here were written by attached dramatists of the company—Shakespeare, Fletcher, and James Shirley. Before making any valid statements about typecasting as a general practice, even in the King's company, one would need information about many more of the role assignments even in these cited plays. Still more essential would be casting information about the scores of plays produced by the company but written by unattached playwrights like Barnaby Barnes, George Wilkins, Tourneur, Middleton, Henry Shirley, Richard Brome, Lodowick Carlell, William Davenant, John Ford, Ben Jonson, and the several anonymous plays in the repertory list of 1641.[25]

On the basis of the evidence now available one can only say

[24] See Bentley, *The Jacobean and Caroline Stage*, IV, 701-705.
[25] See ibid., I, 65-66 and 108-134.

that typecasting seems to have been common for leading comedians. Beyond this there is evidence that for short periods in the Lord Chamberlain-King's company certain specialties like the hungry knave, the handsome young lover, the paired heroines seem to have been exploited by attached dramatists of the company. I have found no evidence of a consistent practice of typecasting for all plays. Certainly the major role in the best-known plays cannot have been typecast, and typecasting cannot have been the controlling principle in the preparation of plays or in the selection of sharers for the King's company or for Queen Henrietta's.

DOUBLING

For the professional players doubling had been a normal feature of casting for generations before Shakespeare came to London. Indeed, doubling was a euphemism: common enough was tripling and quadrupling and even quintupling as shown by the printed casts of Tudor interludes and by a few of the later Plots and prompt manuscripts. Versatility was certainly required of all professional players, men and boys, sharers, hired men, and apprentices.

David Bevington has collected the many examples of Tudor plays written to be performed by touring companies, of limited size, several published with casting charts on the title pages, and he has shown brilliantly how the plays were constructed to facilitate such doubling. He shows how this principle of construction was dominant through the time to Marlowe.[26]

The practice of constructing commercial plays to allow for doubling was still important after Marlowe, even when the acting troupes had grown much larger than six men and a boy. Shakespeare was careful to observe it, as has been demonstrated for his earlier plays.[27] One might have assumed that

[26] David Bevington, *From "Mankind" to Marlowe*, Cambridge, Mass., 1962.
[27] William A. Ringler, Jr., "The Number of Actors in Shakespeare's Early Plays," in *The Seventeenth Century Stage*, ed. G. E. Bentley, Chicago and London, 1968, pp. 110-34.

the doubling was less extensive in Jacobean and Caroline times when the companies were larger and richer than the sixteenth-century strollers had been, but evidently this was not the case. The 1607 quarto of *The Fair Maid of the Exchange* presents a rather elaborate doubling chart; the 1610 quarto of *Mucedorus* carries a chart showing how "Ten persons may easily play it"; and the 1631 prompt manuscript of Massinger's *Believe as You List*, performed by the largest and richest of the Caroline London companies, shows the most complex doubling of all.

Audiences were fully aware of this practice as occasional comments show. In the Induction for Marston's *Antonio and Mellida* Alberto says to Piero "the necessity of the play forceth me to act two parts." In his *Histrio-Mastix* (1633, Li^v, p. 262) William Prynne says that "lascivious love songs" are sung on the stage: "between each several action; both to supply that chasm or vacant interim, which the tiring-house takes up, in changing the actors' robes to fit them for some other part in the ensuing scene. . . ." In Richard Brome's comedy, *The Antipodes*, performed, according to the statement on the title page of the quarto of 1640, by Queen Henrietta's company in 1638, there is a dialogue between Barbara and Blaze in the fourth scene of the fifth act (K3-K3^v).

> *Bar.* O *Tony.*
> I did not see thee act ith' play. *Bla.* O, but
> I did though *Bab*, two Mutes. . . .
> A Mute is one that acteth speakingly,
> And yet says nothing. I did two of them.
> The Sage Man-midwife, and the Basket-maker.

Proper doubling is occasionally noted in published texts. The cast printed in the quarto of Thomas Nabbes' *Hannibal and Scipio* shows William Sherlock in the roles of Maharball and Prusias; Hugh Clark playing Nuntias and Syphax; Robert Axen, Bomilcar and Gisgon. These examples are merely indications that doubling was well known; they are never full casts, for they leave six to twenty roles unassigned.

Far more illuminating than such literary publications or manuscripts intended for patrons are the papers prepared for

use in the theaters where the purpose was aid in the performances, not exploitation of readers. Very enlightening about
the custom of doubling are the seven "Plots" which have been
enumerated and defined above. Though none of these Plots
lists a formal dramatis personae with assigned roles, all of
them give the names of actors, including sharers, hired men,
and boys. Doubling is required of most of these players, usually of the hired men but often sharers as well. In the Plot for
the revival of *The Seven Deadly Sins* II, apparently as revived
by the Lord Strange's men at the Curtain, probably in 1590,
twenty names of performers are recorded, several only nicknames or Christian names, and therefore not always certainly
identifiable, but the evidence of doubling is overwhelming.
Most of the major roles are unassigned, but three sharers are
named, two with a single role, one with a simple double.
Though Richard Burbage (then about seventeen years old) has
only two roles, Richard Cowley was assigned eight parts, John
Duke six, Robert Pallant six, and J. Holland five. The boys,
never given their full names, had only one or two roles apiece.[28]

Though the manuscript of the Plot for *The Battle of Alcazar*
is only a fragment with some pieces missing, it has the advantage of being the only Plot for which a text of the play is also
available, though the printed text is for an abridged version.
Greg thinks the Plot represents a revival of 1598 or 1599 certainly by the Admiral's men. This Plot names ten sharers
(each designated "Mr.") though two of the known sharers are
omitted, seven or eight hired men, and apparently seven boys,
though nicknames may cover some duplication, and the actor
of one female role is omitted. According to this Plot the majority of the players, even the sharers, had more than one role
to play, though for the major characters the second role, if
any, was a slight one. Edward Alleyn, Thomas Doughten,
and Thomas Towne appear not to have doubled at all. The
number of roles assigned each player is smaller than in *The*

[28] Greg, ed., *Dramatic Documents from the Elizabethan Playhouses*, I, 105-122
and II, unpaged.

Seven Deadly Sins II, but "Mr. Sam." has six parts to play, and George Somerset five.

The most intricate doubling is recorded in the prompt manuscript for Philip Massinger's *Believe as You List*, performed by the King's company in 1631. In this very full prompt book twenty-nine roles are assignable from the book keeper's notes, but the players for nineteen other roles are unrecorded in this manuscript; eighteen players of the company are assigned roles but at least eight others known to have been associated with the King's company at about this time fail to appear.[29] Eight of the assignments are to sharers in the company, nine to performers who were probably hired men. Though there are at least seven roles for apprentices in the play, none is assigned by name, though a prompter's note at line 1970 reads: "Harry: Wilson: & Boy ready for the song at ye Arras:" Although the leading sharers like Joseph Taylor, Eyllaerdt Swanston, John Lowin, Richard Robinson, and Robert Benfield have single parts, other sharers like Thomas Pollard, William Penn, and Thomas Hobbes are required to double. But the most surprising feature of the casting for *Believe as You List* is not the number of roles entrusted to individual players; *Tamar Cam I* and *The Battle of Alcazar* both require certain actors to impersonate more characters. But in Massinger's play the same character is sometimes divided between two or even three players.

Such evidence shows that doubling was basic in the casting of Elizabethan, Jacobean, and Caroline troupes, that it could be at least as intricate in the King's company in 1631 as it had been in the Admiral's in 1589, and that less doubling was required of sharers and apprentices than of hired men.

Though only the prompt manuscript of *Believe as You List* shows a single role being performed by two or three different players, it seems likely that expedients resorted to by the

[29] C. J. Sisson, ed., *Believe as You List by Philip Massinger*, Malone Society, Oxford, 1927, pp. xxxi-xxxiv. Of course several of the unnamed players probably took some of the nineteen roles not assigned in the manuscript.

dominant King's men in 1631 would also have been used by poorer and smaller troupes. As Sisson points out, roles so divided can have conveyed little individuality in the performance. It should be noted, however, that such shifting of actors would have been easier in large-cast historic plays using togas and robes than in comedies with contemporary English settings. Comedies of this sort are more usual in late Jacobean and Caroline times than they had been in Elizabethan. Moreover the comedies of Jonson, Middleton, Shirley, and Brome tend to use twenty to twenty-five characters as opposed to the forty-nine of *Believe as You List*.

After the consideration of so much scattered material bearing upon casting, it is chastening to note that the great majority of the evidence which has been found comes from the Lord Admiral's company, the King's company, and Queen Henrietta's men, while very little has been found concerning the more than a dozen other troupes playing in London during the period. Moreover, the evidence is bunched chronologically, coming mostly from plays performed 1589-1602 and 1626-1642. We can only assume that practices of unnoted companies and practices during the unrepresented periods would conform. Perhaps these assumptions are not too hazardous, since the three troupes represented are the major ones, and since the practices apparent in the King's company's prompt manuscript for *Believe as You List* in 1631 do not seem to differ much from those observed in the Plot the Lord Admiral's men had prepared for their performance of *The Battle of Alcazar* in 1598 or 1599.

All the evidence testifies to the dominant importance of the sharers who are almost always given the leading roles. But it is equally notable that very seldom in the extant lists are roles assigned to *all* the men known to have been sharers at the time of performance.

Another feature of performances made apparent in these lists is the comparative prominence of the apprentices; usually two or three of the boys have more lines than any of the hired men. In a few plays, such as *The Merchant of Venice, As You*

Like It, All's Well that Ends Well, and *Cymbeline,* and several of
the plays of Beaumont and Fletcher, the leading role has been
prepared for a boy.

Typecasting, which has been postulated by several theater
historians, is exhibited to only a limited extent in these lists.
Comic roles regularly go to recognized comedians. Also, there
seem to be periods of the exploitation of certain actors in roles
fitted to them, like the "hungry knave" to John Shank in certain Beaumont and Fletcher plays, and the young lover roles
in the years 1638 to 1641 to Stephen Hammerton. But the
habitual selection of new sharers to carry on a standard "line"
as claimed by Baldwin for the Lord Chamberlain-King's company is not confirmed by these casts and lists. Baldwin's detailed fitting of all the leading characters in the plays of Shakespeare and of Beaumont and Fletcher involves far too much
speculation, dubious dating, age approximation, and details
of a player's complexion and coloring to be trusted as far as
he carries it.[30]

[30] Baldwin, *The Organization and Personnel of the Shakespearean Company,* pp.
198-283.

CHAPTER IX

Conclusions

IN THE YEARS between 1590 and 2 September 1642 when
the Lords and Commons issued their order that "publike Stage-
Playes shall cease, and be forborne" the profession of player
flourished in England as never before and seldom since.[1]
Though most of the one thousand and more known professional players in England were poor men frequently without
London employment, the status of the profession improved
in these years and a few of the players accumulated respectable estates as shown by their wills and by occasional allusions. In 1619 Edward Alleyn founded the College of God's
Gift at Dulwich. Sir Richard Baker, a contemporary, said of
Alleyn's action: "This man may be an example, who having
gotten his wealth by stage playing converted it to this pious

[1] . . . annual earnings of actors and actresses are adversely affected by the
frequent periods of unemployment experienced by many. According to

234

use, not without a kind of reputation to the Society of Players."[2] Similarly Ralph Crane wrote in 1621 that his pen had
had employment

> . . . mongst those civil, well deserving men
> That grace the stage with profit and delight.

The rise of the London players from their obsolete classi-
fication in the category of rogues and vagabonds, to which
their enemies still liked to consign them, is also illustrated by
the more elaborate publication of their plays in handsome vol-
umes like the Jonson folio of 1616 and the Shakespeare folio
of 1623, by their official patents as companies of players under the patronage of members of the royal family, by their
livery, by the appointment of most of the sharers as Grooms
of the Chamber in ordinary, by their increasingly frequent
appearances in command performances at court, and by the
appointment of some of them to particular court posts, such
as the appointment of John Lowin to be King's Porter and by
the royal patent issued in 1639 to Joseph Taylor creating him
Yeoman of the Revels to His Majesty.

The organization of these professional troupes was guild-
like, with the sharers, generally named in the company patent
as the legally responsible members, at the top. They shared
the receipts from certain parts of the theater after every performance, and they shared the fees for court performances
which eventually became considerable. In the year March 1638
to January 1638/39 the court performance fees for the King's
players amounted to £300. In this company several sharers—

data obtained by the Actors' Equity Association (which represents actors
who work on the stage) and the Screen Actors Guild, between two-thirds
and three-quarters of their members earned $2,500 or less a year from
acting jobs in 1978, and less than 5 percent earned over $25,000 from such
work. [*Occupational Outlook Handbook*, 1980-81 ed., U.S. Department of
Labor Bureau of Statistics, March 1980, Bulletin 2075, p. 458.]
See also William J. Baumol and William Gordon Bowen, *Performing Arts, the
Economic Dilemma: A Study of Problems Common to the Theater, Opera, Music, and
Dance*, New York, 1966.
  [2] Richard Baker, *A Chronicle of the Kings of England*, London, 1684, p. 423.

Burbage, Shakespeare, Heminges, Condell, Shank, Taylor, Lowin, Ostler, Underwood, Kempe, Phillips, and Pope—also at different times owned shares in the company's two theaters and thereby received a second cut of the daily receipts. This sharers' ownership of the company playhouse was not common, however. It should also be remembered that this troupe of King James and King Charles was the most prosperous one known.

The group of sharers of a troupe selected new patented members, sometimes from other companies, sometimes from the ranks of their own hired men. These new sharers had to pay an entrance fee to cover their part in the company store of costumes and play manuscripts and toward new purchases and new fees and other expenses. This payment for a share is referred to several times, but the total sum is seldom mentioned. In February 1634/35, William Bankes said that he had paid £100 to become a sharer in the company of Prince Charles (II) in the early thirties, and William Bird or Bourne says that he paid £200 to become a sharer in the King's company in about 1640. Some companies, possibly most, had an agreement to return at least part of this fee if the sharer left the company and returned all its property then in his possession. At least some companies acknowledged an obligation to pay back a portion of his entrance fee to the widow of a deceased member.

Sharers selected, or ratified the selection, of new plays. They appear also to have ratified decisions to fine or to dismiss transgressing members. Sharers took most of the principal roles in the plays for which we have casts or lists. But these lists almost never show every sharer assigned to a role.

Employed by the sharers were the hired men: stagekeepers, prompters or book holders, wardrobe keepers or tiremen, musicians, gatherers, and minor players. The number of these hired men in a company increased with increasing prosperity during the period, and it must have varied from the poorest to the richest companies, but we know that on 27 December 1624 the Master of the Revels issued a protection from arrest for twenty-one hired men of King James's company. It is clear that the majority of these men were not primarily players, but most of them could be called upon to appear on the stage in minor roles in plays with large casts. The sharers paid these dependents two to ten shillings a week in prosperous periods. In hard times these hired men took what they could get—sometimes nothing.

Boy players for the female and juvenile roles were apprenticed for varying periods to individual sharers, not to the company; they received board, room, clothing, and professional training, but no wages.

The method of training these boys is not clear. A few of them, but not many, had been in the early boy companies but apparently most of those so trained were no longer juveniles when they transferred. In 1629 Richard Gunnell and William Blagrave were licensed to "train and bring up certain boys in the quality of playing with the intent to be a supply of able actors to your Majesty's servants of Blackfriars." There is some suggestion that the Lady Elizabeth's company in its later days may have had some such function, and there is a similar suggestion for Beeston's Boys. At best these organizations could not have prepared all of the boys needed in the several London troupes of players. Most of the training must have been supervised by the individual sharer to whom the boy was apprenticed.

Within the playing company, notably in the troupe of the Lord Chamberlain-King's men, there is evidence of cordial, even affectionate, relationships, particularly among sharers and between apprentices and their masters, as shown in several wills. Of course there are also examples of discord as in the charges and countercharges at the breakup of organizations, and in the quarrel between John Shank and his fellows Benfield, Pollard, and Swanston over shares in the Globe and Blackfriars theaters.

In the play written for the London companies there are normally fewer roles for the boys than for the adults—usually four to six boys were required though it seems to have been common for some of them to double. Though it was usual for the longest and most difficult roles in the plays of the period to be written for sharers, there are a number of testimonials to the effectiveness of certain boys and in several familiar plays the longest role or the second longest was prepared for an apprentice.

It would seem logical that many of these boy players should eventually have become sharers, but the extant records do not show so many of these logical progressions as one would have expected. The clear examples are Nathan Field, Richard Perkins, John Underwood, William Ostler, Nicholas Tooley, Richard Sharpe, Thomas Holcomb, John Honeyman, John Rice, Theophilus Bird, Hugh Clark, and Nicholas Burt.

The business affairs of these London companies were complex, and they required responsible supervision. Hundreds of costumes had to be ordered and paid for; theater rents had to be paid; plays had to be commissioned, paid for, licensed, and fees paid to the Master of the Revels not only for licenses but for various privileges; court and other private performances had to be arranged and payments collected; transportation to palaces and great houses had to be provided; liveries had to be received and distributed; hired men had to be employed and paid; new properties had to be collected; rehearsals and other meetings of the company had to be scheduled; provincial tours had to be arranged and financed; playbills had to be printed and distributed. The number, complexity, and interdependence of these chores were such that they could not have been divided among six to eighteen sharers without producing chaos. Clearly the administrative affairs of a London company had to be concentrated in the hands of one or two men.

The extant records make it clear that most—probably all—troupes had such an administrator. We should call him an actor-manager since for all but two of these known functionaries (Richard Heton and William Davenant) we have records of their activities as players, but the term actor-manager seems not to have been used for them before 1642. Various designations are found in different records: steward, chief, warden, governor, leader, master.

The most clearly defined of these administrators is John Heminges acting for the Lord Chamberlain-King's company, and succeeded after 1630 by Joseph Taylor and John Lowin; Christopher Beeston, acting for first Queen Anne's company, then for the Lady Elizabeth's, then for Queen Henrietta's, and finally for the King and Queen's Young company or Beeston's Boys; Edward Alleyn for the Admiral's and the Palsgrave's.

Other managers not so fully identified are Thomas Greene acting before Beeston for Queen Anne's men; William Rowley for Prince Charles's (I) men; Richard Gunnell for the Palsgrave's men and later for the Salisbury Court players; William Davenant for a short period for Beeston's Boys, preceded and followed by William Beeston; Ellis Worth and the comedian Andrew Cane for Prince Charles's (II) company at the Salisbury Court and the Red Bull theaters in the thirties; William Cartwright, Senior, in succession to Richard Gunnell at the Fortune theater; and finally Richard Heton for Queen Henrietta's men during their last years.

Though the greatest profit and prestige for all players was to be found in London, circumstances forced every company to go on the road at various times. The commonest cause for such travels was the plague which led to closing orders for the theaters at least fourteen times during the years 1590-1642. Such restraints varied in length according to the death rate, from a few weeks to eighteen months. The playhouses were also closed for periods of mourning for Queen Elizabeth, Queen Anne, and King James, and for varying periods during Lent. Sometimes prohibitions resulted from the exploitation by the players of censorable material, and at other times scanty London audiences prompted travel.

Of course there were scores of provincial troupes on the road at all times; the general appetite for play performances during these years seems insatiable. Such provincial companies provided competition for the touring London troupes not because they played in the same town at the same time but because a very recent visit from provincials made the mayor and council reluctant to grant playing permission to the Londoners.

When the sharers of a London company decided that they must travel, they had to select a reduced repertory and a reduced number of players. Though there are many hundreds of town records of players' visits, disappointingly few of them record the number of players travelling and only one the exact number of plays they carried. From 1590 to 1607, no numbers are mentioned in the reported town records. Between 1607 and 1637 nine accounts give the number of players in the visiting troupe as from nine to twenty.

As to repertories, one account says that four plays were presented by the Lord Derby's men at Londesborough in 1612; another that the King's company performed five plays before the Earl of Cumberland in 1619/20. But the only account known which specifies exactly how many play books were being carried by a touring company is the statement of Richard Kendall at Oxford in 1634. He says that his company, the King's Revels of Salisbury Court theater, was carrying fourteen plays.

When the personnel and the repertory had been selected presumably the gear (costumes and properties) had to be collected, transportation arrangements made, and an itinerary determined. Unfortunately I have no evidence at all about these steps except for a few stray references to horses, wagons, and hampers.

Once on the road and in a selected locality, the leaders of the troupe had to call on local officials to identify themselves and to request permission to perform. The response to their request varied widely from town to town and from year to year: sometimes permission was denied because of hostility; sometimes it was refused for fear of epidemics; sometimes because of apprehension of local disorders which now and then accompanied performances, especially at night. When permission to perform their plays was refused the players were usually given a gratuity out of respect for their royal or noble patron.

If their reception was cordial the players hoped to begin their visit with a performance called "the Mayor's play" before the council and their guests in a civic building. But several communities, though allowing public performances, forbade the use of the town hall. For other performances a convenient place had to be secured. The preferred auditorium seems to have been an inn like the Checkers Inn at Canterbury, or the White Horse or the Red Lion at Norwich, or the King's Arms at Oxford, but other provincial playing places are mentioned, such as common halls, moot halls, schoolhouses, even churches, and at least one provincial playhouse.

When the London companies cast their plays the assignments were normally restricted to those sharers, hired men, and apprentices belonging to the troupe at the time. Such cramping restrictions in casting were alleviated by the fact that many plays (perhaps most of those prepared for the major companies) were written with a particular organization and its personnel in mind. Such anticipation always, during the time of their contract, characterized the work of attached dramatists or poets-in-ordinary, like Heywood, Fletcher, Massinger, Shakespeare, Shirley, William Rowley, and Richard Brome. Even for many unattached playwrights such anticipation was common. *Henslowe's Diary* and his correspondence are replete with records of payments made to dramatists before a play was begun or during the course of its composition.

The sources of our knowledge of casting are very few compared with the large number of plays performed by the London companies during the period. They are seven extant Plots or production synopses of action, a few prompt books, three collections: the Jonson folio of 1616, the Shakespeare folio of 1623, and the Beaumont and Fletcher folio of 1679. In addition there are a few formal manuscripts with incomplete casts and sixteen or seventeen quartos with printed casts, never complete assignments of parts, and all of them after 1618, most of them from 1629 to 1632.

The collective evidence of these casts, lists, and notes make it clear that major roles were generally assigned to sharers; less important parts were given to hired men. The plays of the period in general, cast or uncast, make it clear that boys would have been more conspicuous on the stage than the hired men. In a few plays the longest role was a boy's, but though these roles are conspicuous—Portia, Rosalind, Helena, Imogen, and perhaps a score of others—they are found in a small minority of the 600 or 700 play texts surviving from the period.

Typecasting, though apparent in a number of instances, does not seem to have been the dominant practice among the London companies of the period. Leading comic roles do appear to have gone regularly to the known comedian among the sharers—Kempe, Armin, Shank, Greene, Robbins, Rowley, Cane, Reade. A few other specialities can be observed for limited periods, as the romantic juvenile for Stephen Hammerton in plays of the King's men in the last four or five years before the Civil Wars. Perhaps a few other roles were written for a specific cadaverous player or a notoriously bulky sharer or an unusually talented singing boy, but the regular preparation by attached dramatists of type roles for type actors is not suggested by the available evidence.

One feature of casting among the dramatic companies of the time does appear to have been universal—doubling. Of course this practice had been common among the players for more than a century, as Bevington's *"Mankind" to Marlowe* shows, and it is not yet completely extinct. But the lists, casts, prompt books, and Plots extant for the period 1590-1642 show that all the companies represented must have taken doubling for granted. Not only do the prompt books and Plots show most players assuming more than one role, but several actors were required to represent four or five or even eight different characters. One prompt book shows instances of one role divided among two or three players. Individualization among minor characters, especially in the large-cast historical plays, cannot have been expected.

The profession of player in these years, though too glamorous to please the moralists and the Puritan preachers, was strenuous and uncertain. It was really profitable for only a few, and most of those few were sharers in the Lord Chamberlain-King's company.

APPENDIX

Casts and Lists of Players

THE CASTS set out for reference in this appendix are those found in printed quartos and formal manuscripts; they are the most full, precise, and authentic casts that have come down to us. Here they are organized according to the producing company: Prince Charles's (I), one; King's, ten; Queen Henrietta's, six; Prince Charles's (II), one; King's Revels, two.

PRINCE CHARLES'S (I) COMPANY

The first cast to be printed in a quarto, that for *The Inner Temple Masque, Or Masque of Heroes*, 1619, is, of course, an abnormal piece for professional players since, as a masque, it required far fewer spoken lines than plays and fewer characters. As the title shows, the masque was put on by the lawyers of the Inner Temple; the dancers, always most conspicuous in a masque, were members of the Inner Temple, and the Templars were the producers. The professional players hired to speak Middleton's lines were:

The Parts	The Speakers
D. Almanacke.	Ios. Taylor.
Plumporridge.	W. Rowley.
A Fasting-day.	I. Newton.
New-yeere.	H. Atwell.
Time.	W. Carpenter.
Harmonie	A Boy.

The first four players were sharers in the acting troupe of Prince Charles; Joseph Taylor, the leading performer with the longest role in the masque, was later to become a star performer in the King's company. William Rowley, the dramatist, is assigned his usual part of the fat clown. The only hired man listed is William Carpenter who, as *Time*, had only twelve lines to speak. Perhaps the part was too insignificant for a sharer; or possibly Carpenter was especially good in the role of old men, as Ben Jonson said Salmon Pavy was. Very little is known about Carpenter as an actor but apparently later, before the death of King James, he became a sharer in the company. The boy who played *Harmonie* had no speaking lines, but he sang three important songs. Presumably he was an apprentice in Prince Charles's troupe, since he is listed with the others of the company.

The King's Company

The Duchess of Malfi

The next cast to be printed was that for the 1623 quarto of John Webster's *Duchess of Malfi* as acted by the King's company in 1613 or 1614 with certain cast changes indicated for a revival after 1619. Webster himself must have had something to do with the publication of the play since he signed the dedication, and since the quarto prints commendatory verses by Thomas Middleton, William Rowley, and John Ford; such verses were ordinarily solicited by the author himself. One would assume, therefore, that Webster also recorded the cast, or at least approved of it.

The Actors Names.

Bosola, *I. Lowin.*

Ferdinand, 1 *R. Burbidge,*
   2 *I. Taylor.*

Cardinall, 1 *H. Cundaile.*
   2 *R. Robinson.*

Antonio, 1 *W. Ostler.*
   2 *R. Benfield.*

Delio, *I. Vnderwood.*

Forobosco, *N. Towley.*

Malateste

The Marquesse of Pescara,
   I. Rice.

Siluio, *T. Pollard*

The seuerall mad-men *N. Towley,*
   I. Vnderwood, &c.

The Dutchesse, *R. Sharpe.*

The Cardinals Mis. *I. Tomson.*

The Doctor,
Cariola,   } *R. Pallant*
Court Officers.

Three Young Children.

Two Pilgrims

Though this cast is gratifyingly full, there are certain difficulties about it. The numbers before the actors of the roles Ferdinand, the Cardinal, and Antonio seem to mean that Burbage, Condell, and Ostler created the roles and Taylor, Robinson, and Benfield replaced them in a revival. Since Ostler died late in 1614 and Richard Burbage early in 1619, the opening performance must have taken place before the end of 1614 and the revival between 1619 and the publication date of 1623. But it is difficult to believe that the original performers of all the other roles were still playing them between 1619 and 1623 after an interval of five or more years, especially the three boys Richard Sharpe, John Thompson, and Robert Pallant. Since John Thompson played a female role in *The Swisser* in 1631 it seems unlikely that he could have played the Cardinal's mistress seventeen years before. Furthermore, the bracket enclosing the roles of the Doctor, Cariola, and Court Officers is certainly wrong; Robert Pallant could not have played all six roles. The officers and the Doctor are adult roles and Cariola a boy's role; moreover Cariola and the four officers, all with speeches, appear in the same scene, III, 2. One can only guess that the bracket is a printer's error, that Robert Pallant played only Cariola, and that the roles of the Doctor and the four officers are unassigned. It also seems likely that the cast printed in the 1623 quarto is the cast for the revival, and only Burbage, Condell, and Ostler are singled out for their memorable creation of the roles in the first performance.

If this is correct, the cast for the revival was made up of six sharers, one hired man, Thomas Pollard, and four boys. The unassigned roles of the Doctor, the four officers, and Malateste were presumably also taken by hired men.

As usual, a large number of roles are unassigned or not even mentioned. Besides those named but unassigned, the production required servants, guards, executioners, attendants, ladies-in-waiting, an Old Woman, and Antonio's son. Such omissions are usual in the extant casts. These roles would have required several hired men and boys, and the parts would pretty surely have been doubled or even tripled.

The Roman Actor

Massinger's *The Roman Actor* was licensed for performance by the King's company on 11 October 1626 and published in 1629 in an elaborate quarto with a dedication, six sets of commendatory verses (one by the leading player, Joseph Taylor), and a cast.

The persons presented.	The principall Actors.
Domitianus Caesar	Iohn Lowin.
Paris the Tragædian.	Ioseph Taylor.
Parthenius a free-man of *Caesars*.	Richard Sharpe.
Ælius, Lamia, and *Stephanos*.	Thomas Pollard.
Iunius Rusticus.	Robert Benfield.
Aretinus Clemens, Caesars spie.	Eyllardt Swanstone.
Æsopus a Player.	Richard Robinson.

Philagus a rich Miser.	Anthony Smith.
Palphurius Sura, a Senator.	William Pattricke.
Latinus a Player.	Cvrtise Grevill.
3.Tribunes.	
2.Lictors.	George Vernon.
	Iames Horne
Domitia the wife of *Ælius Lamia*.	Iohn Tompson.
Domitilla cosin germane to *Cæsar*.	Iohn Hvnnieman.
Iulia Titus Daughter.	William Trigge.
Cænis, *Vespatians* Concubine.	Alexander Govgh.

To begin with, the error in lineation must be noted; Vernon and Horne, neither of whom was a boy in 1626, have slipped down among the creators of the female characters. Obviously they should be opposite the Lictors and Tribunes. It could well be that these two hired men handled all the Lictors and Tribunes needed in the play, for the Lictors appear in Act I only and the Tribunes in Act V only. The first Tribune has 90 to 100 lines, but the second only 4 or 5 lines in two scenes; the third Tribune had only 3 lines in one scene; his lines could have been handled by a stagekeeper, or even cut.

The division of the roles in *The Roman Actor* among the different classes of players is similar to that of the other plays of the King's men with casts: eight sharers, four hired men, and four boys. The roles assigned to these hired men, William Patrick, Curtis Greville, George Vernon, and James Horne, are not all negligible. The first Tribune, presumably played by George Vernon, though it could have been James Horne, has nearly 100 lines, and Greville's Latinus about 60.

The Deserving Favorite

The 1629 quarto of *The Deserving Favorite*, written by the courtier-huntsman and amateur dramatist, Lodowick Carlell, is said on the title page to have been acted first before the King, by the King's men, and later by them at Blackfriars.

This is a reversal of the usual order. The date of performance is uncertain; one can be sure only that the piece was performed not later than 1629, and probably not before 1625 when Smith was still a member of another acting company. The cast given is:

THE NAMES OF THE ACTORS.

M^r. *Benfield, the King.*

M^r. *Taylor, the Duke.*

M^r. *Lewin, Iacomo.*

M^r. *Sharpe, Lysander.*

M^r. *Swanstone, the Count Vtrante.*

M^r. *Robinson, Count Orsinio, and Hermite.*

M^r. *Smith, Gerard.*

———————————

Women.

Iohn Honiman, Clarinda.

Iohn Tomson, Cleonarda.

Edward Horton, Mariana.

Iaspero, Bernardo, Seruants, Huntsmen, &c.

This small cast of six or seven sharers (all properly designated as M^r. if Smith was already a sharer) and three boys is not enough to produce the play. Carlell has omitted from his cast three named servants, a messenger, two unnamed but numbered servants, an "Executioner" and "Attendants." None of these characters has any significant number of lines and all are of inferior rank, perhaps therefore not worthy of note by the aristocratic Carlell. Probably three or four hired men could have handled them all, but there is no evidence.

The Lovers' Melancholy

The next recorded cast was printed in the 1629 quarto of Ford's tragedy *The Lovers' Melancholy*, which had been licensed for performance by King Charles's company in November 1628. Though the front matter gives a list of players longer than most, there is no assignment of roles.

The names of such as acted.

Iohn Lowin.	Richard Sharpe.
Ioseph Taylor.	Thomas Pollard.
Robert Benfield.	William Penn.
Iohn Shanck.	Cvrteise Grivill.
Eylyardt Swanston.	George Vernon.
Anthony Smith.	Richard Baxter.

Iohn Tomson.
Iohn Honyman.
Iames Horne.
William Trigg.
Alexander Govgh.

This list has some puzzling aspects: it is longer than most; it names seventeen players, though there are only sixteen named roles in the play; in the usual separation of men and boys, it names five players for the four female roles, including the waiting maid; James Horne was not a boy but a hired man who had received livery for King James's funeral procession four years before and had taken an adult role in *The Roman Actor* two years before. Eight or nine of the adult players were sharers in the King's company: Lowin, Taylor, Benfield, Shank, Swanston, Pollard, Penn, and Sharpe; the status of Anthony Smith in the company at this time is not clear. The hired men listed are Greville, Vernon, Baxter, Horne, and possibly Smith. There are four boys, John Thompson, John Honeyman, William Trigg (who had been apprenticed to John Heminges only the year before), and Alexander Gough.

The number of hired men in this cast is high; it suggests that in 1628 at least four and possibly five of the wage-earning assistants were competent actors, though none attained later prominence.

The Picture

Philip Massinger's tragicomedy, *The Picture*, was licensed for performance by the King's company in June 1629 and published in quarto with a cast and a set of commendatory verses by Thomas Jay in 1630. Jay commends Massinger's modesty in admitting his inferiority to Jonson and Beaumont; it is suggestive of contemporary reputations that Jay does not mention the company's most devoted dramatist, William Shakespeare. The cast reads:

Dramatis personæ.	The Actors names.
Ladislaus King of Hungarie.	*Robert Benfield.*
Eubulus an old Counsaylor.	*Iohn Lewin.*
Ferdinand Generall of the army.	*Richard Sharpe.*
Mathias a knight of *Bohemia.*	*Ioseph Taylor.*
Vbaldo, 2. wild courtiers. *Ricardo,*	*Thomas Pollard.* *Eylardt Swanstone.*
Hilario seruant to *Sophia.*	*Iohn Shanucke.*
Iulio Baptista a great scholler.	*William Pen.*
Honoria the Queene.	*John Tomson.*
Acanthe a maid of honor.	*Alexander Goffe.*
Sophia wife to *Mathias.*	*Iohn Hunnieman.*
Corisca, Sophias woman.	*William Trigge.*

6. Masquers
6. seruants to the Queene
Attendants

According to this list the performance in 1629 used seven sharers, Benfield, Lowin, Sharpe, Taylor, Pollard, Swanston, and Shank; probably one hired man, William Penn; and four apprentices, John Thompson, Alexander Gough, John Honeyman, and William Trigg. But the unassigned roles indicate that at least six more, even assuming extensive doubling, were required. Two of the masquers were boys, one of whom sang and one played the lute. Several of the servants have a few lines to speak, and there is a Poet who is not mentioned at all in the dramatis personae. More than six additional performers must have been needed. Two of them had to be boys with some musical ability. More hired men than William Penn were surely needed even if several of the roles like the messenger and certain of the attendants and servants to the Queen were doubled.

The Wild Goose Chase

The most descriptive of the printed casts for plays of the King's company is that for Fletcher's comedy *The Wild Goose Chase*. The records show that this play was popular[1] and partly for this reason it was not printed for about thirty years after first production. The circumstances of printing throw light on the cast. When Humphry Moseley published the first Beaumont and Fletcher folio in 1647, he claimed to print all the Beaumont and Fletcher plays that had not been published before, but he admitted that there was one play, which in spite of diligent search, he could not find, *The Wild Goose Chase*. Five years later he published an elaborate folio edition of this single play in a size convenient for insertion into the 1647 collection. The title page says that the play was being printed for the "private Benefit" of John Lowin and Joseph Taylor "By a Person of Honour," and Lowin and Taylor wrote an elegiac dedication for the book.

The comedy was probably first produced in 1621 since there is a record of a court performance in the Christmas season of that year. But the cast printed in the 1652 edition is impossible for 1621; Swanston and Penn had not yet joined the company in that year, and Stephen Hammerton had not yet been apprenticed as a boy actor.[2]

The cast is probably that for a revival in the winter of 1632. But the honorific "Mr." was conventionally used then for sharers, and certainly the boy actor of Oriana was not a sharer at that time. A little analysis shows that "A Person of Honour" was using the term for all the players of the company

[1] See G. E. Bentley, *The Jacobean and Caroline Stage*, 7 vols., Oxford, 1941-1968, III, 425-30.
[2] Ibid., and G. E. Bentley, "The Salisbury Court Theatre and Its Boy Players," *Huntington Library Quarterly* 40 (1977), 139-44.

who had become sharers before the closing of the theaters; Hammerton and Honeyman had, and Trigg and Gough had not.

DRAMMATIS PERSONÆ

DE-GARD, A Noble stayd Gentleman that being newly lighted from his Travells, assists his sister *Oriana* in her chase of *Mirabell* the *Wild-Goose*.

Acted by Mr. *Robert Benfield*.

LA-CASTRE, the Indulgent Father to *Mirabell*.

Acted by Mr. *Richard Robinson*.

MIRABELL, the *Wild-Goose*, a Travayl'd Monsieur, and great defyer of all Ladies in the way of Marriage, otherwise their much loose servant, at last caught by the despis'd *Oriana*.

Incomparably Acted by Mr. *Joseph Taylor*.

PINAC, his fellow Traveller, of a lively spirit, and servant to the no lesse sprightly *Lillia-Bianca*.

Admirably well Acted by Mr. *Thomas Pollard*.

BELLEUR, Companion to both, of a stout blunt humor, in love with *Rosalura*.

Most naturally Acted by Mr. *John Lowin*.

NANTOLET, Father to *Rosalura* and *Lillia-Bianca*.

Acted by Mr. *William Penn*.

LUGIER, the rough and confident Tutor to the Ladies, and chiefe Engine to intrap the *Wild-Goose*.

Acted by Mr. *Hilliard Swanston*.

ORIANA, the faire betroth'd of *Mirabell*, and wittie follower of the *Chase*.

Acted by Mr. *Steph. Hammerton*.

ROSALURA | the Aërie Daugh- | *William Trigg*.
LILLIA-BIANCA | ters of *Nantolet*. | *Sander Gough*.

PETELLA, their waiting-woman. Their Servant Mr. *Shanck*.

MARIANA, an English Courtezan.

A Young FACTOR, by Mr. *John Hony-man*.

PAGE.
SERVANTS.
SINGING-BOY.
TWO MERCHANTS.
PRIEST.
FOURE WOMEN.

With the interpretation that the cast dates from 1632 but that the use of "Mr." dates from after 1642, it becomes clear that the profitable revival at Blackfriars in the winter of 1632[3] was performed by twelve named players, eight of whom were sharers at that time, Benfield, Robinson, Taylor, Pollard, Lowin, Penn, Swanston, and Shank. One of the named actors, John Honeyman, was then still in the status of hired man, though he later became a sharer. Three of the players were apprentices, Hammerton, Trigg, and Gough.

Quite a number of additional players would have been needed for the twelve roles not assigned in the printed cast; seven of these parts needed boy actors, Mariana, the Singing Boy, the Four Women, and the Page. Actually the play has two apprentices' roles not listed at all in the dramatis personae, the Post Boy in I, i, and the boy who introduces Mariana in III, i. Without doubling, the juvenile and female roles would have required twelve boy actors; even with doubling it would appear that seven or eight must have been required. Possibly at this time the King's company could draw extra boys from the King's Revels company which had been organized in 1629 to train boy actors for the use of the King's company.[4] The servants, the two merchants, and the Priest would presumably have been assigned to hired men.

The most curious feature of the printed cast is the assignment of the role of Petella, the waiting woman, to John Shank, the leading comedian of the company who had been an actor for at least twenty-two years and had had a son born in 1610. It is even more curious that this well-known patented member

[3] Bentley, *The Jacobean and Caroline Stage*, VI, 22-23.
[4] See *Huntington Library Quarterly* 40 (1977), 137-39.

of the King's company should be assigned a role for which there are no lines in the printed text. Presumably Shank gagged lines, as comedians are known to have done. But there are no scenes that seem to give much scope for Petella, and Shank's assignment here is curious.

Casts in Manuscript: King's Men's

Among the plays of the repertory of the King's company never published in the seventeenth century but still extant in manuscript, there are four that have casts or extensive prompter's notes from which casts can be assembled. They are Fletcher and Massinger's *Sir John van Olden Barnavelt* performed by the company in August 1619; Clavell's *The Soddered Citizen*, probably produced about 1629 or 1630; Arthur Wilson's *The Swisser*, acted at Blackfriars in 1631; and Philip Massinger's *Believe as You List* also performed in 1631.

The character of these manuscripts leaves no doubt that the casts are authentic.

Sir John van Olden Barnavelt

The earliest extant prompt manuscript of the King's company is Fletcher and Massinger's *Sir John van Olden Barnavelt*, never printed until the late nineteenth century but preserved in British Museum MS. Add. 18653. Though the play was written by prominent dramatists attached to the most prominent company, they had the temerity to deal with contemporary religious and political affairs in Holland, and some aspects of this treatment the Master of the Revels, then Sir George Buc, found objectionable. Though the censored material was deleted from the manuscript and the play was performed, publishers may have been wary of it. The manuscript was written out by Ralph Crane, who several times worked for the King's men; there are many prompter's notes.

The play can be securely dated in August 1619, so that it

is earlier than all but one of the printed casts, but by only a few years.[5] As is usual in prompt copies, this manuscript shows the bookholder's concern with minor players and doubled roles, properties, entrances and exits, not with the major characters who would have been sharers. The largest roles in the play are those of Barnavelt, the Prince of Orange, Leidenberch, Vandort, Bredero, and Modesbargen, each of whom has more than 100 lines, but none of the performers of these roles are indicated by the prompter. For the other fifteen or so roles, ten players are named, though generally by abbreviations not always easily expanded. Two of the ten are sharers, Richard Robinson, possibly John Rice and Robert Goffe, and as usual all three of the sharers are given honorific, "M^r." None of these sharers is assigned a major role and at first glance their mention is puzzling. But a little analysis makes their appearance somewhat less abnormal. "Mr Gough" appears only once, and then apparently as an attendant on Leidenberg, surely too small a role for the complete assignment for a sharer. But his name has been crossed out, so that his function in the play, if any, is unknown. "Mr Rob." and "Mr Rice" appear several times as captains, but since the captains are never named, the prompter was presumably trying to keep them straight. Robinson also doubled as an ambassador, and Rice as a servant.

A somewhat unusual feature of this prompt manuscript is the naming of three of the apprentices: Thomas Holcomb, who played the Provost's wife; "G. Lowen," who played Barnavelt's daughter and who is known from this record only; and "Nick," probably Nicholas Underhill,[6] who was assigned the role of Barnavelt's wife. Why the prompter, contrary to the normal practice, needed to be reminded about all the boys in named roles, I do not know.

The other four players identified in these prompt notes are

---

[5] See Bentley, *The Jacobean and Caroline Stage*, III, 415-17.
[6] See ibid., II, 516.

somewhat uncertain because of the use of abbreviations, nick-names, and initials. "Mr Bir" who brings in a chair may have been George Birch; "migh," "mighel" who played a captain, a soldier, and a huntsman cannot be identified; "T.p.," "Tho. po." who played Holderus and a servant was evidently Thomas Pollard; "R.T." who played a messenger, an officer, a servant, and a huntsman cannot be identified.

Obviously the prompt manuscript of *Sir John van Olden Bar-navelt* is much less helpful in understanding casting customs than that of *Believe as You List*.

In the manuscript there is no dramatis personae and no cast. Those given here were compiled by Dr. Wilhelmina Frijlinck for her edition of the play (Amsterdam, 1922), page clx.

The Soddered Citizen

About the same time as they put on Massinger's *Picture* the King's men produced John Clavell's piece *The Soddered Citizen*. Until 1936 this play was known only from Humphry Mose-ley's two entries in the Stationers Register in 1653 and 1660. Both entries were misleading because both gave the wrong author and one was two different plays entered as title and subtitle. The manuscript turned up nearly three hundred years later and was edited by John Henry Pyle Pafford for the Malone Society.

Clavell was an amateur, a gentleman who had turned high-way robber, was captured, convicted, and pardoned by the King. Like a good many modern criminals he exploited his notoriety and published in 1628 a long poem entitled *A Recantation of an ill led life, Or a discouerie of the High-way Law*. The King's men also exploited his notoriety by producing his poor play with a prologue alluding to the author's highway career. The comedy, probably produced in 1629 or 1630[7] carries in the manuscript a cast of King's men.

[7] Ibid., III, 161-65.

THE PERSONS	(AND)	ACTOURS
S^r. Wittworth	A younge gent' of qualitie	Richard Sharpe & Prologue & Epilogue
Makewell	A Doc: of Phisicke	Robert Benfield
Vndermyne	A wealthy Cittizen	John Lowen
Miniona	his Daughter	John Thompson
Modestina	his Orphant	Will: Trigge
Sly	his Servant	John Honyman
Mountayne	A Goldsmith	Curtoys Grivell
Brainsicke	A deboyst young gent' & a Prisoner	Tho: Pollard
ffewtricks	his Boye	Allex: Goffe
Clutch	his Keeper	Anthony Smith
Shackle	his other Keeper	Nich: Vnderhill
Hodge	A countrey fellowe	John Shanke
Birdlyme	A Scrivener	Brain: disguis'd
Brayde	A Haberd: of small ware	Shac: disguis'd
Querpo	A decayde gent'	Clut: disguis'd
A Mayde	Ser: to Miniona	John: Shanks Boy
A Maide	Ser: to Modestina	Mute &c.
	3. Creditors	
	2. Commissioners	
	1. Sollicitor	
	Servants	
	and Mutes	

The thirteen players listed by Clavell are in proportions similar to those in several other casts: six sharers, Sharpe, Benfield, Lowin, Pollard, Smith, and Shank; three hired men, Greville, Honeyman, and Underhill; and four apprentices, Thompson, Trigg, Gough, and the unnamed apprentice of John Shank. At least seven other roles are cited plus an unspecified number of servants and Mutes. In II, 6 there are six servants, all of whom speak; in IV, 2 there are three servants, as well as seven masquers whom Clavell presumably designated as

"Mutes." A certain amount of doubling would have been possible, but in IV, 2 the three servants and the seven masquers are all on stage at the same time. Probably this play would have required the use of a few of the nonacting personnel as well as two or three unnamed hired men.

It is interesting that Clavell wanted to name the player who delivered the prologue and the epilogue. In extant casts this identification is rare, though sometimes the name of the speaker is printed with the text of the prologue or epilogue; more often the character in the play who delivered the epilogue can be deduced from what he says of himself and the play.

The Swisser

Another amateur play acted by the King's men about this time was Arthur Wilson's, *The Swisser*.[8] The piece was never printed in its own time, though listed more than once in the Stationers Register. It remained in manuscript in the British Museum (MS. Add. 36759) until Professor Albert Feuillerat edited it in 1904.

The title page of the manuscript, in the author's hand, reads

THE SWISSER
ACTED
AT THE BLACKFRIARS

1631

The following page of the manuscript lists the cast of King's men:

THE SCÆNE
Lombardie

PERSONS	ACTORS
THE KING OF THE LOMBARDS	*Sharpe.*
ARIOLDUS, a nobleman retir'd	*Taylor.*

[8] Ibid., v, 1267-74.

ANDRUCHO, A Swisser otherwise Count ARIBERT banisht	*Lowin.*
TIMENTES, A fearefull Generall	*Pollard.*
ANTHARIS ⎱ Two old noble men	⎰ *Benfield*
CLEPHIS ⎰ Mortall Enemies	⎱ *Penn.*
ALCIDONUS, Sonne to ANTHARIS	*Swanston.*
ASPRANDUS ⎱ Two Gentlemen	⎰ *Smith.*
ISEAS ⎰	⎱ *Greuill.*
PANOPIA The KINGS sister	*Tomson.*
EURINIA, A Captiue	*Goffe.*
SELINA, Daughter to CLEPHIS	*Trigg.*

1 Gentleman.   4 Souldiers.
1 Gentlewoman.   2 Seruants.
Guard.

As one might have expected from its date—a year or two after *The Soddered Citizen*—this cast is quite similar to that for Clavell's play. The Wilson piece used eight sharers, Sharpe, Taylor, Lowin, Pollard, Benfield, Penn, Swanston, and Anthony Smith; one hired man, Greville; and three apprentices, John Thompson, Alexander Gough, and William Trigg, compared to Clavell's six sharers, three hired men, and four boys. Like *The Soddered Citizen*, *The Swisser* also listed about ten unnamed characters, but most of them appear in only one scene. Again like Clavell's play *The Swisser* also has a song by an unlisted boy. Since the singing boy also appears in Fletcher's *The Wild Goose Chase* revived about the time the others were first produced, it would seem that Blackfriars had a popular boy singer at this time.

Believe as You List

Much more complete casting and more complex doubling is found in Philip Massinger's holograph manuscript with prompter's corrections and additions for his King's men's play *Believe as You List*, licensed for performance by the Master of

263

the Revels on 7 May 1631. This prompt copy was meticulously edited for the Malone Society by Charles J. Sisson in 1927.

This important document is so extensively annotated that the majority of the performers in the production can be identified. The dramatis personae is unusually large for a major company in the 1630s. At least forty-four characters are indicated even allowing for only one Roman soldier; players can be assigned for twenty-nine of these roles, thus giving the largest number of cast assignments we have, even though about nineteen roles are unassigned. More hired men than usual are named, though, as in most prompt manuscripts, the names of fewer principal actors, since an experienced prompter would not need to remind himself of their identity. Indeed, the names of six of the seven sharers who can be cast are not in any stage direction of the prompter. They come from a list of needed properties jotted down after the epilogue, e.g., "Act: 5: A Letter for Mr Benfield," "2 letters for Mr Lowen." Examination of the events in the acts cited shows what roles were taken by Robert Benfield, John Lowin, Eyllaerdt Swanston, Thomas Pollard, Joseph Taylor, and Richard Robinson.

Professor Sisson, who prepared the excellent edition of the play, worked out most of the cast from the author's manuscript and the prompter's notes. At the end of his introduction Sisson printed the following deduced cast, eighteen names if we count "Boy."

LIST OF CHARACTERS AND CAST
in order of appearance.

ANTIOCHUS king of Lower Asia.   Joseph Taylor.
    a Stoic Philosopher

CHRYSALUS ⎫
SYRUS   ⎬ bondmen of   Elyard Swanston.
GETA   ⎭   Antiochus.

BERECINTHIUS, a Flamen of Cy-   Thomas Pollard.
   bele.

first Merchant ⎫
second Merchant ⎬ former subjects
third Merchant ⎭ of Antiochus.

John Honyman.
William Penn.
Curtis Greville.

TITUS FLAMINIUS, Roman Envoy
    to Carthage.

John Lowin.

CALISTUS   ⎱ Freemen of
DEMETRIUS ⎰ Flaminius.

⎧ (1)Richard Baxter.
⎪ (2)Thomas Hobbes.
⎨ (1)William Pattrick.
⎪ (2)Francis Balls.
⎪ (3)'Rowland' (Rowland
⎩   Dowle?)

AMILCAR, Prince of Carthage.
HANNO
ASDRUBAL   Senators of Carthage.
CARTHALO
Carthaginian Officers

⎧ "Rowland"
⎨ William Mago
⎩ "Nick" (Nicholas Burt?)

LENTULUS, Roman Envoy to Car-
    thage in place of Flaminius.

Richard Robinson

TITUS, a spy in the service of
    Flaminius.

Richard Baxter

PRUSIAS, King of Bithynia.
The Queen of Bithynia.
PHILOXENUS, chief counsellor to
    Prusias.
Attendants on Prusias.

⎧ 'Rowland'
⎨ William Mago
⎪ Francis Balls
⎩ 'Nick'

a Lady in attendance on the Queen.
Bithynian Guard
A. METELLUS, Roman Proconsul
    in Asia.
SEMPRONIUS, a Roman Centurion
    under Metellus.
a Jailor at Callipolis.

William Penn

[a Lute Player]	within	Henry Wilson
[a Singer]		'Boy'
a Courtesan from Corinth.		
a Jailor's assistant.		'Rowland'
MARCELLUS, Roman Proconsul in Sicily.		Robert Benfield
Attendants upon Marcellus.		'Rowland'
		Francis Balls
		'Nick'
		Richard Baxter
CORNELIA, wife to Marcellus		
a Moorish Woman, servant to Cornelia.		
a Roman Captain under Marcellus.		William Pattrick
Roman Soldiers.		

The roles which are assigned to no players are ones to which the prompter gives no clue, though several of them are more than bit parts. Amilcar, Prusias, A. Metellus, Sempronius, the Courtesan, and Cornelia each have more than fifty lines to speak.

In addition to the players required for the eighteen or nineteen unassigned roles, two more hired men, probably not actors, are noted as being required for an off-stage function. A stage direction entered by the prompter in IV, 1 reads "*Gascoine: & Hubert below: ready to open the Trap doore for Mr Taylor.*" William Gascoigne was one of the twenty-one men "all imployed by the Kinges Maiesties servants in their quallity of playinge as Musitions and other necessary attendants" in the list of the Master of the Revels dated seven years before, 27 December 1624. Hubert is known only from this prompter's note.

Obviously *Believe as You List* has more characters than the other plays with casts of the King's company during these years. Moreover, the prompter's attention to minor roles gives us a good deal more information about casting plays than the other lists afford.

The seven sharers named here and there by the prompter, Joseph Taylor, Eyllaerdt Swanston, William Penn, Thomas Pollard, John Lowin, Richard Robinson, and Robert Benfield comprise over half of the known patented members in 1631. It seems not unlikely that the roles of Amilcar, A. Metellus, Sempronius, and Prusias were taken by sharers, though there could well have been doubling, as there certainly was among the hired men.

No apprentices are named for the five female roles or for the boy who sang to the accompaniment of Henry Wilson's lute in IV, 2. It is possible that the singer was a musician rather than a boy actor. Doubling among the boys would have been easy, since the Queen of Bithynia and her lady appear only in the third act, the Courtesan only in the fourth act, and Cornelia and her woman only in Act V.

The ten hired men named in this prompt manuscript comprise the largest number identifiable for any play of the period. Evidently not all of them were players. Henry Wilson was a musician attached to the company, and the boy singer may have been one too. The only task assigned to Gascoigne and Hubert was the opening of the trapdoor, a feat which would surely have been assigned to stagekeepers. The other hired men, John Honeyman (recently a boy actor but not yet a sharer), Thomas Hobbes, (possibly a sharer), Curtis Greville, Richard Baxter, William Patrick, Francis Balls, Rowland Dowle [?], William Mago, Nicholas Burt [?] are all known from other documents as players.

One of the most distinctive features of the performance of *Believe as You List* in 1631, as revealed by the prompter's notes, is the intricacy of the doubling. Professor Sisson's careful analysis, though long, is worth quoting.

There can be little doubt that Demetrius is acted by Balls at l. 830, and not by 'Rowland,' who is clearly shown at l.

732 as a Carthaginian officer. This character is thus represented, at different stages, by no less than three actors, and Calistus by two. The confusion in later representations of 'officers' is almost insoluble. But it seems clear that after l. 2556 Baxter ceases to be the officer of Flaminius, whether under the name of Titus (as A. conceives him) or of Demetrius (as M. continues this character eliminated by A.), and becomes an officer of Marcellus at l. 2632. He receives orders from Marcellus as 'servant' l. 2711, is described by Antiochus as servant of Marcellus, l. 2712, and enters in this capacity at l. 2716. Flaminius is reasonably left servantless in this scene of his disgrace. One may fairly conjecture that the missing indication at l. 2861 would show Baxter (or possibly 'Rowland') as the Guard who hales him off to prison, in either case a pretty reversal of function on the part of the actor. These arrangements are all very significant of the want of individuality in such minor parts, even considerable speaking parts, as are those of Calistus and Demetrius. It may be observed that Pattrick and Rowland play Demetrius when he is to speak, and Balls when he has a silent part. Hobbes acts Calistus, ll. 829 sqq., a silent part, and continues it, now a speaking part, in the following scene, ll. 1185 sqq., when Baxter is required for the long-continued part of Titus, ll. 1257 sqq., into which Demetrius seems to be merged by A.

The principal parts are taken by actors who were well-known members of the King's company. Among others available for parts, to which A. gives no clue, were Richard Sharpe, Anthony Smith, John Shanke, George Vernon, James Horne, and for women's parts John Tomson, Alexander Gough, William Triggs, to judge from the casts given in Quartos of plays written by Massinger for the King's company, dated 1629 and 1630. Little is known of Baxter and Mago, and nothing of 'Rowland,' Balls, and 'Nick,' or the lute-player 'Harry Wilson.' . . . 'Rowland' is probably Rowland Dowle, who figures in the list of servants of the King's players granted privileges in 1636. 'Nick' was probably Nicholas Burt, who served under Shanke with the King's men . . . 'Harry Willson' is probably another member of the family of musicians, of whom Nicholas Wilson and the 'Iacke Wilson' mentioned in the quarto of *Much Ado about Nothing* (1600) are recorded. . . .

It must be remembered that the doubling indicated in this quotation still leaves more than thirteen roles unaccounted for. And the number thirteen still allows for only one Roman soldier when more were surely needed. Sisson names eight unassigned players known to have been in the company at the time *Believe as You List* was being prepared for production. Obviously the unassigned roles must have required even more doubling. There can be no doubt that the practice was characteristic of performances throughout the period 1590-1642. What William Ringler has shown so clearly was the custom in Shakespeare's plays of the 1590s,[9] the prompt manuscript of *Believe as You List* shows was still characteristic of the same company thirty to forty years later when it was much richer and thoroughly established as the dominant troupe in the city.

Queen Henrietta's Company

The casts so far considered—except the first for *The Inner Temple Masque*—all come from the same company, the troupe of greatest prestige and greatest wealth in the time. In the reign of Charles I, from which most of the extant casts derive, the second ranking company was that of Queen Henrietta Maria, a troupe which was formed in 1625 or 1626 and acted with success at Christopher Beeston's Phoenix theater in Drury Lane until the owner-manager ousted them during the long plague closing of 1636-37.

The six extant casts for this company were published between 1629 and 1655. Written first was Massinger's *Renegado*, printed in 1630 with a cast that dates from 1625 or 1626,

9 "The Number of Actors in Shakespeare's Early Plays," in *The Seventeenth Century Stage*, ed. G. E. Bentley, Chicago and London, 1968, pp. 110-34.

though the play must have been written a year or two before for the predecessors of the Queen's men at the Phoenix, the Lady Elizabeth's men; James Shirley's *The Wedding*, acted probably in 1626 and printed in 1629; Thomas Heywood's *The Fair Maid of the West*, Part I, probably written before 1610 for another company but revived by Queen Henrietta's men about 1626 with their cast and published in 1631; *The Fair Maid of the West*, Part II, probably first acted about 1629 and published with Part I in 1631; Robert Davenport's *King John and Matilda*, acted some time between 1628 and 1634 but not issued from the press until 1655; and finally Thomas Nabbes's *Hannibal and Scipio*, acted in 1635 and published in 1637.

These casts of Queen Henrietta's men are similar to those for the King's company, and it is noteworthy that the majority of them come from plays first published in the same years as those plays of the King's company which were printed with casts.

The Renegado

The dramatis personae for Philip Massinger's comedy, *The Renegado*, assigned nine named roles to nine players, two of whom were apprentices, Edward Rogers and Theophilus Borne or Bird. Unfortunately the adult players named in these Queen's men's casts are much more difficult to classify as sharers or hired men than those for the King's. The original patent for the Queen's men (which probably named the sharers) has not yet been discovered, and the six extant records of livery allowances made to members of the company do not name the sharers but only a manager or a leading actor who is to receive livery for himself and twelve or thirteen "his fellowes." But the extant evidence suggests that the sharers in the *Renegado* cast were John Blaney, John Sumner, Michael Bowyer, William Allen, and William Robbins. Robbins was a popular comedian who is known to have played comic roles in at least five of this company's plays, *The Renegado*, *The Wedding*, *The Fair Maid of the West* I and II, and *The Changeling*.

The hired men in the cast were William Reynolds and William Shakerley. It is notable that the nine assigned roles are described, but the ten or twelve unassigned roles are not. Though Turk 1 and Turk 2 have a few lines to speak, Turk 3 and the sailors are walk-ons. Some could be doubled.

Dramatis Personæ	The Actors names.
ASAMBEG, *Viceroy* of Tunis.	Iohn Blanye.
MVSTAPHA, *Basha* of Aleppo.	Iohn Sumner.
VITELLI, *A Gentleman of* Venice *disguis'd.*	Michael Bowier.
FRANCISCO, A *Jesuite.*	William Reignalds.
ANTHONIO GRIMALDI, *the* Renegado.	William Allen.
CARAZIE, *an Eunuch.*	William Robins.
GAZET, *seruant to* Vitelli.	Edward Shakerley.
AGA.	
CAPIAGA.	
MASTER.	
BOTESWAINE.	
SAYLORS.	
IAILOR.	
3. TVRKES.	
DONVSA, *neece to* Amvrath.	Edward Rogers.
PAVLINA, *Sister to* Vitelli.	Theo. Bourne.
MANTO, *seruant to* Donusa.	

The Wedding

James Shirley's comedy, *The Wedding*, is more fully cast than Massinger's play; fourteen players are named as compared with nine for *The Renegado*. Seven of the named actors were sharers: Richard Perkins, Michael Bowyer, John Sumner, William Robbins, William Sherlock, Anthony Turner, and William Allen; three were hired men, William Wilbraham, John Young, and John Dobson, who is known as an actor from this record only. Somewhat exceptionally, all four boy actors for the female roles are named: Hugh Clark, John Page, Edward Rogers, and Timothy Reade. In this play the unassigned roles number less than half those for *The Renegado*. Only one of them, the Surgeon, has as many as twenty-five lines and though most of the others speak a few lines, their scenes are so few and so scattered that these unassigned roles could easily be doubled.

William Robbins has a comic role again, a rather substantial part of nearly 200 lines. Robbins also speaks the epilogue, and in character. This assignment and its nature suggest that he had already begun to achieve a reputation, that he could rely upon a favorable reception, and that he was able to cajole an audience effectively.

The Actors Names.

Sir *Iohn Belfare*.	*Richard Perkins*.
Beauford, a passionate louer of *Gratiana*.	*Michael Bowyer*.
Marwood, friend to *Beauford*,	*Iohn Sumpner*.
Rawbone, a thin Citizen.	*William Robins*.
Lodam, a fat Gentleman,	*William Sherlock*.
Iustice *Landby*.	*Anthony Turner*.
Captaine *Landby*.	*William Allin*.
Isaac, Sir *Iohns* man.	*William Wilbraham*.
Hauer, a young Gentleman, louer of mistresse *Iane*.	*Iohn Yong*.
Camelion, *Rawbones* man,	*Iohn Dobson*.
Physician Surgeon	
Keeper Seruants.	

Gratiana, Sir *Iohns* Daughter.	*Hugh Clarke*
Iane, Iustice *Landbyes* daughter,	*Iohn Page*.
Millicent, *Cardona's* daughter,	*Edward Rogers*
Cardona,	*Tymothy Read*.

The Fair Maid of the West, I and II

The casts for the two parts of Thomas Heywood's *The Fair Maid of the West, or A Girl Worth Gold* are somewhat confusing at first glance. Part I and Part II were published together in 1631, when Part I was more than twenty years old, though Part II, obviously a sequel, appears to have been first produced only a year or so before publication.[10] The fact that both title pages boast of a court performance suggests that they were acted together, a suggestion apparently confirmed by the fact that there is no epilogue for Part I and no prologue for Part II, but only a prologue addressed to the court before Part I and an epilogue obviously to the court for Part II.

The fairly full cast (ten actors) before Part I must be that for the revival with Part II, for the players named are the familiar members of Queen Henrietta's company, a troupe which was not organized until fifteen or more years after Part I first appeared, but which inherited a number of the plays written (as this one was) for the old Queen Anne's troupe. The five actors named in the dramatis personae for Part II must be those who had no recorded roles in Part I or whose parts were changed for Part II.

The cast for Part I names ten players for the twenty-seven named roles, in addition to "Petitioners, Mutes, personated." It is noteworthy that Christopher Goad is assigned two roles, one of the few instances in which doubling is specified in a printed cast.

Since Part I and Part II appear to have been acted together, it is probably best to consider them as one cast. Thus we have altogether ten actors named for Part I, Michael Bowyer, Richard Perkins, Hugh Clark, Christopher Goad, William Sherlock, William Robbins[on], Anthony F[T]urner, Robert Axell, William Allen, William Wilbraham; and for Part II five actors named, Theophilus Borne or Bird, Anthony Turner, John Sumner, Robert Axell, and Christopher Goad. But three of the five also appear in Part I though in different roles, so that we have a cast for the double feature of twelve Queen Henrietta's men. Seven of them were sharers at the time, Michael Bowyer, Richard Perkins, William Sherlock, William

[10] See Bentley, *The Jacobean and Caroline Stage*, IV, 568-71.

Robbins, Anthony Turner, William Allen, and John Sumner; three were hired men, Christopher Goad, Robert Axen (or Axell), and William Wilbraham; two—Theophilus Borne and Hugh Clark—were apprentices.

But in Part I there are about seventeen unassigned roles. In Part II there are about ten, but they ought not to be added together. In the first place, it is not absolutely certain whether the unassigned roles in Part II were simply played by the actors who had taken them in Part I or whether they were thought not worth recording. In the second place, all the extras available for Part I were also available for Part II if Part I and Part II were presented together.

There are two or three oddities about these two casts for *The Fair Maid of the West*. In the dramatis personae for Part I six of the ten named players are given the honorific "M^r": Bowyer, Perkins, Robbins[on], F[T]urner, Allen, and Wilbraham. In most of the various theatrical documents of the time this title, when it is used, designates a sharer; in such documents those actors not given the title were usualy hired men or boys. But here Wilbraham is called "M^r" though I can find no other evidence that he was ever a sharer in this company, while Sherlock is not so honored here though other documents show that he *was* a sharer. I can only suggest an error, though I am unhappy to question old documents to cover my own ignorance.

Another oddity is the assignment of "A kitching Maid" to Anthony Turner. Why should a sharer have played a female role? And since the character appears in only one scene and speaks only five lines, why should the actor be mentioned at all?

Another minor puzzle: since Wilbraham played Bashaw Alcade in Part I, why was the role given to Turner in Part II? In neither part does the role of Bashaw Alcade amount to much.

Again, the ordering of the characters is highly abnormal. The men's roles are not separated from the boys' roles in the usual manner, nor are the characters listed in roughly the order of importance. The lineation in the quarto dramatis personae is very odd. One wonders what sort of a manuscript the printer had, and who listed these roles.

The Fair Maid of the West
Part I

Two Sea Captains.

Mr. Caroll, A Gentleman.

Mr. Spencer. By Mr. Michael Bowyer.

Captain Goodlack, Spencers friend; by Mr. Rich. Perkins.

Two Vintners boyes.

Besse Bridges, The fair Maid of the west; by Hugh Clark.

Mr. Forest, a Gentleman; by Christoph. Goad.

Mr. Ruffman, a swaggering Gentleman; by William Shearlock.

Clem, a drawer of wine under Besse Bridges; by Mr. William Robinson.

Three Saylers. A Surgeon.

A kitching Maid; by Mr. Anthony Furner.

The Maior of Foy, an Alderman, and a servant.

A Spanish Cap. by C. Goad.

An English Merchant; by Rob. Axell.

Mullisheg, K. of Fesse, by Mr. Will. Allen.

Bashaw Alcade; by Mr. Wilbraham.

Bashaw Ioffer.

Two Spanish Captains.

A French Merchant.

An Italian Merchant.

A Chorus.

The Earl of Essex going to Cales: the Maior of Plimoth, with Petitioners, Mutes, personated.

The Fair Maid of the West
Part II
Dramatis Personae

Toota, Queen of Fesse, and wife of Mullisheg. By Theophilus Bourne.

Bashaw Ioffer.

Ruffman.

Clem, the Clown.

Mullisheg, King of Fesse

Bashaw Alcade. By Mr. Anthonie Turner.

A Guard.

A Negro.

A Chorus.

A Captain of the Bandetti.

The D. of Florence, with followers. By Mr. Joh. Somner.

The Duke of Mantua. By Rob. Axall.

Mr. Spencer.
Capt. Goodlacke.
Forset.
Besse Bridges.
A Porter of the kings gate.
A Lieutenant of Moors.

The D. of Farara. By Christoph. Goad.
An English Merchant.
Two Florentine lords.
Pedro Venture, *Generall at Sea for the D. of Florence.*

King John and Matilda

Robert Davenport's historical tragedy, *King John and Matilda*, can be dated only not earlier than about 1628, since Hugh Clark had had a boy's role in 1626, and since the list of "the Actors that first Acted it on the Stage" includes the names of Christopher Goad and John Young who are known to have been no longer members of Queen Henrietta's company in July 1634, not later than early 1634. I think, however, it belongs late in that six-year period, since Hugh Clark who played the large and demanding role of Bess Bridges in *A Fair Maid of the West* in 1626 must have had time to become not only an adult but a sharer in the company.

This quarto has certain affinities with the handsome folio edition of John Fletcher's *The Wild Goose Chase* published three years earlier in 1652 with a cast of King's men. As the Fletcher comedy was published for the "private Benefit" of the actors John Lowin and Joseph Taylor, this one was "Printed for *Andrew Pennycuicke*." As Lowin and Taylor signed the dedication of *The Wild Goose Chase*, so Pennycuicke signed the epistle to the Earl of Lindsey in *King John and Matilda* in which he says "*my selfe being the last that that* [sic] *acted Matilda in it.*" Moreover, the cast printed for the Davenport play singles out for praise Richard Perkins and William Sherlock as that for *The Wild Goose Chase* had singled out Joseph Taylor, Thomas Pollard, and John Lowin.

The cast itself is somewhat odd and perhaps not entirely trustworthy. No apprentices are named for the female roles of Queen Isabel, Matilda, Ladies of honor, and Lady Abbess. All ten players named are given the title "M." generally reserved for sharers. But it is unusual for sharers to have taken

all the leading roles with none carried by hired men. Furthermore, if Robert Axen ["Iackson"], Christopher Goad, and John
Young were ever sharers in Queen Henrietta's company this
is the only evidence of it. Both Goad and Young were members of a lesser company by July 1634. Pennycuicke does not
appear to have been infallibly honest,[11] and I suspect that
Axen, Goad, and Young were really hired men when they
played in *King John and Matilda*.

"Other Lords and Gentlemen, Attendants on the *King*" would
include three characters named in the text but not in the cast,
Richmond, Winchester and Mowbray, who have ten to sixty-
five lines each, and a child called merely "Boy" in the text
who has about fifty lines. All in all the cast Pennycuicke presents with his edition seems rather careless and one wonders
how much to rely upon it.

There is a big scene in the fifth act which would seem to
require several extra "Barrons" and four or six "Virgins" to
carry Matilda's hearse. This act also has "The Song in Parts"
which would require at least two singers in addition to musicians for the "Hoboyes" and "Flutes" who play for the
procession.

The Names of the Persons in the Play,
And of the Actors that first Acted it on the
Stage, and often before their *Majesties*.

King *John*.	M. *Bowyer*.	
Fitzwater,	M. *Perkins*,	{ Whose action gave Grace to the Play.
Old Lord *Bruce*,	M. *Turner*.	
Young *Bruce*,	M. *Sumner*.	
Chester,	M. *Iackson*.	
Oxford,	M. *Goat*.	
Leister.	M. *Young*.	
Hubert,	M. *Clarke*.	
Pandolph,	M. *Allen*.	

[11] See ibid., II, 524-25, and Rudolph Kirk, ed., *Philip Massinger's The City
Madam*, Princeton, 1934, pp. 9-15.

Brand,   M. *Shirelock*, who performed
                            excellently well.

Other Lords and
    Gentlemen, At-
    tendants on the
    King.

                    Queen *Isabel*.
                    Matilda.
                    Ladies of honour.
                    Lady *Abbesse*.

Hannibal and Scipio

The last Queen Henrietta's men's cast which has been pre-
served in a quarto is that for Thomas Nabbes's historical tragedy, *Hannibal and Scipio*, "Acted in the yeare 1635. by the
Queenes Majesties Servants, at their Private house in *Drury
Lane*" according to the 1637 title page. The cast names seven
sharers, William Sherlock, John Sumner, William Allen, Hugh
Clark, Anthony Turner, Michael Bowyer, and Richard Per-
kins; four hired men, George Stutville, Robert Axen, John
Page, and Theophilus Bird; and one apprentice, Ezekiel Fenn.
Four of the players named in the cast, two sharers and two
hired men, are given double roles: Sherlock played Maharball
and Prusias, Clark played Nuntius and Syphax, Stutfield played
Soldier and Bostar, and Axen played Bomicar and Gisgon.
The amount of doubling is not unusual, but it is uncommon
for so much to be indicated in the cast of principal players.
Another oddity is the single boy named, Ezekiel Fenn, who
played Sophonisba.

This play uses a large number of characters, notably four
female roles plus "Ladies" in addition to Ezekiel Fenn's role
of Sophonisba. There are four adult roles not in the cast plus
Soldiers and "A full Senate." Obviously *Hannibal and Scipio*
required a good deal of doubling in addition to the eight roles
listed as doubled in the cast. The Soldiers, Attendants, and
the Senators do not speak; evidently they are the "Mutes"

who need not have been players at all. As in *King John and Matilda*, there is vocal music, a song with a chorus in Act I, Act II, and Act IV. Apparently Queen Henrietta's men could rely on their musicians in 1635.

The speaking persons.

Maharball.	By *William Shurlock.*
Himulco.	By *John Sumner.*
Souldier.	By *George Slutfield.*
A Lady.	
Hannibal	By *William Allen.*
2. other Ladies.	
Nuntius.	By *Hugh Clerke.*
Bomilcar.	By *Robert Axen.*
Syphax.	By *Hugh Clerke.*
Piston.	By *Anthony Turner.*
Crates.	
Messenger.	
Scipio.	By *Michael Bowyer.*
Lelius.	By *Iohn Page.*
Sophonisba.	By *Ezekiel Fenn.*
Massanissa	By *Theophilus Bird.*
Hanno.	By *Richard Perkins.*
Gisgon.	By *Robert Axen.*
Bostar.	By *George Stutfield.*
Lucius.	
A young Lady.	
Prusias.	By *William Shurlock.*
	Mutes.

Ladies. Souldiers.
Attendants. Senators.

PRINCE CHARLES'S (II) COMPANY

Holland's Leaguer

This troupe was much less important than the King's company or Queen Henrietta's men and much less is known of it;

for most of its members our information is less secure than for their more established competitors. Only one of their casts is known, that for the performance of Shakerley Marmion's *Holland's Leaguer* produced at the Salisbury Court theater in December 1631 shortly after the company had been licensed.

Probably the most unusual feature of this cast is the large number of apprentices. One wonders if some of the boys had been held over from the previous tenants of the Salisbury Court theater (the speaker of the prologue says that Prince Charles's company was "New planted in this soile"). The previous occupants of the theater had been the King's Revels company, a kind of training school to provide apprentices for the King's company. A lawsuit in the Court of Requests in 1632 carries the statement that the King's Revels was organized,

> . . . to train and bring up certain boys in the quality of playing not only with intent to be a supply of able actors to his Majesty's servants of the Black Friars when there should be occasion as by the said bill of complaint is suggested but the solace of his Royal Majesty when his Majesty should please to see them and also for the recreation of his Majesty's loving subjects.

At one time this King's Revels troupe consisted of at least fourteen boy actors. Possibly some of them had been left at the Salisbury Court theater when Prince Charles's (II) company moved in.[12]

Dramatis Personae

Philautus, a Lord inamored of himselfe.	William Browne.
Ardelio, his parasite.	Ellis Worth.
Trimalchio, a humorous gallant.	Andrew Keyne.
Agurtes, an Impostor.	Mathew Smith.
Autolicus, his disciple.	Iames Sneller.
Capritio, a young Novice.	Henry Gradwell.
Miscellanio, his Tutor.	Thomas Bond.

[12] See the *Huntington Library Quarterly* 40 (1977), 129-49.

Snarle, ⎫ *friends to Philautus*	Richard Fowler.
Fidelio. ⎭	Edward May.
Ieffery, tenant to Philautus	Robert Huyt.
Triphœna, wife to Philautus.	Robert Stratford.
Faustina, sister to Philautus.	Richard Godwin.
Millecent, daughter to Agurtes.	Iohn Wright.
Margery her maid.	Richard Fouch.
Quartilla, Gentlewoman to Tripœna.	Arthur Savill.
Bawd.	Samuell Mannery.
2 Whores. Pander. Officers.	

The cast for Marmion's play is fuller than most, sixteen players. The first eight, Browne, Worth, Keyne, Smith, Sneller, Gradwell, Bond, Fowler, were presumably sharers at this time, since all appeared in the list of Prince's players made Grooms of the Chamber five months later. The next two in the list, Edward May and Robert "Huyt," were probably hired men, since they do not appear in the list of Grooms. The last six players were assigned female roles and were presumably apprentices, though none had appeared in theatrical records before, and only Wright and Mannery later. The two whores for whom no actors are named, could be doubled by two of the boys listed, as could "Boy," who appears in I, 5.

Andrew Keyne (Cane) who had a reputation as a comedian and who was one of the leaders of the troupe has a rather long comic role, nearly 400 lines.

THE KING'S REVELS COMPANY

Another company with a single certain London cast is the one called the King's Revels, or sometimes the Children of the Revels. It is now known that the company was established in 1629 to train boy players for the premier royal troupe, King Charles's company, and that in 1630 there were at least fourteen boys attached to the Children of the Revels.[13] But the

---

[13] See ibid.

character of the company obviously changed, for in July 1634, when they visited Oxford, there were at least eleven adults in the organization.[14] It is to this later period that *The Tragedy of Messallina* must belong.

The Tragedy of Messallina, The Roman Empress

The *Messallina* cast, published in the quarto of 1640, presumably the one for the first performance of the play, must date after 18 July 1634, when William Cartwright, Sr., was a member of another company, and before 12 May 1636, when all theaters were closed by plague to remain so about eighteen months; besides, the boy performer of the role of Messallina had a son christened in November 1637.[15]

Since the extant records of this company are scanty, one cannot be too sure about the status of the individual members of the cast, but it would appear that the first four named were sharers, William Cartwright, Sr., Christopher Goad, John Robinson, and Samuel Thompson. The fifth and sixth men in the cast, Richard Johnson and William Hall, were hired men, and Barrett, Jordan, and Morris were apprentices.

Even with extensive doubling, however, it would seem next to impossible for a second-rate company like the King's Revels to stage this play in its printed form. Besides the roles cast, there are over thirty other characters (most of whom speak), dances, processions, and spectacles, including Messallina and Silius appearing aloft in a cloud and then descending as in a masque. Surely the play must have been cut for this company. Indeed, after the duet by two spirits near the end of the fifth act, appears this comment in a stage direction: "*After this song (which was left out of the Play in regard there was none could sing in Parts). . . .*" Since this play is such an amateur composition obviously brought to the press by the author, it is not unlikely that other parts of the play were cut for the performance.

[14] See Bentley, *The Jacobean and Caroline Stage*, II, 688-89.
[15] See ibid., V, 1002-1004 and II, 359.

The Actors Names.

Claudius Emperour—*Will. Cartwright Sen.*

Silius chiefe Favorite   *Christopher Goad.*
   to the Empresse.

Saufellus chiefe of Counsell   *Iohn Robinson*
   to *Silius* and *Messallina*

Valens }
Proculus }   Of the same faction and favorites.

Menester an actor and Favorite }
  compel'd by the Empresse. }   *Sam. Tomson.*

Montanus a Knight in *Rome* }
  defence vertuously inclined. }   *Rich. Iohnson.*

Mela Seneca's Brother—*Will. Hall.*

Virgilianus and }
Calphurnianus }   Senators of *Messallinas* Faction.

Sulpitius of the same Faction.

Narcissus }
Pollas }   Minnions to the Emperour of his faction.
Calistus }

Evodius a Souldier.

Messallina Empresse—*Iohn Barret.*
Lepida mother to *Messallina*—*Tho. Iordan.*
Sylana wife to *Silius*—*Mathias Morris.*
Vibidia matron of the Vestalls.
Calphurnia a Curtizan.
Hem and *Stitch*, two Panders.
Three murdered *Roman* Dames.
Manutius and *Folio*, Servants to *Lepida.*
Three Spirits.
Two severall Antimasques of Spirits and Bachinalls.

Money Is an Ass

Another play with which the King's Revels company seems to have been associated, though the evidence is incomplete, is Thomas Jordan's *Money Is an Ass.* The first 1668 issue calls the piece "A Comedy, As it hath been Acted with good Applause." But no name of either company or theater is to be found on the title page.

Most of what is known of this comedy comes from the front matter of the two issues of the play, the second of which is also dated 1668, but is entitled *Wealth Outwitted, or Money Is an Ass.*

In the second issue is Jordan's dedicatory epistle with the lines:

> This Play was writ by *Me* & pleas'd the Stage,
> When I was not full fifteen Years of Age.

The prologue "Spoken by Night" makes assertions which seem to show that all the players were boys:

> *Tis new, Ime sure, nere Acted, There's none know it*
> *We never had more Tutor then the Poet.*
> *Since it is thus, Let us harsh censures 'scape.*
> *Had every Actor been some others Ape,*
> *Seen his part Plaid before him, you might say,*
> *We had been Children, not to Act the Play;*
> ....
> *We are but Eight in Number, therefore he,*
> *That drew this piece, being confin'd not free*
> *Could not so well declare himself as when*
> *He shall confine, his Persons to his Pen.*
> *Accept of this, next time, we shall prepare*
> *To feast your Senses with more curious fare.*

All of this is somewhat confusing, especially since Jordan is known to have been a rather slippery character. Of the eight boys named in the cast two are otherwise unknown, but six of them are included in a list of players copied into the town records at Norwich on 10 March 1634/35, and a good many of these Norwich players appear elsewhere in connection with the King's Revels company. I can only conjecture that while Jordan was a boy actor in the King's Revels company "he wrote a play which the adult actors allowed the boys to present entirely on their own, probably under private auspices, since the performance took place at night."[16]

Though Jordan's play is poor stuff, he showed far greater dramatic economy than did Nathanael Richards in *Messallina*. Jordan assigned one character to each player and had to rely on extras for only Silver and Hammerhead and their wives. These characters appear only in Act IV, scene 3; they have only six or seven lines among them, and they never appear again. But none of the eight named actors could have played the roles since all eight appear in this scene. The four tiny roles would have been no strain for the most inexperienced boy actors.

The Actors Names.	
Captain Penniless.	*Tho. Jordain.*
Mr. Featherbrain.	*Wal. Williams.*
Clutch.	*Tho. Loveday.*
Money.	*Tho. Lovel.*
Credit.	*Nich. Lowe.*
Callumney.	*Tho. Sandes.*
Felixina.	*Amb. Matchit.*
Feminia.	*Wil. Cherrington.*

The Wasp, or Subject's Precedent

A third play which has been associated, with some show of plausibility, with the King's Revels Company is a manuscript of the otherwise unknown piece, *The Wasp*. Though the manuscript bears no ascription to company or theater, it is a prompt manuscript with a few inserted names which suggest the King's Revels troupe.

The existence of this manuscript play in the Alnwick Castle collection had been known to several scholars, but its details were not generally available until the appearance in 1976 of the edition of the late Professor J. W. Lever for the Malone Society. Besides the usual prompt manuscript modifications,

[16] See ibid., IV, 678-81 and 685-87.

additional stage directions, property warnings, and notes, the names of six players appear: "Iorden, Barot, Morris, Ellis, Ambros, Noble." Lever identifies all but the last (who does not appear elsewhere): Thomas Jordan, John Barrett, Mathias Morris, Ellis Bedowe, and Ambrose Matchit. The first three had taken women's roles in the King's Revels' performance of Richards' *Messallina*; Bedowe and Matchit are also associated with the King's Revels company. In *The Wasp* manuscript all six actors named have minor adult roles, except "Ambros," who as the young son of Archibald ("filius") has fifty-five or sixty lines.

The King's Revels company, in which all the named players except "Noble" had appeared, was founded in 1629 as a group to train boy actors for the King's company.[17] The troupe is not well known, and the manuscript of *The Wasp* adds little to our knowledge of its management and casting practices. Apparently five of the six actors named were hired men, one was a boy, and none were sharers.

Casts Dubious or Uncertain

There are a certain number of casts that do not have the authenticity of those printed above, but that may have some value for occasional consultation. Most of them are manuscript additions or annotations of early editions; the difficulty is that there is usually no evidence as to who wrote the annotations. Was it one of the players? Was it a spectator who had witnessed an early performance? Was it someone drawing on his memories of what his father or grandfather had told him? Was it a guesser? Was it a nineteenth- or twentieth-century reader or scholar exhibiting his ingenuity? Or was it a well-informed forger, like Collier? Or even James Orchard Halliwell-Phillipps who, though certainly a vandal and apparently a thief, has not, I think, been demonstrated a forger?

[17] See "The Salisbury Court Theatre and Its Boy Players," pp. 129-49.

Philaster, or Love Lies a Bleeding

The prolific nineteenth-century scholar, James Orchard Halliwell-Phillipps, developed a crude and destructive predecessor of the useful photocopying machine. He kept his notes by cutting pages from sixteenth- and seventeenth-century books and manuscripts and pasting them into his properly classified scrapbooks, even going so far, in one instance I remember, as to cut out the Induction to *Bartholomew Fair* from four different copies of the Jonson folio in order to have it handily classified under four heads in four different scrapbooks.

In one of these scrapbooks, of which there are more than one hundred in the Folger Shakespeare Library, there is pasted signature A3 of the 1634 quarto of Beaumont and Fletcher's *Philaster*. This popular play, first acted by the King's men about 1609 but kept in active repertory by the company for over thirty years, was printed in 1620, 1622, 1628, 1634, 1639, 1652, [1663], 1679, and 1687. It was from a copy of the fourth quarto that Halliwell-Phillipps clipped for his scrapbook the page in which the players' names have been added in manuscript.

This cast as transcribed by David George in his article in *Theatre Notebook*[18] is as follows:

The King.	Benfield
PHILASTER, heire to the Crowne.	Ey Clarke
PHARAMOND, Prince of Spaine.	Pollard
DION, a Lord.	Lowin
CLEREMONT, ⎫	Pen
	Noble Gentlemen his Associates.
THRASALINE, ⎭	Bird
ARETHVSA, the Kings daughter.	Wat

[18] "Early Cast Lists for two Beaumont and Fletcher Plays," *Theatre Notebook* 28 (1974), 9.

GALLATEA, a wise mod-   White
   est Lady attending
   the Princesse.

MEGRA, A Lascivious   Thomas
   Lady.

and old Wanton Lady,
   or croane.

Another Lady attending
   the Princesse.

EVPHRASIA, Daughter of   Charles
   Dion but disguised
   like a Page called *Bel-*
   lario.

An old Captaine.   Patrick

Fiue Citizens:

A Countrey fellow.   Patricke

Two Woodmen.

The Kings Guard and
   Traine.

Expanding the names, one finds that the King is asserted to have been played by Robert Benfield, Philaster by Hugh Clark, Pharamond by Thomas Pollard, Dion by John Lowin, Claremont by William Penn, and Thrasaline by Theophilus Bird. All six of these players are known to have been sharers in the King's company 1640-1642. The parts of an old Captaine and a Countrey Fellow are said to have been doubled by William Patrick known to have been a hired man in the company at least as late as January 1636/37. The four roles assigned to apprentices were Arethusa to Walter Clun, and the page called Bellario to Charles Hart, both of whom are said by Wright to have been "bred up Boys at the *Blackfriars*; and Acted Women's Parts," though there is no extant contemporary evidence of their attachment to the King's company. The other two boys are less certain. Gallatea is said to have been played by White [?] and Megra by Thomas, but no apprentices with such names can be assigned to King Charles's company at present. Several boy players of the period are possibilities, but none can be associated with the company. This fact is not necessarily a contradiction of the authenticity of this cast, for certainly the King's men had more apprentice actors than we can name now.

In sum, this cast seems a likely one for a performance of *Philaster* by the King's company in 1641, 1642, or 1643, but its authenticity cannot be assumed.

The Maid's Tragedy

This exceedingly popular play of Beaumont and Fletcher's was printed at least ten times in the seventeenth century, though the first edition did not appear until eight years or more after the first performance. In the Folger Shakespeare Library is a copy of the quarto of 1630 (the third) in which there appears to have been at some time a manuscript cast. On the verso of the title page in this edition appears a dramatis personae under the head SPEAKERS. Unfortunately the Folger copy has been very heavily cropped at some time, so that the players' names which had been written in front of, not behind, the characters' names, have been mostly trimmed away. In an article in *Theatre Notebook*[19] David George has transcribed the dramatis personae with what remains of the casting and has expanded these remains to assign players of the King's company in about 1630 to certain roles.

[Benfiel]d	King
[Tay]lor	Amintor
[Grev]ill	Diphilus
S[hank]	Diagoras
E[dward] C[ollins]	Antiphila
S[harp]	Night

The evidence for these identifications seems to me much too slight to give them any standing. One would have to assume an annotator who used a most eccentric system of abbrevia-

---

[19] David George, "Pre-1642 Cast-Lists and a New One for 'The Maid's Tragedy,'" *Theatre Notebook* 31 (1977), 22-27.

tions; too many of his abbreviated names, seven of thirteen, even Mr. George cannot assign to any known member of King Charles's company; the fact that the names appear in the 1630 quarto is no evidence for any particular date; they might have been intended for a performance of 1650 or 1680. Furthermore we have no evidence that the original annotations were intended for members of the King's company at all. They could have been made for some amateur performance in the country, like those of Mildmay Fane at Apthorpe, or those which Arthur Wilson says took place with some regularity at Draiton and Chartley.[20]

All things considered, this copy of *The Maid's Tragedy* at the Folger has not really yielded any information about the casting of their plays by the King's company.

The Shoemakers' Holiday

In *The Shakespeare Society's Papers* is an article signed "Dramaticus" and dated 7th November 1848, which gives an alleged cast of about 1600 for Dekker's play.[21]

"Dramaticus" begins by asserting that Robert Wilson collaborated with Dekker in the play, and continues:

> My reason for stating that Robert Wilson, as well as Thomas Dekker, was engaged upon "The Shoemakers' Holiday" is, that a friend of mine, who really does not know the value of it, but who, at the same time, is unwilling to part with it, has a copy (in a tattered condition, I am sorry to say) with the names of the two dramatists at the end of the preliminary address. The names are not printed, but they have been added in manuscript in a hand-writing coeval, I think, with the date of publication, but, at all events, very little posterior to it; moreover, (and this is quite as curious, though, perhaps, not quite as important) with the names of the actors against all the principal parts, as they were sus-

---

[20] See Bentley, *The Jacobean and Caroline Stage*, II, 292-99 and V, 1267-69.
[21] *Shakespeare Society Papers* 40, (1849), 110-22.

tained when the comedy was first brought out. These are
not made to precede the play in a regular list of the *dramatis
personae*, as has been usual since the Restoration, but they
are inserted in the margin as the piece proceeds, and as the
different performers enter. . . . I have extracted the names
of the characters, and I have placed after them, in the in-
telligible fashion of a modern play-bill, the names of the
different actors, showing precisely the parts they filled.

King of England	Jones.
Nobleman, his attendant	H. Jeffes.
Earl of Lincoln	Rowley.
Lord Mayor of London	Shawe.
Rowland Lacy	Massy.
Simon Eyre, Shoemaker	Dowton.
Hodge, his foreman	Singer
Firke, his man	Wilson
Ralph, a soldier	Jewby.
Hammond, a city merchant	Towne.
Warner, his friend	Flower.
Scott, friend to the Lord Mayor	Price.
Askew, friend to Lacy	A. Jeffes.
Dodger, the Earl of Lincoln's man	Jones.
Lovell, an officer	Day.
Dame Eyre	Birde.
Jane, wife to Ralphe	H. Jeffes.
Rose, daughter to the Lord mayor	Dowton's boy, Ned.
Sibill, servant to Rose	Alleine.

To various historians and bibliographers (Fleay, Chambers,
Greg), these additions in "a hand-writing coeval, I think, with
the date of publication" have smelled fishy and there are several touches in the style of John Payne Collier, the most adept
literary forger of his time and an active member of the Shakespeare Society. Sure enough, about a century later the copy
"in a tattered condition" turned up in the Houghton Library
at Harvard. On the title page is the autograph of J. Payne

Collier and inserted into the volume is a sheet of paper in Collier's own hand with the list of actors, though in a different order from the one he used in his article.[22] Collier knew a great deal about Elizabethan plays and stage history, and the cast he invented is not an impossible one. Unfortunately its only authority is Collier's active and scheming imagination.

Volpone and *The Alchemist*

Other manuscript casts in printed plays have been reported by James A. Riddell.[23] In a copy of the Jonson Folio of 1616, once owned by Robert Browning, there are manuscript assignments in what appears to be a seventeenth-century hand of nine roles in *Volpone*, two in *The Silent Woman*, nine in *The Alchemist*. The two assigned in *The Silent Woman* are Sir Amorous to Hugh Attawell and Morose to Will. Barksted. These are too few to mean much in a study of casting.

In *Volpone* and *The Alchemist* the majority of the leading roles are assigned to the principal players of the King's company as follows:

Volpone		*The Alchemist*	
Volpone	*Richard Bur-badge*	Subtle	*Richard Bur-badge*
Mosca	*Henry Condell*	Face	*Nat: Feild*
Voltore	*Nath: Feild*	Dol. Com-mon	*Richard Birch*
Corbaccio	*John Hemings*	Dapper	*John Vnder-wood*
Corvino	*Nich: Tooly*	Drugger	
Avocatori		Love-Wit	*Bentley*
Notario		Epicure Mam-mon	*John Lowin*

[22] Fredson Bowers, "Thomas Dekker, Robert Wilson, and *The Shoemaker's Holiday*," *Modern Language Notes* 64 (1949), 517-19.

[23] "Some Actors in Ben Jonson's Plays," *Shakespeare Studies* 5 (1969), 285-98.

Nano		Surley	*Hen: Condell*
Castrone		Tribulation	
Grege		Ananias	*Nich: Tooly*
Politique- Would-Bee	*John Lowin*	Kastrill	*Will: Eglestone*
Peregrine	*Goffe*	Da. Pliant	
Bonario	*John Vnderwood*	Neighbours.	
Fine Madame Would-bee	*Richard Birch*	Officers.	
Celia		Mutes.	
Commandadori			
Mercatori			
Androgyno			
Servitore			
Women			

In the light of our knowledge of the personnel of the Shake-spearean company these castings for *Volpone* and *The Alchemist* are all plausible except for "Bently" in the role of Love-Wit. As Dr. Riddell points out, no actor named Bently is known in the reign of James I or Charles I. A member of Queen Elizabeth's company, John Bentley, seems to have been fairly well known in the early 1580s, but he died in 1585.[24] Riddell conjectures that "Bently" is a lapse for "Benfield" who appears in a number of casts of the company and had become a sharer by 1619. The role of Love-Wit is not unlike others Benfield assumed later but his participation in this performance can be only a guess.

If the two casts are genuine and accurate except for the lapse of "*Bently*" they must date before 16 March 1618/19 when Richard Burbage was buried and after 1615 or 1616 when Nathan Field joined the company. In this period of about three years Burbage, Condell, Field, Heminges, Tooley, Lowin, Goffe (Robert) and Underwood of the *Volpone* cast

[24] See Edwin Nungezer, *A Dictionary of Actors and of Other Persons Associated with the Public Representation of Plays in England before 1642*, New Haven, 1929, pp. 44-45.

were sharers in the company. The player *"Richard Birch,"* an apprentice, presumably, who took the female roles of Doll Common and "Fine Madam Would-bee" is found in no other record of this or of any other company. A *George* Birch was a member of the company in the 1620s but he does not seem likely to have been an apprentice 1616-1619 since he was married to Richard Cowley's daughter in January 1618/19. Conceivably a young adult could have played the hoyden Doll or the virago Madam Would-bee, but the name "Richard" is used twice. It seems to me more likely that the roles in this performance of *Volpone* were taken by eight sharers and an hitherto unknown boy, Richard Birch, for there had to be a good many more boy actors than we know by name now.

The cast for *The Alchemist* is very similar to the one for *Volpone*: eight sharers and a boy. John Heminges and Robert Goffe are omitted; *"Bently"* and William Eccleston are added. If *"Bently"* was meant for Benfield, we again have eight sharers and a boy. It is notable that no hired men are in either cast.[25]

It seems a plausible conclusion that these two casts derive from revivals of the two Jonson plays by their owner, the King's company, some time between 1615 and January 1618/19. The fact that the book in which the notes are written was not published until 1616 does not necessarily mean that the performance noted took place after that date; the writer might simply have remembered a performance he had seen a year or so before he wrote.

But there is no evidence of the identity or trustworthiness of the writer.

AMATEUR CASTS

A number of casts for the productions of plays by amateurs are extant for the period 1590-1642, some in print and some

---

[25] See Bentley, *The Jacobean and Caroline Stage*, II, under each player's name.

in manuscript. Obviously they are of no value for an under-standing of the profession of player in the time. Most of them come from productions at the colleges of Oxford or Cam-bridge; one or two from schools; and a few from amateur performances at great houses or even at court.

Index

Library of Congress Cataloging in Publication Data

Bentley, Gerald Eades, 1901-
The profession of player in Shakespeare's time, 1590-1642.

Includes bibliographical references and index.
1. Theater—England—History. 2. Actors—England. I. Title.
PN2589.B46   1984   792'.028'0942   83-43059
ISBN 0-691-06596-9

Gerald Eades Bentley is Murray Professor of English Emeritus
at Princeton University and author of the seven-volume
Jacobean and Caroline Stage (Clarendon Press), *Shakespeare
and Jonson* (Chicago), and other works.

DATE DUE

FEB 11 1998			
MAR 0 3 1998			
MAR 1 9 1998			
OCT 3 0 2003			
NOV 2 5 2003			
DEC 1 1 2003			
APR 2 4 2007			

WITHDRAWN